LAP OF THE GODS

JILL DUDLEY

TRAVELS IN CRETE
AND THE AEGEAN ISLANDS

Published by
Orpington Publishers

Origination by
Creeds, Bridport, Dorset
01308 423411

Cover design and map by
Creeds
Cover based on an original concept by
Clare Taylor

Printed and bound in the UK by
Berforts Information Press

ISBN 10: 0-9553834-6-3
ISBN 13: 978-0-9553834-6-5

CONTENTS

		Page
	Introduction	
1.	Crete	1
2.	Naxos	35
3.	Delos	51
4.	Santorini (Thira)	59
5.	Samos	79
6.	Patmos	99
7.	Paros and Tinos	111
8.	Kos	133
9.	Rhodes	155
10.	Lesbos (Mytilene)	181
11.	Chios	207
	Glossary of Gods & Heroes	227
	Bibliography	233
	Index	235

INTRODUCTION

Those who have read my earlier books on Greece, *Ye Gods!* and *Ye Gods! II*, will know that Harry and I are not the intrepid travellers we would like to be but travel warily, fearful of disaster striking while abroad and being carted home on stretchers.

I am, however, single minded when I have a plan. My trips to the islands have never been for the sun and the sea (though they are a bonus) but to experience at first-hand the locations of the myths and legends of the islands.

There are eleven islands in this book, each one chosen for a specific pagan god, historical character or legendary story which has caught the world's imagination. I write about the ancient sites, about early Byzantine churches and festivals, and about the characters we meet. I make no apology for lifting three chapters from *Ye Gods!* (Delos, Patmos, and Paros combined with Tinos) because it seems to me sensible to have all the Aegean islands I have found of particular interest together in one book. Paros and Tinos are interesting for their miracle icons, and anyone who has read *Ye Gods!* will see that here I have expanded on Paros and put a little more of interest into Tinos.

Those who have enjoyed Harry in my earlier titles will be glad to know he is still with me. He comes to keep an eye on me, though often the eye is shut – well, both eyes really – his idea for every trip being to have it over and done with and then get home again. He is, of course, at a disadvantage as he never speaks to foreigners which cuts out nearly everyone we meet abroad.

As with all my books I am searching for enlightenment, questioning impossible to believe matters in the Christian faith, and making comparisons with ancient worship. Harry is my sparring partner in such matters, though he prefers to take Christianity and the Church's teachings on trust. I hope that anyone of strong convictions feeling sorry for my agnostic, near-atheistic plight will not feel it necessary to shower me with pamphlets, but accept the fact I am quite happy in my unbelief as Harry is in his blind belief. If there is God, then I can see no reason why he cannot enlighten me himself, and if there is not, then that explains everything.

My enthusiasm for Greece has never flagged over the years and, although I start each journey with some apprehension, even pessimism, I am glad to say I've ended each triumphantly having side-stepped the obstacles and somehow overcome the challenges each trip has placed before me. I hope whoever reads *Lap of the Gods* will enjoy the humour and be inspired by the imaginative mind of Greek antiquity.

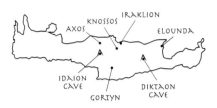

CRETE

On the short flight from Athens to Iraklion, a curve of moon was visible low in the night sky. It was the colour of burnished gold and shaped like the horn of a bull. Harry saw it first and drew my attention to it.

"A good omen," I said. I was ridiculously aware of good or bad omens – flying magpies, black cats and suchlike. To see a horn-of-a-bull moon on my way to Crete, seemed to me eminently satisfactory.

"It all began with a bull," I explained to Harry.

"A bull?" Harry enquired, turning over a page of his paper which was full of depressing news.

"Well, the Minotaur – although he wasn't altogether a bull, he was a monster who was half man, half bull."

"Oh, that. Old Zoos again?" he enquired. He turned another page of his paper to look for more depressing news.

"Well, no. Not on that occasion. Though, come to think of it, Zeus did turn himself into a bull to attract the attention of Europa whom he then ravished." I told him the story of Europa, daughter of a Phoenician king, and how she had first been spotted by Zeus playing with her friends on the seashore; in order to attract her attention, Zeus had promptly turned himself into a majestic snow-white and friendly bull. Europa had been so enchanted with him that she'd climbed onto his back, whereupon he'd swum away with her to Crete where they'd consequently had three sons, the eldest of whom had been Minos who was to become king of Crete.

My horn-of-a-bull moon appeared to be sinking into the sea or, rather, over its horizon. In the dark the sea was just blackness, so it was all very mysterious as we flew through the night.

Harry turned another page. Depressing news always gave him a corresponding feeling of well-being. A bull market would have been appropriate to the moment, but shares had tumbled and all was doom and gloom. The stewardess passed with a black plastic bag in which to put our rubbish, and the newspaper was deposited into its depths.

It was announced that we were to fasten our seat-belts as we were approaching Iraklion. Not long afterwards the lights of the airport raced up to meet us and the bouncing thud as we hit the runway reassured me that we were safely on the ground. My plan to visit Knossos and several other important landmarks in Crete was now a decided possibility instead of an uncertain hope.

It was a day to take stock; a day to recover our travelling wits and acclimatize from the cold September wind and drizzle of England to the thirty-five degrees centigrade and cloudless blue skies of Crete. It was a day to idle and admire the architecture of Iraklion whose many buildings showed signs of Venetian influence.

My primary goal that day was the church dedicated to St. Titus. He was the first bishop of Crete who'd come to the island with St. Paul in the first century. It had been St. Paul who'd appointed him bishop, and St. Titus who'd set about converting the Cretans.

The inside of the church I found disappointingly dull. Under the Turks the original Byzantine church had been turned into a mosque and had then been rebuilt in the nineteenth century following an earthquake.

I asked to see the skull of the saint which had been brought back to Crete a few decades earlier having been taken away by the Venetians for safe-keeping when the island fell to the Turks. I was escorted to a side chapel where it was pointed out to me.

I peered down at the bejewelled dome-shaped bishop's mitre. The crown had a hole cut in it to reveal a small portion of skull. I sat down on a bench and waited for some sort of mystical happening, but felt quite unmoved and slightly bored which I thought shameful.

We walked on to the tiny domed Church of Agios Minas, a late Byzantine gem which, because of its diminutiveness, had been allowed by the Turks to remain standing as their mosques stood higher.

The interior of this small church was exquisite with its ancient icons, its ornate pulpit and bishop's throne. St. Minas had been an Egyptian martyr of the third century whose name was really only one vowel different from King Minos. As far as I knew the saint had had nothing to do with Crete, so I could think of no reason for this dedication except as a deliberate attempt to hook the pagan mind with its legends of King Minos to the new Christian religion.

Iraklion was a major port and we soon took ourselves down to the harbour. The sky was blue, paling towards the horizon; the sea was shades of turquoise. A picturesque schooner full of holiday makers was sailing into port. We passed colourful fishing boats moored up along the quayside, and stepped over and around fishing nets, then walked out along the mole towards the massive grey stone crenellated Venetian fortress. In contrast to the calm waters of the harbour on our right, the open sea to our left was being whipped up by a strong wind, sending waves crashing against the rocks there.

At the end of this extensive mole which stretched far beyond the fortress, we found a small café where we sat with Coca Colas. From there we could see a marina with yachts nestling at anchor with the buildings of Iraklion rising elegantly behind them. Far beyond against the skyline was Mt. Jouktas, its peak shaped curiously like the profile of a bearded man in repose. The Cretans said it was the head of the dead Zeus, and it marked the site of his tomb, which to me, of course, made no sense at all because no god can die.

When I mentioned this to Harry he said pagan gods were only illusions so of course they could die, to which I said that if they were only illusions then God needn't have bothered with his 'thou shalt have no other gods but me' commandment; either way, I said, it made no sense to have a tomb since gods were immortal. To this Harry said 'Of course it makes sense', then 'maybe it doesn't', and finally 'Oh, I don't know'.

A ferry-boat of the Minoan Line came sailing in to port, and our attention was drawn to it: "That's probably coming in from Santorini," he said. He was quite keen to visit the famous island renowned for its great volcanic eruption which had caused the tsunami that had engulfed Knossos.

But Santorini wasn't on the agenda yet. What was on the agenda were the great discoveries and excavations at Knossos the following day, and we were both looking forward to that.

Our second day on Crete and we were at the ancient Palace of King Minos. Harry pointed to the site-plan and decided that we should head up some steps to the Central Court. We sat in the shade of an olive tree while taking stock of our surroundings. It was midday and the heat was intense, making this shady area with a warm breeze blowing a pleasant respite from wandering amongst the excavations. Knossos had been built in a prime location, close to the sea but not visible from it.

"So what about the Minotaur?" asked Harry. He screwed the cap back on his bottled water which was already half empty.

"It's a long story," I said. "It all originated as a result of King Minos needing to establish his right to the throne and, for some reason best known to himself, setting up an altar to Poseidon and praying for a suitable sacrifice worthy of the god to be sent to him. His prayer was answered by a magnificent bull appearing from the sea – a gift from Poseidon who was god of the sea. The animal was so impressive that Minos couldn't bear to kill it, so sacrificed a bull from his own herd instead. Poseidon was furious and, in order to teach King Minos a lesson, caused his wife to become besotted with the creature. The result of this somewhat unsavoury love affair was the birth of the Minotaur who had the head of a bull and the body of a man."

"Not exactly what you want your relatives to see in the nursery," Harry remarked.

"Absolutely not. It's why he was hidden away in the heart of a labyrinth."

"So where's the labyrinth?" Harry pored over the site-plan. I told him that there wasn't one marked and the whole of Knossos could be considered a labyrinth.

I went on to tell him how Theseus, son of Aegeus (King of Athens), had set out to kill the Minotaur. At the time there'd been an annual tribute of seven youths and seven maidens paid by Athens to King Minos of Crete who fed them to the Minotaur. Theseus had been determined to put an end to this barbaric practice and heroically volunteered to be one of the youths with the intention of killing the monster. "Then Ariadne, King Minos' daughter, fell head over heels in love with Theseus," I told Harry. "And, in order to save his life, she gave him a ball of gold thread to unravel as he found his way through the labyrinth to the Minotaur's lair. After killing the Minotaur he was then able to find his way back to the arms of Ariadne, after which they sailed away together to the island of Naxos," I said.

We left the peace and shade of our tree and went up to view the ante-room to the Throne Room with its frescoed walls of plants and griffins. In it there was a large libation bowl and a throne. I tried to imagine how King Minos must have felt when he found out his daughter had eloped.

During the different Minoan periods religion had been Mother Goddess centred. The Mother Goddess of the Olympian gods had been Rhea, and a temple in her honour had been built at Knossos. Zeus was her youngest son and she had given birth to him here in Crete.

To identify the temple of Rhea at Knossos became a bewildering impossibility, and I asked one of the site attendants, a rather plump resigned-to-this-boring-job young man, if he could speak English? Yes, he replied, showing signs of cautious interest. That was a relief as it was too hot to exert myself with the Greek language. The temple of Rhea, I enquired? He got up from his seat. "Over there," he said, pointing to something which bore no resemblance to a temple. "Where are you from?" he asked. "From England," I answered. He then informed me with pride that he'd studied English for a year in Manchester. "Ah, Manchester, how interesting! How did you like the English rain?" I enquired. "Oh, very much. We would like to see rain here in Crete," he said solemnly.

I asked him what an enormous Henry Moore type sculpture was, consisting of two thick grey prongs rising from a heavy base. Those, he said, represented the powerful horns of a bull. One was symbolic of the religious authority of the king, the other his political authority. He then went on to explain how the double-headed axe (two axes joined together back to back) was also an emblem of Cretan sovereignty, and represented the same thing as the horns of a bull, but with the added symbolism of the waxing and waning moon. He showed me a photograph of a gold double-headed axe in our booklet which demonstrated clearly what he meant.

Whilst talking he kept his eyes on the visitors trailing around the ruins. He suddenly excused himself, put a whistle to his lips and gave a number of shrill blasts, at the same time waving an arm at some students, one of whom had leapt onto a wall. The whistle was effective and the young man jumped down obediently. We left the young attendant to his duties.

Having wandered over and under and around royal roads, palaces, royal villas, crypts, shrines, court rooms, stairways and corridors, we finally flopped down on the stone seats of a theatre where religious rites had once been performed.

King Minos had been a just and wise king, and had been spoken of very favourably by such authors as Homer and by such philosophers as Plato. According to *The Odyssey* King Minos and his brother Rhadamanthys, had been so well thought of that they'd been appointed judges of the souls of the dead in the underworld, directing them to Tartarus or to the Isles of the Blest.

I gave one last look around the labyrinthine site, and noted the far distant hills where single trees set at regular intervals were silhouetted against the skyline looking like a crenellated fortress. But it was time to catch the bus back to Iraklion. I followed Harry to the exit.

Harry and I weren't the most harmonious couple when driving together as he constantly kept nagging me to keep my eye on the speedometer, while I thought he'd drive better if he kept his eye on the road.

To keep the peace we'd asked the Stoic to join us – she was our long-standing friend from Cyprus, and an expert at smoothing things over when Harry and I became enraged with one another. For Harry's birthday I'd given him a road map of Crete to encourage him to become navigator rather than driver. I'd highlighted my top priority sites to be visited and, as they also covered the places in World War II, where the British had lain low with their V.I.P. captive General Kreipe (a wartime adventure Harry was fascinated by), we were in agreement over the route to be taken.

And now here through the arrivals gate came the Stoic, a large unflappable figure having flown in from Larnaka. I could have kissed her when we stood before the car and she said (I had already briefed her to say this as part of my subtle planning): "My dears, don't ask me to map-read, I don't know my west from my east and if I sit in the back I'll get car sick."

"Harry's a great map-reader," I added.

"Yes, your wife's told me you're a wizard with a map," said the Stoic enthusiastically. And Harry, who had absolutely no faith in my ability to navigate or drive, thought it his duty to sit in the front with the map open on his lap.

"So where's the brake, I wonder? Where are the indicators? Horn?" The Stoic adjusted the seat and made herself comfortable. She turned on the ignition and gave a few revs, and we were off. Well, fairly off, because we got stuck in a traffic jam almost at once. Harry's directions were meticulous. "Ease in to the right now. The next turning should say – "

I sat in the back amongst pieces of luggage; the bigger suitcases were in the boot. My job was to translate signposts if they were in Greek, and shout out if I saw the name of the next village when Harry called it out to me from the map. But, as most of the major place names were in English as well as Greek, I really had very little to do but look out of the window.

The Stoic's driving was, like herself, unflappable. Whenever Harry said: "Right here – no, not here, next turning," she obeyed instructions. When he said: "Go straight over now," she stopped and allowed the car speeding across our path to get by first. When he told her to turn right, and then changed his mind half a mile on, she turned about without a murmur.

We reached Kritsa by late afternoon and found a pension almost immediately. For someone who never expects plans to be achievable, I was well content that we had arrived at our first destination and were on course to see the Diktaon Cave the following day. It was there that it was said Rhea (the great Mother Goddess) had given birth to Zeus.

The Diktaon Cave was a worthy cavern for the nativity of the supreme god of the ancient world. Rhea knew what was fitting for the birth of her immortal son; it had to be somewhere out of sight of her husband Kronos because an oracle had warned him that his supremacy would be overthrown by one of his offspring. In order to prevent such a calamity Kronos had swallowed his children as soon as they were born. Rhea became increasingly enraged by such paranoid behaviour so, with the birth of Zeus, she hid him in the Diktaon Cave and gave her husband a stone wrapped in swaddling-clothes to swallow instead.

In the Diktaon Cave Zeus was guarded by the Curetes (minor Cretan gods) who drowned his infant cries by clashing their weapons and shields together, and he was suckled by the goat Amalthea whose horns overflowed with nectar and ambrosia (the food of the gods).

When I told Harry and the Stoic the story of Zeus' birth, the Stoic immediately enquired about the children Kronos had already swallowed. "What happened to them? Who were they? Were they ever born again?" Once the Stoic became curious she wanted instant answers.

"Ah. Good question," I said with regards to the last, and I told her how, when Zeus had eventually learned about his other brothers and sisters inside his father, he'd arranged for an emetic to be given him, and each child was consequently spewed out one after another – Hestia, Demeter, Hera, Hades and Poseidon.

The rebirth of these siblings resulted in the Battle of the Gods when Zeus called on the Hundred-handed giants and the Cyclopes to help overthrow his father. After a long war waged on Mt. Olympus, Zeus finally won, thanks to his thunderbolts made for him by the Cyclopes, and the multiple rocks hurled by the Hundred-handed giants.

"With his defeat, poor old Kronos was condemned to eke out eternity deep down in the depths of the earth, in Tartarus," I said.

"Not a nice story," Harry declared.

"I wonder why he swallowed his children and didn't just kill them," mused the Stoic.

"Because they were immortal," I said immediately.

"Yes, I suppose that would make sense. To have all those immortal babies inside you. Too dreadful."

"Typical pagan story," Harry remarked. He was studying the open map on his lap, his finger marking our progress up this spiralling mountain road. "You'll see a turning any moment now," he told the Stoic. After a few metres we saw the signpost to the right, and in no time we'd arrived.

The parking area was filled with cars, and several restaurants were doing brisk business. At the bottom of the mountain track two mules and a muleteer were waiting under a tree hoping for a fee to carry anyone up the rocky ascent to the mouth of the cave.

"A mule? I wouldn't want the animal to buckle under my weight," declared the Stoic. "No, my legs are used to taking me, so I'll spare the poor beast."

I was glad of the walk after the long drive, and followed Harry who was already leading the way up the stony path. Five minutes afterwards one of the mules could be seen below us mounting the twisting track with a woman beside it steadying a toddler sitting astride the animal; the muleteer walked ahead, and the child's father followed behind. Another young couple strode up, the father with a baby sleeping soundly strapped to his back with a dummy in its mouth. Zeus should have had a dummy to stop him crying, I thought, then the Curetes wouldn't have had to do so much banging and crashing of their weapons to drown his wailing.

The mouth of the cave yawned at us as we approached. At its entrance steep wooden steps with a hand-rail descended into its depths. Exhausted visitors were arriving up them, and either smiled triumphantly or were so wearied by their exertions they could only pause to get their breath. One woman collapsed on the rocky ledge beside us, incapable of further movement. She was sweating profusely and quite speechless as she looked at us, her chest heaving. I asked her if she had water, but she had nothing and I offered her my bottle. She took it, though her hand was shaking so violently she found it difficult to put it to her lips. The Stoic ordered her to stay where she was until she felt better. When at last the woman was able to speak we learned she was English. She had to get down to the car park immediately, she said, or her coach would leave without her. She was in such a state I told her to keep the bottle as I could share Harry's. We left her and began our own descent into the cave.

Awesome was the best word to describe its interior; a Gothic cathedral in which you could almost hear the shudder and crescendo of organ music. The cave walls were sculpted by nature in perpendicular patterns, and were of an oily dark hue in sombre shades of jade and deep amber. Its lofty height and width were astonishing. Spiritually uplifting? Yes.

Long before Greek influence had brought the supreme god Zeus to the Cretans, the Minoans had gone there to honour a young boy god, son of the Mother Goddess of fertility. When the Hellenes had arrived in Crete they'd brought their Olympian gods with them, and the story of Rhea giving birth to Zeus became the accepted story at the Diktaon Cave.

The cave was lit at strategic points revealing its vaults and niches and marbled columns shaped by nature. I'd brought my torch which I shone around the walls and crevices. As we got lower into its depth my eye was drawn to a great rounded stalagmite below; it reminded me of a gigantic misshapen *omphalos* such as the one at Delphi, said to be the navel of the world. The *omphalos* here was to me the navel of the god.

We descended to the rock-floor of the cave where there was a small lake; its waters were as clear as glass and revealed the numerous coins which people had thrown in, using it as a wishing-well for their own unspoken hopes and fears.

We could only stand and stare around in silence. A cathedral demands silence and hushed whispers. It was believed that King Minos, wise and just king, had come to this cave and had spent nine years learning about law and justice from Zeus (his father) who, as supreme god, had been the giver of laws and dispenser of justice.

Another story concerning the cave was of Epimenides, a semi-legendary poet-prophet of the sixth century B.C., who was said to have fallen into a deep sleep in this cave lasting fifty-seven years. When he awoke he found he had the gift of prophecy. In a poem, attributed to Epimenides, King Minos addresses Zeus:

> *But thou art not dead: thou livest and abidest forever,*
> *For in thee we live and move and have our being.*

The first line I supposed must refer to the Cretan idea that Zeus had died and Mt. Jouktas was his tomb. But to me the fascination was the last line which was quoted by St. Paul when he'd addressed the Athenians (Acts 17: 28), using the words to refer to God, not Zeus.

One last look around the dark majesty of this lofty cavern; another glance at the sheet of perpendicular folds said to be the shawl of the infant Zeus, and we began the steep climb up the numerous steps towards the light again – from the dark and the ancient past, we came up to the sunlight and the present.

Antiquity was now behind us as we emerged and moved on to the future.

The scenery in Crete was incredibly rugged with its mountains and hills and gorges and sea. On our drive back to Kritsa from the Diktaon Cave we had to cross the Lasithi plain, an extensive upland plateau with scattered villages. It had once had many picturesque windmills, each one with four or more triangular white cloth sails. Now only a few remained, most were mere rusty metal skeletons with long spikes where the sails had once been.

The Lasithi plain was encircled by mountains and could only be exited through one of the mountain passes. Whilst Harry gave the Stoic directions, I opened my notebook and began to make rapid notes like an artist with a sketch-book, recording each detail of the landscape.

"How would you describe those mountains?" I asked. "Rolling? Undulating? Mounds of mountains?"

"Waves of them," said the Stoic.

I scribbled: 'In distance faced with gigantic waves of grey mountains.'

We took a mountain pass and after a while the terrain on our right fell away sharply, deepening to a gorge full of holm oak and cypresses. The Stoic kept her eye mostly on the road but occasionally came out with: "Oh, look! Do you see that little white church on its ledge over there?" Whereupon she removed her driving spectacles for a better look.

The 'ledge over there' with its little white church overlooking the gorge was behind us by the time I'd caught sight of it. I saw below its ledge a cluster of whitewashed houses clinging to a precipice. It all looked precarious and, from a daily living point of view, totally impracticable.

We came to a village called Zenia and skirted alongside a gorge which was here filled with olive trees and, as this opened up, a mountain came into view crowned with a massive craggy lump of rock.

The Stoic stopped in a layby. She tended to do this every now and then in order to take photographs. The craggy-lump-of-rock-topped mountain sloped down to a long jagged ridge beyond which we could glimpse the sea. In the foreground were loops of grey, treeless bent-pin mountains with lower pyramid shaped ones in front. Stretching away from the roadside there were broom and sun-dried wild flowers and grasses.

"You can understand how the British managed to hide out with General Kreipe," Harry said, using his binoculars to scan the scenery.

"I don't understand at all how they did," I said. "They were completely dependent on the Cretan peasants bringing them food and leading them up goat-tracks from cave to cave. I think it amazing that nobody betrayed them."

The Stoic whom we had briefed to read the book *Ill Met by Moonlight* by W. Stanley Moss, one of the British army officers involved, said: "The Cretans are staunchly loyal once they've identified their friends. They're great survivors and great fighters. Besides, they were really suffering under the German occupation."

We drove on down to another village and were soon in a valley where there was again a spread of olive groves. Beyond were enormous grey-brown mountain mounds like elephants lying on their sides. I almost expected to see ears and trunks languidly waving in the air. I noticed it was getting warmer as we got lower.

Driving on we were for a while hemmed in on all sides by high hills, before breaking free and entering olive groves again. The sun was going down casting long shadows.

"Lato!" Harry announced, and pointed to a mountain.

We had started that morning with a visit to Lato. It was only a few miles from Kritsa and was a remarkable and important Hellenistic city covering the slopes of two mountains. We'd spent several hours scrambling about its ruins, climbing the steps to its *prytaneum,* the administration centre, and its *hestaenum,* the important sacred site dedicated to Hestia, goddess of the hearth and family, whose sacred flame burned continuously at Olympia, and from which all others were lit. Located about ten miles from the sea, from the port of Agios Nikolaos, it was well placed for trade with Asia, North Africa and Europe.

For us the enjoyment of Lato had been its isolation and solitude. There had been no other person there as we'd climbed up its steep and stony track to a temple above, though to which god it was dedicated is not known.

"Look at that small church there!" cried the Stoic. From the road we briefly caught sight of a small whitewashed church far across the mountain below the ancient Lato excavations. We hadn't noticed it when we'd been at the site that morning, and it was so isolated I couldn't see how anybody could get to it.

We drove on and eventually saw Kritsa with its tiered white houses tucked into its hillside. We arrived back at our pension and found our landlady, her mother and her husband in their courtyard shelling chick-peas. The old mother was seated regally between them dressed entirely in black, with a black hood-like head scarf fastened under her chin; her weather-beaten, fine-boned face looked up at us as we approached. She had a calm expression and a gentle smile of welcome.

I asked our landlady about the small white church below Lato. Did anybody ever go there, and how could they get to it, I asked? She said that there was a track that people could take from the road. It was open once a year for the feast-day of – and I thought she said St. Adonis. Adonis, I queried? Yes, yes, Adonis! To have a church dedicated to a saint with the name of Aphrodite's lover?

"It is open every year on 17th January," she went on.

I have since discovered that that day is the feast-day of St. Anthony and that it must have been the Cretan accent that had made the 'nt' sound like a 'd'.

I also asked her about a nearby twelfth century church dedicated to Panagia Kera. What did Kera mean, I enquired? She struggled to find the right English words to explain it. It meant, she began, the special woman of a home, the special woman of religion – the lady in the heavens.

What? Immediately I made the connection with the Mother Goddess of the ancient past. The Church, of course would deny any connection, and raise its hands in horror at the word 'goddess' applied to the Virgin Mary; only the words Panagia (All Holy) and Theotokos (God bearer) were acceptable. Yet the Virgin Mary had undoubtedly slipped into the Mother Goddess role and was beseeched for fertility problems just as the earlier Mother Goddess had been.

The 12th century Church of Panagia Kera was set back from the road, its whitewashed exterior visible through pine trees. It had a cylindrical central dome with a winkle-shaped terracotta tiled roof, and three similar shorter ones in front, each with a narrow window not much larger than an arrow-slit. The flanking buttresses were like outstretched wings.

Inside its cool and shadowed interior, the thick walls, arches and domes were smothered in frescoes depicting important early Christian saints, and events from the Gospels. I'd read somewhere that frescoes had formerly been for the benefit of the illiterate, for those unable to read the stories in the New Testament for themselves.

For one who was able to read the Gospels, my problem was my inability to interpret the frescoes, and I badly needed a dedicated fresco scholar to tell me what was what. I left Harry wandering around and went to the nearby church shop where I bought a book about the history of the church; it had in it a detailed plan of the frescoes. I then sat on a stone ledge and marked the ones that I thought I'd find interesting. I had my small torch and shone it into the dark corners of the church where the rich colours glowed at me in the semi-darkness.

I learned from the book it had originally been a single-aisled church with a dome. Side aisles had been added later making it a three-aisled church. It was the middle aisle, the oldest part, which attracted me. It had a fascinating, ancient looking dome with crossed poros stone ribs in high relief looking not unlike a cross on a hot-cross bun; the dark colours and glaze completed the hot-cross bun effect. Such a dome construction suggested a much earlier date than the twelfth century.

The quartered areas between the raised intersections on the dome were themselves divided into three horizontal tiers, each depicting a scene from Christ's life – his presentation in the temple, his baptism, the raising of Lazarus and other Gospel stories.

I moved on to the sanctuary which, because the church was now a museum, had no *iconostasis* (altar screen). The altar was very small, built of stone with a flat slab on top. I turned my attention to the apse. Most of the plaster there had fallen away; what was left was the blue robe of the Virgin Mary and traces of the Archangels Gabriel and Michael.

The presence of the Virgin Mary in the apse, I'd just read, was to emphasise the divine and mortal nature of Jesus, the link between Man and God. This imagery had, apparently, come into use in the fifth century when the Monophysite heresy had been threatening Church unity. Monophysites had insisted that Christ was wholly divine, unlike the Orthodox/Catholic claim that he was both Man and God.

I discovered a number of other memorable frescoes, such as The Massacre of the Innocents in which Herod was seated on his throne and Herod's soldiers held up to him babies skewered on the end of their lances.

Another was The Descent into Hell. According to the Apocryphal Gospel of Bartholomew, when he (Bartholomew) had met Christ after his Resurrection, he'd asked him where he'd gone after he'd vanished from the tomb, and his reply had been that he'd gone down to hell to bring those who were there back to life and resurrection. I'd often wondered why the Apostles' Creed had in it the words, 'and he descended into hell', especially as St. Luke's Gospel had Christ saying to the good thief who was crucified with him: '"Truly, I say to you, today you will be with me in Paradise."' In the dictionary the word 'apocryphal' means 'of doubtful authenticity', 'sham', 'false'. I wondered why the words 'descended into hell' from the Apocryphal Gospel of Bartholomew had got into the Apostles' Creed at all. I supposed the Church would have its reason for it, but I had yet to ask someone.

A memorable fresco was The Last Supper. The table was spread with a white cloth on which were wine flasks, ornate drinking vessels, knives and, somewhat unusually, large white radishes. Centrally placed was a pedestalled bowl containing a single fish. Unlike the Da Vinci's Last Supper which had Jesus centrally placed at table, this fresco had him to the left end with all the disciples with haloes, and faces half turned looking towards him. Judas was the only one in profile with one hand reaching out to the fish. Strangely, Judas too had a halo. In the 1970s a work called the *Gospel of Judas* was discovered. It was linked to a Gnostic sect ('gnostic' is 'to know' as opposed to 'agnostic' which is 'not to know'). In this Coptic manuscript, dating from the third or fourth century, it is claimed that Judas was only doing what Jesus had requested him to do in order to fulfil his (Jesus') destiny. Far from being the villain of the piece, here Judas was the hero. It's interesting that many of such early circulating manuscripts regarding Christianity, were condemned, sifted out and hidden from the public gaze by those early Christian Fathers, and the four Synoptic Gospels (believable-only-with-faith) were the only ones selected.

I came to a fresco called The Elevation of the Cross, depicting St. Constantine and St. Helena, (his mother). The Elevation (or Exaltation) of the Cross was a major feast of the Orthodox Church. It commemorated the finding of the cross of Christ's crucifixion by Constantine's mother. In the fourth century Helena had travelled to the Holy Land and with extraordinary Poirot-like detective work, had managed to discover the major locations of Christ's life on which Constantine then built majestic churches. Helena had also managed to locate the actual cross on which Jesus had been crucified. Before coming out I'd done some research on Church festivals and had discovered that in the third century Christians had had only two major spring festivals, Easter and Pentecost – both of them had been taken from Judaism – Easter from the Passover, and Pentecost from the Jewish Feast of Weeks.

When Christmas was added to the Church calendar at a later date, the Church had then felt an autumn one was needed. The annual Jewish autumn festival was Yom Kippur, the Day of Atonement, when a goat was sent off into the desert bearing all the sins of the Jews (where our word 'scapegoat' comes from). Christians claim that Jesus died for our sins and, like the Yom Kippur scapegoat, took the sins of the world upon himself. In the fourth century, the Church thought that the Christian equivalent of Yom Kippur should be instituted, and so the Exaltation of the Cross became its autumn festival. The date chosen was the day of the dedication of the newly built Church of the Holy Sepulchre in Jerusalem.

By now I'd become bog-eyed with frescoes, and Harry was more than ready to leave. It was time to walk back up to Kritsa to catch a bus for Agios Nikolaos, and from there another on to Elounda. The Stoic had declared she would like a day of rest, and Harry too didn't feel inclined to tramp around looking for archaeological remains of a temple I wanted to find.

One last look at the interior; another glance at the church's pure white exterior against the deep blue sky; a brief stop to admire a nearby ancient olive tree, the gnarled and hollow trunk of which had a massive girth, its silver-grey-green leaves casting dappled shadows on the dried grasses and wild flowers beneath; one final look back at the white church glimpsed between the bottle-green of the conifers, and we finally left.

It is evening and I am back at the pension with Harry. I am writing up my notes on my solo trip to Elounda. It occurs to me that life is very odd the way at one moment you have a plan, and in the course of the day you put the plan into action and then, hey presto! what has so far been imagined has happened – you've broken through from the unknown to the known. The mind which imagines, and the memory which recalls, are altogether weird and an integral part of being human.

My plan for today was to take the bus to the port of Agios Nikolaos, and another on to Elounda some twelve kilometres along the coast, because I understood there was an ancient temple of Zeus there, now submerged in the sea, but the ruins of which could still be seen. Near to it I'd read there were the remains of a very early Byzantine church.

Elounda turned out to be a tourist paradise, with its harbour of yachts and small boats, and its cruise boats advertising trips to the small island of Spinalonga, the Venetian leper colony, whose fortress was visible from the mainland.

I followed the instructions in my guide-book and walked up the town to the outskirts where I found a signpost pointing down a path to the archaeological site. I thought I'd better fortify myself with food before setting out, so took myself down some steps to a taverna whose terrace overlooked the sea.

Here a thirty year old with red hair and a glum expression served me with a salad. I asked him about the Zeus sanctuary; I didn't want to walk further than was necessary in a temperature of thirty-five degrees centigrade.

He was very dismissive. He'd never ever found the ruins, he said. He'd lived there three years, had snorkelled all around the coast and had never caught sight of any archaeological remains. It was nonsense having that signpost, and high time it was taken down, he grumbled. To my question regarding an early church, he agreed there was one, but really it was extraordinarily boring. Oh, well.

I discovered he was from London, and had no intention of ever returning to live there again. I thought he looked as though he'd like to pick a quarrel; his army regulations hair-cut made him look thuggish. He seemed dismissive of all things in London and equally dismissive of things here in Elounda.

When I was preparing to leave, I was approached by an elderly man who said very ingratiatingly: "Can I help you, madam?"

Yes, he could, I told him. Did he know where this temple of Zeus was?

"Oh, yes, madam." And he went to great lengths to draw me a simple diagram which would help me locate it.

"The waiter has just told me it doesn't exist," I said.

"Oh, don't worry about him, madam. His girlfriend's just gone back to England and he's in a huff. I'm his father, madam." And using 'madam' every time he drew breath, he pointed out exactly where I should walk in order to find this submerged temple.

I followed the man's directions – it really couldn't have been easier. I walked along the tarmac road beside the shore, along the isthmus to the Peninsula of Spinalonga. The isthmus had a canal cut through it to save a long sail around the peninsula.

The sea was a shimmering royal blue, with patches of turquoise. The landscape consisted of low, dark grey hills descending to the terracotta coloured shoreline. Leaving the tarmac road I walked on hard-packed terra-cotta soil. Two stone-built defunct windmills flanked the bridge across the canal. I made for a scruffy café with a reed-covered area under which were tables and chairs beside the sea. I asked the character at the bar, who looked like a pirate, if he could tell me where the early church was, and he pointed me in the right direction.

So there it was! A great length of fine mosaic floor belonging to an early Christian basilica. I noticed that its sanctuary was aligned with a conical hill to the east. So many pagan temples were aligned with a conical hill, believed to have been volcanic, or the source of hidden energy; cult statues looked towards the east; churches also had their sanctuaries to the east.

I left the church and clambered over the rocks along the shore. A heavy swell brought waves up over the rocks, then away again revealing stone foundations of the ancient city of Olous. Tantalizingly, somewhere amongst these ruins was the ancient temple of Zeus and also of Britomartis, a Cretan divinity, thought by some to have been a fertility goddess. Legend has it that King Minos had been besotted by her and the poor girl had leapt into the sea to escape him.

This submerged city of Olous had once been the port used by the important Doric city of Dreros some ten kilometres inland. We had earlier climbed up through its ruins, hoping to reach the temple of Apollo. But, not really knowing where the temple was, we had settled on believing that some massive foundations three-quarters of the way up the hill had been the temple. It was thoroughly unsatisfactory, but it had been too hot to climb higher, or to worry whether or not we'd found it. As we'd driven away we could see from the road a massive structure on the summit, but too late.

I left the rocks and the submerged ruins and returned to the nearby café where I bought a Coke from the wild pirate at the bar, and sat with it under the reed shelter beside the sea. An English couple was seated nearby and expressed their bemusement by what they'd been expecting and what they'd seen, or rather hadn't seen. I told them about the church floor mosaics which seemed to please them. We watched several small colourful boats chugging along the canal and making their way to the open sea. All was tranquil and lethargic.

It had only been a small plan, but I was ridiculously pleased that I'd done what I'd set out to do. It was really very curious that things come to pass, but only if you bestir yourself enough to make them happen.

So here I am now, my plan of the morning having been fulfilled. The sun is setting and I'm staring out from our bedroom balcony to distant ghosts of mountains. Closer lower ones slope down towards each other and between them just visible is a misty coloured sea. The sky is darkening, and a white half moon can be seen through the silhouetted leaves and uplifted branches of a nearby tree.

Harry has enjoyed his day of rest. I have enjoyed my day of action. We've both fulfilled our dreams. I see the Stoic wander out to the dining area below. Tables and chairs are laid for customers under a vine trellis from which hang clusters of black and green grapes. Lights hang suspended from the length of this canopy of vines; it looks picturesque and romantic. The family cat is curled up on a cushion. The landlady can be seen moving about at the back of a nearby building where she cooks for her guests. She has declared herself to be the best cook of Cretan dishes on the island. She little realizes that this alarms Harry. The Stoic, however, has more than made up for Harry's suspicious toying with his food, by giving gasps of joy, and asking numerous questions regarding the ingredients of her Cretan cuisine.

It is time to go down and face the dish of the day. The landlady has a plan whilst for the moment we have none, except to fall in as well as we are able with whatever she has dreamed up for us tonight.

Our new accommodation at the small town of Zaros had bougainvillaea cascading in purple and scarlet from the balconies. On our arrival an elderly landlady with very swollen ankles and dressed in black, with a black headscarf was called from her kitchen by a man whom I took to be a porter seated by the window. The woman had a welcoming, smiling face as she greeted us, and handed us the keys to our rooms, huge and heavy antiquated iron ones which were impossible to lose.

Several daughters and their babies gathered in the dining-room later that afternoon; the babies were bounced on maternal laps and smiled and drooled. The Stoic was expert at baby talk and delighted the mothers. To me one baby looked much like another and I was full of admiration when the Stoic the day after was able to remember which infant was which, and which one was whose. To me each toothless smile and gurgle was just an anonymous plump baby.

The following day was the 14th of September, the day of the Orthodox Church's celebration of the Exaltation of the Cross. I was early for breakfast that morning because I wanted to get up to a monastery where I'd been told the festival would be celebrated. I asked our landlady if I could take a taxi there, but was told that her daughter and husband would give me a lift as they were going. She began to serve me breakfast and I begged her to let me have just a piece of toast and marmalade. But, no, she wouldn't listen, and soon my table had on it a plate of apple pie, cheese pie, cheese omelette, fig rolls, honeyed cakes, goat cheese pie, grapes, slices of sweet bread – but no plain toast! No marmalade!

The landlady's daughter arrived and I was put in the back seat of the car where yet another infant in a small white frock and a dummy in her mouth sat on her grandfather's knee beside me. She looked like any other child with a dummy.

"Look, Sophia remembers you! She is smiling at YOU! Eh, eh, Sophia? Tidddly, tidddly, teeek, teeek!" The child was tickled under her chin. The grandfather, in fact, was our landlady's husband who was the same man I took to be the hotel porter. He was very much part of this happy family.

"Hello! Hellllooo!" I said to the child who gave a big squirm in return. "So you're Sophiaaa-ha-ha-ha!" And so the trip up into the mountains passed with smiling child-centred nonsense talk.

I told the family that I only wanted to stay a short while and would walk back to Zaros. That was fine, they said. The Monastery of Agios Nikolaos was a large domed building still under construction. Those coming for the liturgy were walking down to a small church on a lower level from which I could hear the thin wailing chant of a few people.

Far from being the great festival I'd been expecting, it turned out to be a small gathering of a few faithful. A man beckoned me to sit on a rush-seated chair in a very ancient looking side chapel with a barrel roof. A large iced cake decorated with almonds and silver balls was centrally placed, and near it were plastic bags of bread.

I felt no spark of religious or spiritual empathy with what was taking place. Exaltation of the Cross, so what? I slipped away after about ten minutes and gave a great sigh of relief as I emerged into the sunlight. It was still not yet ten o'clock. There was a cool breeze, the sky was a deep blue as I began the long descent down the tarmac road. Olive trees grew on either side and the melodious sound of a goat-bell drew my attention to a flock of goats dispersed amongst the olive trees. The lead billy goat with the bell was a handsome, long-haired, long-horned beast of a light tan colour with a broad cream band around its nether parts. It leapt from a rock to a mound and grazed busily at some dried thistles. A young man in a red T-shirt kept vigil over his animals.

It was a simple hike which took about an hour, and I was glad I'd left the church when I had because it was just beginning to get really hot by the time I arrived back at our hotel.

"So tell us about the place we're going to," said the Stoic. We were on our way to Gortyn from Zaros.

I leaned forward from my back seat. "What do you want to know, the pagan part or Christian?"

"Oh, pagan. We have to start with the pagan as that came first."

"Well, it was at Gortyn that Zeus ravished Europa," I said, and I told her what I'd already told Harry on the plane, how Zeus had transformed himself into a majestic white and friendly bull in order to seduce the beautiful young girl he'd spotted.

"Yet another bull story!" sighed the Stoic, "Such unsavoury goings on! It's no wonder people turned to Christianity!"

"It's what I'm always telling my wife," said Harry. "She loves these idiotic legends which have nothing believable to them. She gets quite cross when I remind her of what she herself told me, that the early Christian Fathers called the pagan gods mere 'poetic fancies', which they were." He had a finger on the open map following the route to Gortyn. "When you come to a main road you turn left," he instructed.

"Isn't all religion 'poetic fancy'?" enquired the Stoic vaguely, overtaking an elderly peasant woman wearing a printed cotton dress and black head scarf, and leading a donkey laden with brushwood.

"Yes, isn't it?" I asked, glad to have the Stoic's support. "Isn't religion just imagination at work in human consciousness?"

"Explain imagination," said the Stoic. "Explain consciousness," she added.

For a while we bandied the words 'consciousness' and 'imagination' around but got nowhere with our attempts to fathom or define them. Maybe our inability to give them some comprehensible meaning was precisely because they lay in the realm of incomprehensibility.

We overtook a contraption chugging along slowly which revealed peasant resourcefulness. We had seen several such conveyances whilst in Crete – a rotovator to which a seat was attached for the driver who could then sit comfortably holding the handlebars of the machine; this one pulled a small trailer in which a goat was standing placidly, its big green goat eyes staring ahead. The roar of a motorbike overtaking it and us didn't worry the beast, as it shot past with two unhelmeted young men whose black locks flew in the wind, and whose third pillion passenger was a small boy seated on the motorcyclist's lap. What were rules and regulations for but to be broken?

We arrived at the Gortyn archaeological site, bought our tickets and entered.

One of the few things at Gortyn which was easily identified was the great sixth century Byzantine cathedral dedicated to St. Titus. Its lofty ruins stood out on the landscape demanding attention. Titus had been the son of an illustrious pagan, some say a descendant of King Minos no less. When rumour spread to Crete about Jesus the miracle-worker and teacher in Judaea and Galilee, Titus' uncle had sent him to investigate, or so the story goes.

Some believe Titus had been present at Christ's crucifixion and his ascension to heaven, but it isn't known for sure. It is a fact, though, that Titus had been baptised and had accompanied St. Paul on many of his missionary journeys. He'd been, apparently, with St. Paul in Jerusalem when St. Paul had declared himself against compulsory circumcision for those Gentiles who wanted to convert to Christianity; he could see no point in burdening Gentiles with such Jewish requirements when they would find their souls saved by the simple act of becoming followers of Christ.

St. Paul had come to Crete more by accident than intention due to a severe storm which had driven his ship to seek shelter at Kali Limenes, a small haven on the south coast of Crete, not far from where we were. There is no definite evidence but it is thought St. Paul might well have come and preached at Gortyn which at the time had been the capital city of Crete. What is known is that St. Paul appointed Titus bishop of Crete.

In *The Letter of Paul to Titus* in the New Testament he exhorts him to spread the word by example, by leading a sober, upright, and godly life.

Reading up about Titus, I learned that he was said by early Christians to have performed wonders by faith and prayer, such as that described when he'd been at a feast of the goddess Artemis and had prayed for a sign to be sent by God, consequently the cult statue of the goddess had crashed down and shattered. Similarly, his prayers had been answered when a temple of Zeus which had been under construction, had collapsed at his bidding. Whether these Christian stories were true, or pious frauds to advance Christianity, is not known.

We stared up at what remained of the triple apses of the great three-aisled Byzantine cathedral. Apart from that east end there was nothing left but ruined foundations and prostrate stumps of columns. St. Titus had died at the age of ninety-four and had been buried here.

We went on down to the Roman Odeon built around a concave ancient wall bearing the Hellenic Law Code of Gortyn. It was inscribed on stone blocks, written from left to right and back again from right to left; it had originally been installed in a circular assembly hall. This unique code covered all aspects of the judicial law and dated from the fifth century B.C.

Because legend had it that King Minos had learned about law and justice from his father Zeus at the Diktaon Cave, I thought it significant that the Law Code of Gortyn had been constructed right there beside the plane tree under which King Minos had been conceived. It is said that the tree had remained evergreen from that time on in honour of the occasion.

"Just another tree," scoffed Harry when I prepared to take a photograph of it.

"Not just another tree at all," I replied, "it's where King Minos was born. Well, where he was conceived."

The ancient acropolis was visible in the far distance beyond the Odeon. There the earliest city of Gortyn had existed together with an all important temple of Athena on its summit. The temple had been the main centre of worship before the city had extended down to the Mesara plain and another temple had been built and dedicated to Apollo Pythios.

I wanted to see this later temple, but Harry said it was far too hot to exert himself further. The Stoic, who was puce in the face, also declared herself against it. "A fresh, cold orange juice, that's what I need, not more wanderings," she proclaimed. She sat down on a stone wall and was clearly not going to move. "Just looking at the ancient olive trees here is enough for me!" She waved an arm at some nearby trees with gnarled trunks some of which were known to be over a thousand years old.

I asked a girl in an office the way to the temple of Apollo, and was told it was quite difficult to find but if I crossed the main road, and if I persevered – What I wasn't told was that, in fact, anyone exploring that part of ancient Gortyn needed a guide.

"Follow the road," she said, "and after two hundred and fifty metres you will see a wire mesh fence and the sign."

I did what I was told but, as the wire mesh fencing began quite soon and then stopped, and there was a notice to Agia Triada after a hundred metres, I supposed I was already there. I clambered over stony terrain amongst olive trees. It didn't need much imagination for each new pile of stones to represent a newly excavated ancient site. Common sense eventually told me that I was wasting my time, so I turned back. I met a young couple who were also picking their way over the stones and we all agreed we'd gone wrong. The young girl said she really wanted to get up to the acropolis, and I left the two of them arguing which direction to take. I told them I would shout if I came across the notice for the temple.

I walked further on along the main road and was about to give up when I came to the notice board I'd been told about. I was too far away by then to shout, so saved my energy. Here there was a good track to follow and I came first to the *nymphaion*, then the Roman *praetorium* and Imperial Temple. All these were easily identified by a notice board and a wire mesh fence surrounding the excavations.

The path wound on through olive groves, but there were no more notices. I saw a parked car and found a man reading a book. Did he know where the temple of Apollo was, I asked? He was, in fact, English, and told me he had no idea, but his wife and daughter had set off together to find it.

I pressed on, and soon saw the distant figures of the mother and daughter. I followed them and left the track, scrambling over stony banks and ditches. I then lost sight of the two others and, by pure chance, found myself beside a fenced off area of ruins and fallen column drums where a small notice announced the temple of Apollo Pythios. The title Apollo Pythios originated when Apollo killed the Python, the evil dragon he'd found at Delphi.

My fascination with this temple was that in the second century it had been converted to a three-aisled Christian basilica, and had remained in use until the sixth century when the great cathedral dedicated to St. Titus had been founded by the Emperor Justinian.

I wondered whether St. Paul had stood beside this pagan temple. It was very curious how St. Paul had become so one-eyed about the absolute necessity to spread Christianity. It wasn't as though he'd been a disciple of Christ and had followed him around. Rather, as a Jew he had been an enemy of all Christians. Then wham! his sudden conversion and conviction.

It was time to find my way back. It was only a matter of returning to the path which led to the main road, and it surely wouldn't be too difficult. I started to walk over the stony ground amongst the olive trees. I felt amazingly competent taking my bearings from the afternoon sun as I headed east. In reality I was extremely incompetent as I should have gone north – Harry knew exactly what I should have done when we were reunited several hours later. Lost in an olive grove! Impossible!

Fortunately, I had my bottled water. I walked and clambered over stony mounds, and came up repeatedly against meshed fencing, so had constantly to retrace my steps. I kept stumbling round and back and up and down, and unhooking one wire fencing in order to get through, only to come up against more of it. It was a nightmare and I expected any moment to become dehydrated.

Eventually, I saw in the distance through the olive trees farming allotments, and a peasant feeding his goats. I asked him for the main road, and he pointed towards some houses. But I didn't want that village or that road, and was convinced I needed to get back to the original path and the original main road where I could make my way back to the main Gortyn site.

Returning the way I'd come I immediately got lost again. I continued scrambling over stones and banks and heading blindly onwards. Talk of labyrinths! I'd read that it had been in the fields at Gortyn that King Minos' wife, Pasiphae, had had her fling with the majestic bull sent by Poseidon for sacrifice, but which King Minos had kept alive much to Poseidon's fury. Pasiphae, it was said, was the daughter of the sun. Was she just! I was so hot, I was so lost!

Tramping in thirty-five degrees centigrade addled my brain and I just kept walking blindly (I'd forgotten about walking east by now). I was expecting at any moment that my legs would turn to jelly and I'd collapse in a heap. I prayed to all the gods to get me out of this never ending olive grove. I was aware that maybe – yes, maybe! I was being taught a lesson in humility. I shouldn't have had that inclination to scoff at a convent we'd visited a few days back where I'd thought the nuns slightly senile, and where I'd fobbed off a geriatric nun who'd wanted to sell me an elastic bracelet and had given me a sweet, with a mere smile and a wave of dismissal. Nor should I have thought the nun who'd unlocked the church the most bored-out-of-her-mind nun I'd ever had the misfortune to meet. Nor had I had proper respect at the Church of Agios Titos at Iraklion where I'd seen his skull, or at his church here, for that matter. Here I was, the great unbeliever, sort of saying sorry, and praying to be helped now.

But the powers that be were saying: 'There she goes calling on us to help her. But she doesn't believe in us so she can jolly well help herself.' What could I do but get on with it? There was no alternative.

Consciousness – imagination – the fine line between standing aloof from deity, defying it even, then finding oneself alone and having to cope. One part of my conscious self told me that whether I believed or didn't, I would still have to help myself by my own actions; another part was aware that outside assistance from unseen powers might make things easier and be a consolation because I wouldn't be so alone.

Not a soul to be seen, not a track to be found, only stony ground and olive trees. I comforted myself that at least they offered spasmodic pools of shade. I decided to bypass God and appeal to Apollo. "Come on Apollo! Here's your chance! YOU get me out of here!"

Having unwound more wire tying yet another length of mesh fencing, I squeezed through the gap and continued to tramp and stumble over stones when quite suddenly I saw a motorbike at the far end of an open stretch of ground. Heading for it I saw a man far beyond bent over a line of vegetables. I called out and the figure slowly stood up. The man shaded his eyes against the glare of the sun to see who it was disturbing his peaceful occupation. I wished he would walk towards me; instead I had to walk the several hundred yards to him. Where, oh, where, was the main road, I asked him in Greek. He waved an arm in the direction I had come. No, please, I said, I didn't want him to point, he had to take me. I was a helpless woman in danger of spontaneous combustion, and very tired and very lost, I said. He could see at a glance I wasn't lying.

I held money out to him. "I will give you five euros if you will take me on the back of your motorbike," I implored.

The elderly peasant looked at me as though I'd made an indecent suggestion, or he feared his wife might catch him with a female pillion passenger. He said words to the effect that he thought my extra weight on this stony terrain wouldn't do his motorbike any good. I waved the money at him and said he absolutely, positively had to lead me to the road. I had walked too far in too many circles to be given only vague directions.

The man obviously realized that he could only get rid of me if he did as I asked. I promised him a sainthood, a place in the Elysium Fields, everything which would be good for him, so long as he took me to the main road where I could find my way back to the St. Titus cathedral ruins at Gortyn.

We started to walk – very slowly. All Cretan peasants move slowly to conserve energy in the heat of the day. In fact, most of them lie inert when the sun is at its height. After an interminably slow tramp, during which I glanced frequently at my watch and saw it was long past the time I'd told Harry I'd be back, I was at last put on the track I needed. The man told me to keep straight and I would find the road. I again offered him the money for his help, but he wouldn't hear of it. No, no, it was nothing, he said.

It was everything. I thanked him profusely and set off along the path. I began to hear the sound of speeding cars along the main road. What a joyful sound! I came to a small building and saw another man watering some plants. I double checked that when I came to the main road I needed to turn left. Yes, yes, you turn left, the man assured me, as though I were asking the most ridiculous question. It is very near now, he said encouragingly.

I reached the main road and turned left. About a hundred yards along the road I passed a wayside shrine. I hesitated, then turned back to it. I felt slightly ridiculous as well as conspicuous to passing motorists as I stood before the shrine, made the sign of the cross (Greek Orthodox way) in a very unobtrusive, surreptitious manner, and said I was sorry for being such an unbeliever; I sent up a prayer of thanks for my safe return, promising to mend my ways for ever after. I then continued on my way and promptly forgot my promise as I sank back into the comforting knowledge that I was safely back where I wanted to be.

Several hundred yards on I rounded a bend and saw Harry. Until then I was still only hoping I was heading in the right direction. He was standing at the turning to the Gortyn site, his hand shielding his eyes against the setting sun.

"Where in heaven's name have you been?" he demanded.

"God alone knows!" I answered.

I never let on that I'd stopped at a wayside shrine, and had almost grovelled in gratitude to the unseen powers who'd helped me from the olive grove and put me back on the right path for the road. Or had I in reality just helped myself?

The kitten followed us from the courtyard up four steep stone steps before turning back down again. We were being taken to our new apartment rooms at Axos by Maria, a youngish woman in tight fitting knee-length stretch trousers and a loose fitting T-shirt. We'd parked on a level high above her house and I'd walked down the short steep driveway to find out if we'd come to the right place. Seeing a woman seated at a kitchen table preparing vegetables with both feet soaking in a washing-up bowl of water, I'd called out to her from the open door. She'd been quite unflustered at being caught out like that, and had calmly removed her feet from the bowl, and put on her sandals. Yes, we'd come to the right place and she was Maria, she'd said.

She took us to our rooms at the top of her house. She lived on the outskirts of the village of Axos, on a steep rocky hillside. From our balcony we were able to look out over the village to the distant mountains. Somewhere out there was the Idaion Cave, my last planned destination for this trip.

"After you have unpacked you must please come down, and I will welcome you with a drink," Maria said.

Our welcoming drink turned out to be nothing less than a feast. We drank raki and helped ourselves from a bowl of yoghurt made from goat's milk, mixed with chopped cucumber and tomatoes.

Maria told us her husband was the village priest. They had three sons, one newly married, and the younger one still at school. The village priest? Maybe I would at last be able to discuss the Orthodox Church festivals and glean more how Christianity had grown out of paganism.

But it was not to be. Her husband would be in Iraklion over the next few days in order to settle their second son into his new college, we were told.

Photographs were brought out for our inspection – Maria's husband, her children, her eldest son's recent wedding. There was Maria looking very unlike herself in a low-cut bright red silk dress and well coiffured hair. There stood the bride and groom. She showed us her daughter-in-law with a baby boy seated on her lap. When I expressed surprise that the bride already had a child, she laughed. It was the custom, she said, for a bride to have a baby placed on her lap as it would bring her a fruitful marriage. I passed the photo to the Stoic who made the appropriate cooing sounds at the sight of the baby, while I turned my attention to the little kitten playing around my feet.

Maria continued telling us about the wedding. It was clearly one of the great events of her life. How many people had there been, I enquired? Two thousand five hundred and fifty, came the reply. What? The whole village, she explained. They all pulled together for the occasion, and she brought out for our inspection the most beautiful large, silky textured gold paper napkins with the monogram of the bride and groom's initials entwined in one corner. I only wished we had been there those three weeks earlier so we could have joined in the celebrations.

That evening we were sitting out on our balcony having our pre-supper glass of wine, when we were visited by the kitten. It stared at us with its round green eyes, then bolted into our bedroom. Harry managed to shoo it out and closed the balcony door, whereupon the kitten crouched and mewed disconsolately by my chair. What else could I do but pick it up and hold it on the palm of my hand and place it on my lap. It sucked at my index finger – suck, suck, suck suck. It then began to purr. Suck, suck, suck – gradually its eyes began to close and the sucking grew less as it fell asleep. I stroked it gently and felt ridiculously attached to it.

"And she has the temerity to make fun of me when I coo over babies!" scoffed the Stoic. "Look at her with that kitten, just look at her!"

I had to admit I was enchanted by the little creature. It was so minute, so helpless. Yet it had such an instinct and urge to live. Where did this will and energy for survival come from?

When we went down to Maria we found her cooking our supper. I had the sleeping kitten and told her how hungry the little creature had been. She told me it was a stray and had only appeared three days earlier. No, it wasn't the offspring of her big tabby cat, she didn't know where it had come from. She gave it a handful of dried food (something I thought small kittens shouldn't eat) but I was surprised to see how it gobbled it, making kitten crunching sounds.

The following morning we woke up to the sound of distant cocks crowing, dogs barking, sheep bleating and a donkey braying. Out on our balcony I found my little kitten curled up asleep on a chair.

It was the day for the Idaion Cave.

"So remind me why we're going to this cave?" asked the Stoic as she took a wide berth to pass four black, long-horned cows tethered by four lengthy ropes attached to a farm truck which was being driven at the slow plodding speed of the animals.

"The Idaion Cave is said to be where Zeus grew up amongst the shepherds," I said. I was really looking forward to seeing it, especially as I'd overheard a girl remark when we'd been emerging from the Diktaon Cave that the Diktaon wasn't a patch on the Idaion. The one we were heading for must surely be superlative.

We were soon serpenting our way up through the Idaion mountain range. Here the scenery was of voluminous mountains and valleys which looked as though a pale grey-green Victorian coverlet had been thrown over them, woven with a design of scattered dark green woollen tufts where trees grew.

We suddenly broke through the mountain pass and saw the Nida plateau far below ringed around by mountains. The plateau was a wide, flat stretch of terrain the colour of dark tan suede shoes; the landscape reminded me of the Sinai peninsula where the Israelites had wandered forty years in the wilderness.

Mount Ida, the highest mountain in Crete rising to 2456 metres, had been considered holy in Minoan times. It had also once been wooded. Legend has it that on Mount Ida Zeus had continued to be defended by the Curetes clashing their shields, and had also been surrounded by what were known as the Dactyloi who'd lived in the mountain woods and had been regarded as good spirits.

There was no other car on the road which seemed surprising. We'd come a very long way and had added two days to the journey for the sole purpose of visiting this cave.

We saw in the distance a solitary and dreary stone building, the tourist pavilion mentioned in my guide-book, where refreshments were supposed to be available. It was closed and deserted; there was no vehicle in the car park, and no human being in sight. We were alone.

"Well, here we are," announced the Stoic. "Now we've arrived we'd better get up to this cave. It had better be good!" she warned. Harry's grunt was an even greater warning.

It was mid-morning and getting hot. We put on our sun-hats and carried our water as we began to follow the zigzagging stony path up the mountainside. The few trees that grew gave no shade, and the stony track was flanked by pillow-sized plants like pin cushions with fiercely sharp prickles and tiny pale yellow flowers.

Above us on the mountain we saw a number of goats whose agility had to be admired as they leapt nimbly from rock to rock and nibbled inedible looking thistles and thorns. The lead goat had a large melodious bell around his neck. The flock consisted of silky, long-haired creatures of different colours: tan, black, cream, and some a mix of all three. Goat hair was used for weaving for which the Cretan villagers were famous. I'd read in a book that the wild goats of Mount Ida when struck by poisoned arrows would immediately munch a healing herb growing on the mountain called dictamnon which would miraculously cause the arrows to fall from their bodies, and their wounds to heal.

We came to a small stone-built chapel and found it was unlocked. The interior was sparsely furnished and I lit a candle in honour of the occasion, but was thinking of Zeus whose childhood had been spent here on the mountain.

I remembered that I'd read that on the highest point of Mount Ida, instead of the usual chapel of the Profitis Ilias replacing the customary shrine of Zeus on mountain peaks, there was now a church dedicated to Timios Stavros (the Honoured or Precious Cross). Every 13th September (on the eve of the festival) those who were keen, healthy and strong came from all parts of Crete to climb to the summit, accompanied by a priest. The upward trek took about four to five hours, and they spent the night up there. On the morning of the festival there was a service in the church to celebrate the Exaltation of the Cross. It was the final triumph of Christianity over paganism.

It was something I would have liked to have done, but to get up there, and the lack of creature comforts or any privacy during the night, were things I didn't particularly want to endure, and certainly not something Harry would have put up with.

Now in the small stone-built chapel I said: "I've read that on the eve of the festival of the Exaltation of the Cross on the peak of Mount Ida, true believers – and only true believers, mind you – see the heavens open and a shining cross appear in the night sky."

The Stoic regarded me thoughtfully. "To be a true believer – so difficult. I wonder how many see it?"

We left the chapel and continued on our way up. At one point we turned to look down at the Nida plateau stretching away to the surrounding mountain ranges, and saw a red car draw up beside ours. So we were to have company after all? Down there on the plateau we could also make out what we took to be a thick, dark irregular line imperceptibly moving across the terrain, followed by what appeared to be a dot. Harry raised his binoculars and declared it to be a flock of goats with a small boy taking up the rear.

We continued our climb. I was on the look-out for a tree where, apparently, pilgrims had once hung their votive offerings, but I could see nothing that looked worthy of the word 'tree'.

Another zigzag and we could see the mouth of a low-hung cave. Steel tracks led to its entrance, presumably for the benefit of the archaeologists removing artefacts from the cave. There had been discoveries dating to as early as Minoan times when it had been a place of pilgrimage. Amongst the treasures removed had been terracotta and bronze figurines, tripod cauldrons, ivory objects, fragments of large statues, jewellery and Roman lamps, indicating that the cave had still been of importance at the time of the Romans. There had also been bronze shields. A bronze cymbal depicting Zeus between two Curetes had been a prize find and was now exhibited at the Iraklion Archaeological Museum. I'd seen it myself there. A notice forbidding all flash photography had been prominent in the museum, but I'd very much wanted a photo of it, so had told the young girl attendant that I didn't know whether my camera would flash or not. When I'd taken the photo it had gone off like a blinding light on the road to Damascus. "Sorry," I'd said, and the girl had cautioned me with a look of reproach. The photo had, in fact, been one of my more disastrous, as the metal had reflected the flash a hundredfold, and the result was a featureless round burst of light.

So there we were at the mouth of this cave. There was nothing I could say which could remotely make up for the effort and expense of getting there. There were railway sleepers set at regular intervals down the steep descent inside it to help visitors down the twenty or so feet to what appeared to be an extraordinarily unsafe looking platform consisting of splintered wooden planks. Harry forbade me to go down to it, and I had no wish to plummet through the flimsy looking wood. I could see no exotic stalagmites or stalactites to entice me further than the tenth sleeper. There was no holy 'feel', no sense of wonder. It was merely a rocky cave and a monstrous disappointment.*

I wished I could trigger some thought to stimulate Harry into believing it had all been worthwhile.

But Harry got in first. "I knew it was a gross waste of money coming here," he said with convenient hindsight.

"But what could be more important," said the Stoic soothingly, "than to let your wife find out for herself?"

Harry was in no mood to be soothed. "My wife – " he said (he always began a sentence with 'my wife' when he was displeased) – "My wife has an uncanny knack of making plans without any thought as to whether they are feasible or what extra expense will be involved."

"Oh, I wouldn't say that!" I said defensively.

"My wife," went on Harry revealing controlled exasperation, "never pays the bills."

"And why is that?" I countered. "Because *my husband*," I said with emphasis, "insists on paying them! *My husband*," I continued, "thinks I'm incapable of adding up or subtracting." By now we were ignoring each other and addressing our remarks to the Stoic.

"*My wife* does NOT know how to subtract, only how to add and how to multiply! She knows how to add on the noughts, *my wife* does!" snorted Harry.

"But if he only trusted me to pay the bills, he just might find I would make huge efforts to take off some of the noughts," I countered.

"Oh, I am quite sure *she'd* do that! *She'd* practise every possible deceit to disguise the true facts!"

"As all good financiers do," I said with aplomb. "It's what's known as 'massaging the truth'."

"My dears! all this unseemly talk about money! So vulgar!" declared

---

* Since then I have seen photos of its interior. Its 40 by 50 metres chamber is full of stalactites and stalagmites, mostly beige but some hues of red and blue. I should have looked out for an ancient cult altar at the mouth of the cave cut into the rock but knew nothing of it. Tradition has it that King Minos came as a pilgrim to the cave every nine years to recall the laws of his father Zeus.

the Stoic calmly. "I, personally, have loved this expedition. Just look at the view! Look at those mountains! And look, a cloud!"

It was a small cloud poised above a distant mountain peak, hanging in the air against the blue sky like a silver barrage balloon. Clouds in Crete were a rarity. I thought how Zeus 'the cloud gatherer' (as he'd been known in antiquity) had lost his powers and seemed no longer able to gather them. Cretans now prayed to God for cloud and rain, but God wasn't responding here in Crete. In England they prayed for sun, but God didn't respond much there either.

Four perspiring individuals trudged up towards us along the stony track. They must have arrived in the little red car. We exchanged greetings, but said little – there was nothing we could say to encourage them regarding the cave; we merely nodded and smiled as we passed.

We are on our way back to Iraklion, and Harry is again map-reading; he has quite forgotten his 'my wife' exasperation. We will soon be home and he is looking forward to being able to speak his own language and to understand what those around are saying. We should reach Iraklion by early afternoon in good time for the Stoic's flight first, and ours later that evening.

We've been several hours on the road and now, quite suddenly and unexpectedly, far below in the distance we get a panoramic view of Iraklion spreadeagled around its wide curve of bay, with a flotilla of small white sailing boats speckling the sea.

My mind drifts back to the past few days, to Maria in her kitchen and to my little tabby pussycat with his two pointed ears which looked too big for his head, his little pink nose and round green eyes. Last night, seated out on our balcony, he again curled up on my lap and suck, suck, sucked my finger trying to satisfy his hunger. Purring and sucking he finally fell asleep. At supper when I took him down again to the kitchen, Maria's big tabby cat had decided to teach him a lesson and went in to the attack. Poor little mite squealed and spat and stood his ground. Although so small he showed the greatest will to survive. The will to live is amazing in everything that has been given life. So odd. If you come to think of it, no living creature, human or animal, ever stops drawing breath from the moment of birth till the time of death, and between those two poles of existence they do everything in their power to keep breathing, to keep that pulse of life beating.

After the Idaion Cave débacle, we'd stopped for lunch at Anoyeia.

It was a village which had suffered terribly in World War II. When the Germans suspected villagers to be helping the British officers who'd captured General Kreipe, they'd destroyed the village and every man or boy caught within a mile of it had been shot. Today nobody would guess such atrocities had occurred. The village has been rebuilt, people go about their work, the tavernas are busy, and the shops open for customers. The remarkable thing is that normality ever returns after war and such barbarities.

Good heavens! We are arriving at the airport, and here we have to hand back the car...

It has been a long wait at the airport but at last we are in the air and heading for home. The twinkling lights of Iraklion are things of the past as we fly through the night. Pin-pricks of light far below reveal a ferry-boat on the blackness of the sea. And suddenly, hanging there in the night sky is a pure round, burnished gold full moon.

I draw Harry's attention to it. "A golden guinea of a moon," I say. I actually think it looks like an orange, but I think a golden guinea sounds more romantic than an orange.

We appear to be flying alongside the moon which seems very odd as normally a moon is up above in the sky. But then, I suppose, we ourselves are high in the sky. The moon is telling us how long we've been away. When we flew to Crete it was a horn-of-a-bull moon, and now it's a full moon.

I sit back and begin to make plans. I think a trip to Naxos should come next.

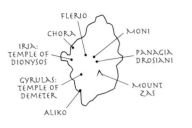

FLERIO

CHORA

MONI

IRIA:
TEMPLE OF
DIONYSOS

PANAGIA
DROSIANI

GYRULAS:
TEMPLE OF
DEMETER

MOUNT
ZAS

ALIKO

2

NAXOS

A ding-dong sounded alerting passengers to pay attention, and a moment later the public address system announced that we would soon be arriving at Naxos, the island to which Theseus and Ariadne eloped after Theseus killed the Minotaur on Crete. I left my seat and went and stood by the railings to get my first glimpse of the island. Houses straggled along the pale sandy shoreline with mountainous hills rising behind. The sun shone, and the sea was a glittering sapphire-blue. We were heading for a promontory, and a moment later we had rounded it and saw the picturesque port with its white flat-roofed houses climbing the hillside to the massive stone-built *kastro* (the Venetian castle) on top. But standing out supremely as the island's major landmark was the Portara, two monumental white marble uprights joined by a lintel, which rose up from the small offshore islet of Palatia beside the port. The word Portara means 'great doorway', and what is seen is all that remains of the building of a temple which was begun in 530 B.C. but never completed.

We went down into the hold where people were preparing to disembark. A repetitive ditty was played on the loud speaker as the ramp was lowered to the quayside with a great clattering of chains. When all was secure for passengers to leave, solemn chords sounded.

We had booked into a small hotel up near the *kastro*, and were met by a strong young man holding up a placard with the name of our hotel on it. He told us we could only get to the hotel on foot, and offered to carry our larger bags.

"Is it true that in England you do not say you walk with the feet, but with the one foot?" he asked pleasantly.

"That's right." I'd never thought about it before.

"Why is that?" he asked. "Why do you walk with the foot and not with the feet?"

"Not with but on foot," I corrected.

"You walk on the foot?" the young man looked puzzled.

"No, you walk on foot," I said, beginning to feel puzzled myself.

"Then I walk on foot and take you," said the man. He turned and started the ascent.

We strained to keep up with him as he corkscrewed up the narrow flagged alleyways, pausing at strategic points as he waited for us to catch up with him. We climbed steps, passed small souvenir shops, grocers, barrows of fruit and vegetables, and on up and up and up. Eventually we came to our hotel where we were welcomed with glasses of iced water.

More climbing of stairs to get to our room, but oh, how worthwhile the climb! From our bedroom balcony we looked out over the white flat-roofed houses to the port and sparkling sea where the ferry-boat we'd arrived on was now taking on fresh passengers and cargo. Best of all from here was a bird's eye view of the marble Portara on its islet which could be reached from the port by way of a long causeway. Scholars believe the temple had been in honour of Apollo because it was aligned with Delos, the tiny island and birthplace of Apollo. Others believe equally that it was intended as a temple of Dionysos. Legend has it that Dionysos, god of wine and drama, ordered Theseus in a dream to leave Naxos because he wanted Ariadne for himself. Since Dionysos is said to have married Ariadne, and was also patron god of Naxos, I felt that a temple dedicated to him in so prominent a place was the more likely. Another legend has it that Theseus (the rat) grew bored with Ariadne and so abandoned her, and Dionysos found her languishing and married her.

We watched the ferry-boat leave port with its new load of passengers. When Theseus obeyed the god's command to leave the island, he'd sailed first to Delos before going on to Athens where his father, King Aegeas, was awaiting his return. His homecoming, however, turned to tragedy. It had been agreed with his father that, if he was successful in killing the Minotaur, he would return with a white sail hoisted, but if he failed, then the boat would return with a black sail as a sign of mourning at his death. But on arrival Theseus forgot to hoist the white sail and King Aegeus, supposing that Theseus had been killed, cast himself off a cliff into the sea and was drowned – hence the name the Aegean Sea. I closed my eyes, enjoying the warmth of the sun on my face.

"I suppose having a god for a lover could be quite something," I murmured. "Dionysos gave her a crown which, when she eventually died, was placed in the heavens and became a constellation – the Corona, I believe. Don't you think that rather nice?"

A grunt was all I got from Harry whose eyes I saw were closed.

Later that afternoon we wandered down through the maze of alleyways to the port. From there we were able to walk along the causeway which connected Naxos with the islet where the huge marble uprights and lintel stood against the skyline. To our right waves crashed on rocks and sent spray into the air and over the concrete walkway.

Once on the islet we followed a well-worn track through low patches of cushiony scrub to the comparatively level area prepared for the never-completed temple. It had been the dream of the tyrant, Lygdamis, at a time when Naxos had been flourishing. He'd wanted to build the highest and the most majestic temple ever, and had begun it in 530 B.C. It had never been completed because war had broken out with the island of Samos. Scattered pieces lay around, such as column drums and marble blocks. From the further side of the great marble doorway you could look through it towards the town climbing the hillside to the *kastro,* framing it like a picture. Several domed churches near the port were within this framework.

We sat down on a rock and I pondered the events which had taken place here millennia ago. I told Harry about Homer's *Hymn to Dionysos* in which the god was captured by pirates who'd spotted him on mainland Greece disguised as a handsome youth and, thinking him the son of a king, had seized and bound him. Much to their consternation the bindings wouldn't hold, and worse still wine began to flood over the deck, a vine grew from the sail heavy with bunches of grapes, and ivy began to twine around the mast. To their absolute horror their captive then turned into a lion and roared at the crew who by now realized the handsome youth must be a god. Eventually they were all so terror-stricken they dived overboard, except for the helmsman whom Dionysos commanded to sail on to this island and he became his priest.

"Of course, the Christians countered Homer's Dionysos god-story with a saint one," I told Harry. "In that the Christian saint was called St. Dionysios and came from Mt. Olympus."

"Oh, yes?"

"The story goes that at Olympus he was sitting idly on a rock one day just like we are now, when he spotted a small plant growing at his feet, and it looked so beautiful that he dug it up. He was on his way to Naxos for some reason, though I don't know why. Anyway, to keep the plant from withering he put it in the leg-bone of a bird – a rather odd thing to do, but never mind. The plant loved this and outgrew the bird's leg-bone, so the saint next placed it in the bone of a lion. Then, outgrowing that, it was finally placed in the bone of an ass. And so it arrived here, and the saint planted it and it bore magnificent bunches of grapes – hence Naxos became famous for its wine not, according to the Church, because of the pagan god of wine, but because of their saint."

We got up and began to walk around the circumference of Palatia, peering down into the peacock blue sea and its submerged slate-grey rocks. Another ferry-boat was sailing into port from the island of Paros which was faintly discernible on the horizon.

"It's strange," I began.

"What's strange?"

"Well, all those bull stories on Crete."

"What about them?"

"Ariadne was the grand-daughter of Zeus who disguised himself as a bull when he wanted to have his wicked way with Europa, and then Ariadne became the wife of Dionysos who was associated with bulls. Well, his followers identified him with the power and fertility of a bull. Don't you think that's interesting?"

"Hum."

"His worshippers would go wild and tear bulls apart with their bare hands, and devour the flesh because they believed they were gaining inner strength from doing it. Imbibing the god," I said. "Rather like taking the sacraments today, I suppose. Gaining strength from it," I added.

"No comparison!"

"I suppose not, since the sacraments are handed to you, and you don't have to fight for them. To be able to catch a bull and tear it to pieces, though! I'd have thought it an impossibility, frankly. You'd have to have supernatural strength and speed to manage it. I've never been able to catch a bull, let alone tear it to shreds. I could barely corner a bullock, but to catch and hold a bull? Impossible!"

But Harry had more imminent matters to be concerned about than bull stories. "Which way for our hotel?" he asked.

"Well, it's upwards, that's all I know."

We started to climb, zigzagged, lost ourselves, enquired, zigzagged further and, after nearly half an hour and ten further enquiries arrived at our destination. More climbing of stairs, and once again we were looking out over roof tops. Lights were coming on in the port, and prominent and serene was the Portara whose marble uprights and lintel gleamed white with a touch of rose pink in the evening light.

It was a fine day and Harry was driving (much to my anxiety), and I was map-reading (much to his). We passed what seemed to be a plantation of bamboo, then fields of baled straw. Gentle hills rose up in the distance.

Amazingly, we reached our destination, the small enclosed sanctuary of Dionysos, not far from the village of Iria. A pleasant young man was pushing a wheelbarrow and appeared to be familiar with the site, and I asked him in Greek what he could tell me about it. I managed to glean that there had been several temples built one after another, the first one being ninth century B.C., and the last fifth century. Apparently, the temple had not been aligned to the east as was normal with temples but towards a nearby river because the river was regarded as a source of energy.

He pointed to a large rectangular area which had several broken columns, one with an Ionic capital. The flooding of the river, I was told, had destroyed the first temple, which was why they'd had to rebuild it. Finally, the last temple had been destroyed by the Christians who'd constructed a church on the site dedicating it to St. George. That too had been destroyed by the river bursting its banks, and had now been rebuilt a mile or so away using the marble from this site.

"Flood damage to the pagan site, and then to the Christian church!" I said to Harry. We were seated in the shade of tamarisk trees where a gentle, cooling breeze fanned us. Here the ground was higher so we were looking down at the slabbed walkway around the temple, with its few white marble column drums rising stark against the grey-green mountainous hill beyond. "You'd have thought whichever god was in power – Dionysos, I suppose, and then the Almighty – would have prevented the destruction of holy places built in their honour. Or, perhaps, they just like to see men bewailing and running about like ants to rebuild temples and churches."

"Well, whatever." Harry was not inclined to give the matter much thought.

For a while we watched the young man trundling his wheelbarrow around, though what exactly he was doing, I wasn't sure. I unscrewed the cap from our bottle of water and took a few sips.

"You remember Cadmus who sowed the dragon's teeth which sprang up as armed men, and all that?" I asked Harry, as we idled and cooled ourselves on the seat.

"What about him?" He took the bottle from me and drank.

"Well, his daughter was Semele. Semele was the mother of Dionysos, which makes Cadmus his grandfather."

"If you say so," said Harry idly.

"But in an odd way Semele was only partly his mother," I went on. "She didn't actually give birth."

"Another weird Greek story?"

"Absolutely. Couldn't be weirder. When Hera, Zeus' long-suffering wife, learned that Zeus was having a fling with Semele, she persuaded her to ask Zeus to reveal himself to her in his full glory as a god. This he did which had the disastrous effect of reducing her to a cinder."

"I remember that part. And old Zoos put the embryo in his leg – "

"Thigh," I corrected.

"Where it remained till the god was ready to be born."

"A son of god, if ever there was one, if you think of it," I added.

"There were hundreds of sons of those old gods," Harry remarked.

"Don't you think it's odd that they had so many, and God only had one?"

"Not at all odd."

"I mean, he could have immaculately conceived lots of sons. He could have peopled the world with sons – and with daughters too, come to that. In that way we'd have no doubt of God's existence because it would be obvious – tangible sons and daughters of God all walking around and giving Sermons on the Mount. Instead, it's said by Christians that God had one Son – though Jews and Moslems say he didn't. They deny that God could ever have a Son. And God himself said that to Muhammad. Amazing. The mind and its imaginings! I mean, why do we imagine there is deity at all? What is in us to even suppose there is a God and, therefore, a Son?"

"No idea."

"It all presumably has to start with Mind and Memory. Without Mind one couldn't possibly think at all. And without Memory one would be quite unable to recall what one has thought in the past, or what others tell you. There would be nothing but the immediate – a day to day dullness. Without Mind there could be no thought for the future, so no planning – just existence. And you can thank old Zeus for that too! He had a fling with Mnemosyne, whose name means 'memory', and the result was the nine Muses responsible for literature, art, history and whatever else that makes life interesting."

"Hm. Are we moving on?"

"Yes, I suppose we have to," I said lazily, moving one foot into the getting up position, then reluctantly the other, before finally standing. More map-reading was required.

I dithered over the road map for some while, then gave Harry directions for the village of Apo Sangri near which was Gyroulas and the sanctuary of Demeter, goddess of corn. Both she and Dionysos were to do with growth, vegetation and fruition.

Demeter's daughter, best known as Persephone, but who is also often referred to as Kore, was the one whom Hades abducted and dragged screaming down to his subterranean kingdom. Some say that Zeus, unknown to Demeter, had given her as bride to Hades. This tragedy occurred at Eleusis on the outskirts of Athens. Poor Demeter, anguished by her daughter's disappearance, searched the world for her. While she sorrowed nothing grew and everything began to wither and perish. With nothing to eat the human race was dying, and the gods themselves were suffering because men had nothing to sacrifice to them – what was the point of gods if there was no one to honour them?

In time Zeus realized he must intervene, and ordered Hades to release Kore to her mother for two thirds of the year, and he could have her for the other third. Demeter was overjoyed to see her daughter once more and everything flourished and was fertile again – a sort of death and resurrection idea.

In one other ancient story concerning the birth of Dionysos it was Kore who'd been impregnated by Zeus and had given birth to Dionysos. This had so angered Hera that she had the child torn limb from limb by the Titans who had then been blasted by the supreme god's lightning. The heart of Dionysos, however, was saved and given by Zeus to Semele to eat, whereupon Dionysos became known as Dionysos the 'twice born'. It was thought to be a story that expressed the dark forces of nature.

The sixth century B.C. temple of Demeter was a conspicuous,

white Naxian marble edifice raised on a platform with several tall columns, some with lintels, rising against a backdrop of distant rounded mountains. Alongside it were two pits that had been dug out and were linked by a channel; they were for the juices of plants which had once been offered to the much earlier agricultural fertility deities. The temple was on the customary west-east orientation, symbolizing the connection between life and death, decay and renewal. The worship of Demeter here had brought together the scattered rural communities of Naxos who were dependent for their survival on the fertility of the land.

The temple had been converted to a Christian basilica in the early years of Christianity, but had then been destroyed by the Moslems in the seventh century. Later, a small stone church had been built to the west of the temple, with an attractive gently arching terra-cotta roof.

We followed the flagged pathway to the museum where there were various statue bases with inscriptions to Demeter, Kore and Zeus. Fourth century dedications showed a close relationship between the cult there and the Eleusian Mysteries on mainland Greece.

We had done more than I'd hoped to achieve that morning, and now more map-reading was required to find our way to our next hotel at Aliko where we planned to stay the next few days.

From the balcony of our new hotel we could see across the hotel complex and swimming pool to sand dunes and blue sea. On the horizon was the hazy outline of Paros.

I didn't like to mention the word 'cave' after our disappointment with the Idaion Cave on Crete, but there was one I was hoping to see. I simplified matters by merely telling Harry that there was a track I wanted to walk along on Mount Zas, "We have to drive to a place called Filoti to do it," I said.

"Where's this Filly place?" Harry had his map open on the balcony table. I pointed out the village to him.

"Well, that shouldn't be too difficult," he said. "Why do you want to go there?" he asked suspiciously.

"Oh, it's just a mountain where Zeus was said to have spent his childhood – or so they like to claim here on Naxos." I pretended to be sceptical.

"Hum. Well, I suppose there's no harm in walking along a track. We have to do what you've come out for."

★⟫

So here we are on Mount Zas walking along a goat-track flanked by low scrubby bushes. The scenery is increasingly spectacular as we make our way upwards alongside a narrowing gorge. Looking back we can see how the gorge opens up to a wide plateau where there are silver-grey olive groves punctured here and there with bottle-green cypresses. A small white building, maybe a chapel, squats amongst them. To the south and west we can see the distant sea and an island. Across the gorge the mountain is rugged with a solitary small tree on its ridge. The crags are pure white marble which gleam when the sun comes out from behind high scudding clouds. Naxos, of course, is famous for its white marble. We can hear the sound of goat bells, and see agile, long-haired goats jumping from one craggy marble rock to another across the gorge.

Thank God I haven't mentioned the cave to Harry. Because he's unaware of it he hasn't fretted or objected to this walk but, oh, dear! the path now suddenly ends in a dense thicket, and there seems to be no way through or around it. I am quite defeated in this my secret aim to reach the cave.

We turn back and I sit on a boulder feeling thwarted and in a stubborn frame of mind. I have to overcome my frustration and decide to enjoy the extreme tranquillity of the scenery. I give myself up to imagining Zeus here as a young god.

"Zeus is said to have grown up on this mountain," I remind Harry.

"Do gods grow up? I always think of them as mature from the start," Harry says.

I give the matter some thought and realize that quite a number of them were never babies, but born fully grown – Aphrodite from the waves, or Athena fully armed from Zeus' head. I've never heard of the goddess Demeter as ever being a baby, nor Hera, nor Poseidon. They were all swallowed at birth by their father, so presumably grew to maturity inside him.

I spot an eagle, equated with Zeus, which I regard as a good omen, though in my thwarted state the omen is pointless. But I look on the bright side and realize this obstructed walk gives me more time for the next place I hope to see that day.

"So where to now?" Harry demands. He is standing leaning on his trekking stick, striking a pose as if ready for action though uncertain which direction to take. We can only go one way, and that is back the way we've come.

"Well –" I begin, but hesitate. I don't want to say what I am hoping to see, so I just say: "I'll take you on a mystery tour."

Unlike many other islands Naxos is well watered with springs and streams, and is very fertile. On our way to my next goal we passed many goats, and several flocks of sheep and cattle. We were driving through the central Tragea region, and I was aiming for the Church of Panagia Drosiani, one of the earliest churches on Naxos, near the village of Moni.

On our way I glimpsed a signpost pointing down a pathway which looked interesting. Harry, who was in control of matters since he was driving, stopped obligingly when I called to him to stop. He backed into a layby, and I saw that the signpost was to Agios Georgios, an eleventh century church.

We walked down a pathway flanked by orchards and a low stone wall. The branches of trees hung over the path offering us their fruit: figs, pears, pomegranates, as well as brambles with blackberries and vines with wizened grapes, possibly intended as sultanas. Scuttling into the crevices between the stones of the wall, or else sunning themselves, were lizards of varying colours from lime green to russet.

We found the tiny eleventh century church closed, but charming in its tranquil setting. Outside in its courtyard were two ancient olive trees, one quite hollow, and the other split wide enough to sit in comfortably.

That church was a small unexpected surprise, but it was the next one which was of greatest interest, being from the sixth century. The Panagia Drosiani was a small hunched grey-stone building with a grey lichen-coloured roof like an old-fashioned beehive with a small window overlooking a round bun-shaped dome topping a rounded stone wall.

Harry was quite taken with it. "Panagia Drosiani," I told him. "Panagia meaning 'All Holy', and 'Drosiani' meaning 'refreshment', or 'dew', or something of the sort."

"A bit peculiar for a name, isn't it?"

"Some say it's because the icon of the Virgin Mary in the church weeps dewy tears whenever the nearby village of Moni is in danger; others that people pray to her in a drought and she brings rain."

We entered this gem of antiquity which had three small chapels and a central dome. Ancient faded-with-age frescoes covered the walls, and in the dome was Christ Pantocrator (Christ the all powerful) with his hand up in blessing. There was a modern altar in the sanctuary, and faint traces of frescoes either side of the apse. On the apse itself was the Virgin Mary.

I shone my torch into nooks and crannies and saw small barred-to-visitor rooms, and an ancient crucifix of Christ whose feet were nailed together in the Roman Catholic manner, the Orthodox Church has the feet of the crucified Christ separate.

On our way back to the car we met a couple of Dutchmen who were the sort of confident young men who were able to get to places others couldn't – the cave on Mount Zas for example. Yes, it had been an easy walk, though the cave itself was hardly worth the effort, they told me. Clearly we had taken a wrong track.

"Cave?" said Harry afterwards. "I didn't know you were aiming for a cave?"

"I didn't know either," I lied.

"Thank God for that!" Harry said.

"Had I known I would have tried to get to it," I added compounding the deceit. The Virgin Mary would surely have shed tears on hearing me.

We sat beneath an oak tree and had a picnic lunch. The oak tree was sacred to Zeus. On the ground were outsize acorn cups about two inches in diameter containing large acorns. I gathered several of them to take home as a memento of our time on Naxos.

"We're now going to see a young man," I said.

"What young man? Who?" Harry demanded.

I told him about the *kouros* of Flerio, a large recumbent figure of a young male figure, a sleeping giant, who had lain in the same spot for over two thousand five hundred years. There were several such *kouroi* on Naxos, and this one was on our way back to Aliko bay by another route.

I gave up on trying to map-read since Harry always double-checked on whatever I said, looking sideways at the map while driving. Instead, I looked at the view, the widening gorge from the village of Moni, the fertile valley and plateau, the pattern of mountains in the distance and the sea beyond. We began to pass hills with marble quarries gouged out of their sides, and saw a great rectangular block of pure white marble ready to be transported to some destination for architectural or sculptural purposes, no doubt.

At last a signpost pointed to the site we were looking for. We followed a path amongst oleanders (it was on private property, but open to the public). And there it was! Just inside an open gateway, lying against a stone wall, was a large archaic, mid-sixth century B.C. figure of a nude male nearly six metres long. I wasn't sure if he was of marble, but visible through the grey grime of centuries were traces of white. One leg was broken off below the thigh which was why maybe it had been left lying where it had fallen. Some believe the figure had been intended to be sculpted into a statue of Apollo, or possibly a statue of Theseus – or Dionysos.

We wandered on to a sanctuary, or rather several small religious sites on a low hill which dated back to the eighth century B.C. A notice-board described how this ancient site had been used by the marble quarry workers for the worship of chthonic deities (subterranean gods). It was miniscule in comparison to the great sanctuary of the goddess Demeter.

Higher up the slope amongst a marble outcrop we came across a diminutive seventh century B.C. rectangular temple, said to be the earliest ever temple made of marble. There was also a great marble block which dominated the site believed to embody the divine power of those deities and heroes who protected the quarry workers. A marble threshold to a new temple with slots cut in it ready for its marble uprights was considered the prototype for later ones, the Portara at Chora being one of them.

We had done all I had planned that day (except the cave), and were soon back at Aliko where the sea sparkled in the late afternoon sun. We walked barefoot along the pale sandy shore. Later we sat out on our balcony with glasses of wine, and watched the glow of the evening light where a few gleaming shreds of cloud hung in the pale amber sky like the hair of Angora goats.

We are back in Chora seated at a taverna in a relaxed post-food state. We have just finished a bottle of wine – and quite right too since this is the island of Dionysos, god of wine. Amongst the plates and glasses are a china salt cellar and pepper pot designed as a man and woman clasped together in an embrace.

With nothing better to do, Harry takes the pepper pot (man) and starts to tap the table with it.

With nothing better to do either, I pick up the salt cellar (woman) and make her dance seductively before the pepper pot.

"Ariadne and Theseus," I say, and Harry smiles silently.

We weave the two pieces around each other, in and out the plates. Ariadne hides behind the empty wine bottle, and Theseus looks for her. For some reason we find this intensely amusing. Dionysos was god of drama as well as wine.

A couple close by are chain smokers and, with every puff, cigarette smoke wafts in our direction which I fan away with my hand. Harry now makes a paper boat out of his table-napkin. He places Theseus on it and draws him to the side of the table. "He's sailing away to – well, wherever he sailed," he remarks. In response I make Ariadne throw herself face down weeping. Salt dribbles from the hole in her head, three pinches of which I promptly throw over my left shoulder for luck.

The man at the next table, who is at that moment the one blowing smoke at us, leans across and says: "It is good to see two older people, shall we say, indulging in their private amusement. It is rare in a married couple. You are husband and wife?"

Harry remains silent because the man, although his English is excellent, is clearly foreign.

"You have visited Naxos before?" the woman asks, but she gives us no time to answer and instead tells us that she and her husband come every year because they have fallen in love with the island.

"You like to travel?" the man asks Harry.

Harry looks to me to answer for him.

"We love the myths and legends of Greece," I say. "There's such drama and tragedy in the Theseus and Ariadne story."

"So many tragic events as a result of human passion," says the wife.

"My wife's a writer!" Harry makes this sudden and unexpected pronouncement.

"Is that so?" the man enquires, drawing deeply on his cigarette and exhaling it in my face. "What is it you write? You write novels?"

"Travel books," I reply. And I tell them of my interest in how Christianity took over from the old pagan gods, and the various subtleties that have been used to make the religious change-over easier for pagans, such as the old gods becoming saints – Dionysos, for example, St. Dionysios – Demeter, St. Demetrios.

"And St. Ariadne," adds the man.

"Really? A St. Ariadne?" I ask.

"She died in 130 A.D. She was a slave girl who refused to accompany her master to a pagan temple on the occasion of his son's birthday. For this she was flogged and scraped with an iron claw," the man says.

"And then she escaped," says his wife, "but they followed her, and she prayed by a rock which opened up to receive her, is that not correct, Otto?" His wife has her head back and blows out another lungful of smoke which, because of a light breeze, immediately engulfs me.

"The name Ariadne," her husband says, "means 'holy'. *Ari-* I would suggest being a cognate of the Greek word *ierós*, 'holy'."

"The great tragedy, of course," the woman adds, "is that Ariadne's mother, Pasiphae, is in love with Poseidon's white bull and gives birth to the Minotaur. Another disaster because of human passion."

"Pasiphae was the daughter of the Sun. Her name means wide-shining," the man remarks.

"Didn't you tell me, Otto, there was a St. Apollo?" The woman asks.

"I did indeed, Renata. His mother and father were very devout and prayed every day to have a son. Then one night they both dreamed that a shining man planted a tree in their house."

"Yes, yes, I remember you telling me. And then St. Apollo was born." She draws deeply on her cigarette, then turns to me. "Please to write your name and the titles of your books." She rummages in her bag and hands me a pen and notepad.

I scribble them down, during which time they stub out their old cigarettes and light new ones and, out of the corner of my eye, I notice Harry picking up Ariadne and placing her back in the embrace of Theseus, then giving her a kindly pat on the head.

The hour is late, and we gather our belongings and say our farewells to the German couple.

We leave them contentedly inhaling deeply, and exhaling together. The smoke wafts up into the air from each of them and entwines above their heads – in my present frame of mind I see it as yet another depiction of Theseus and Ariadne embracing.

We are very happy with Chora and want to explore it more thoroughly. It is amusing winding our way through vaulted alleyways, up steps and around corners where we come across marble plaques and coats of arms above old mansion doorways.

We arrive at the Roman Catholic cathedral in the square before the *kastro*. To my surprise I think the interior is more beautiful than the Greek Orthodox cathedral down near the port. It is baroque and much of it is in white Naxian marble. It has a central pure white dome with arched windows through which bright sunlight floods in, and a barrel-roofed recess containing the altar, behind which is a magnificent ornate gilded and carved icon of the Virgin and Child. Quiet organ music is being played. But I am not here for the Venetian influence, or for Catholicism, but for the pagan past and the Greek Orthodox early Byzantine churches.

We return through the vaulted alleyways, down steps, and find ourselves buying fruit, cheese and bread at a grocer's shop, before returning to our hotel where we picnic up on the flat roof. From here we have a stupendous view over the whitewashed parapet to shades of grey mountains on one side, the Venetian castle behind, and before us the white cubic houses descending to the deep blue sea where a few yachts lie at anchor, and the Blue Star ferry-boat is disgorging its passengers.

And, of course, nearby is the amazing Portara, starkly white against the sea and sky. I can spot a few people wandering about there. I would like to be there too, but I was there early this morning while Harry was still in bed. As ever it was curiously haunting with its ancient legends.

Returning from my visit to Portara I'd heard chanting from a tiny church nearby. It was the Church of Agios Nicholaos, one of the earliest, built over a fourth century one. I'd crept inside and found it charming, entirely whitewashed with a barrel roof. After about five minutes I'd crept away again and came out to a wide levelled area on which were a few scattered marble column drums and capitals. This, according to a notice board, were the finds from a recent archaeological dig. Before the excavations anyone going to the little Church of Agios Nicholaos would have had to have gone down a number of steps to it but, because of the excavations outside, the ground level had been lowered considerably. Nearby on a higher elevation, and approached by wide shallow steps, was the late eighteenth century, brilliantly white Greek Orthodox cathedral with its bell tower of four bells. It also had been built on the site of a much earlier church, the Zoodochos Pigis (the Life-giving Source or Spring).

So here we are with a light breeze fanning us on the rooftop of our hotel, looking down on what was once pagan and now Christian. One religion dies – or, perhaps, I should say it is eclipsed – and

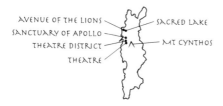

CHAPTER

3

DELOS

The *meltemi,* a persistent north wind, blew strongly, lifting the small boat high on the waves and hurling it down into troughs like a demented elevator. Those who started optimistically on deck were soon drenched by the waves crashing over the bows. Hanging onto rails and girders we staggered below to the warmth of the cabin. In due course the boat steadied as it gained the lee of the land and we returned on deck to savour the moment of arrival.

It was the light that first struck me, a brilliance that overlay the tiny island of Delos set in its turquoise and sapphire sea.

"Light?" said Harry, who never had any sense of the mystique. "In the middle of August in the middle of the day it's what you'd expect in Greece."

It was the dolphins too, symbol of Apollo. A party of French children pointed fingers and cried out repeatedly, *'Voila! Voila! Un dauphin! Un dauphin!'* A member of the crew obligingly hung over the bow railings and banged on the hull to encourage these inquisitive creatures to leap from the waves before arching back into the sea's depths. Dark forms could be seen moving swiftly below the surface of the water.

To me the legends of Delos were exciting; they set the mind alight and brought meaning to everything as the boat headed for the ancient port. The white marble of the ruined temples rose against the mushroom-grey of the island.

According to legend the beautiful Leto, an immortal Titaness, had been loved by Zeus and had become pregnant with twins by him. When Hera, wife of Zeus, learned of it she was furious and forbade the earth to allow Leto to give birth anywhere under the sun. Leto wandered far and wide searching for a place willing to receive her and risk Hera's wrath. Lord Zeus eventually requested help from his brother Poseidon.

Poseidon told Zeus of this small island which until then had been submerged and drifted aimlessly, an island known as *A-delos* meaning 'invisible'. In response to the call for assistance, Poseidon brought the island to the surface and secured it on four columns of diamonds. *A-delos* now became Delos ('visible', 'manifest').

The small island, however, was afraid that Hera would take revenge and kick her back under the sea. It was not until Leto swore an oath on the River Styx (the greatest oath possible to be taken by an immortal) that the god to be born would build a temple on her soil and, in consequence, Delos would become the most revered island in the Hellenic world, that Delos agreed to the birth taking place there.

Leto's promise to make Delos famous throughout the world was kept and for centuries this small island was a centre for pilgrimage. Even today boatloads of enthusiasts come daily so that the authorities ration visitors to a few hours only on the island.

I was helped from the boat by a strong, swarthy seaman and was very conscious that I was now stepping onto hallowed ground.

"Hallowed ground?" queried Harry when I told him what I thought, "It looks more barren than hallowed."

"How sad for you," I said, "that you can only see a barren island with ruins, whereas by using a bit of imagination you'd see colonnades and temples!"

We decided to separate so that Harry could dawdle at the museum whilst I hurried to the north-east of the island. I would then collect him so he could come up Mt. Cynthos with me in the south-east.

I followed a dusty track and headed for the palm tree which could be seen from the sea. It marked the spot where Apollo had been born. I passed a notice which said 'Temple of Poseidon' and duly noted the four remaining columns which rose against the blue sky. On my way I passed the Terrace of the Lions, large sculpted marble beasts squatting on their haunches, their front legs upright and facing east towards the Sacred Lake and rising sun.

Arriving at the palm tree I found it ringed by a low stone wall. The palm tree was close to the Sacred Lake which was now dry. At the time of Apollo's birth the Sacred Lake had been filled with water, fed by the river Inopeus which flowed down Mt. Cynthos, a low mountain in the south-east of the island. Its source was said to have been the Nile, no less.

Leto's confinement had lasted nine days and as her birth pangs had increased she'd clung to the palm tree that grew there. Several goddesses had attended Leto but Hera, continuing her fit of jealousy, had kept Eileithyia, goddess of childbirth, hidden in a cloud on Mt. Olympus – not a difficult thing to do in our experience of Olympus.

Eventually Iris, goddess of the rainbow, had been sent to fetch Eileithyia with a bribe of a gold necklace and they had managed to escape from Hera and get back to Delos in time to help with the immortal birth.

According to Homer's *Hymn to Apollo* when Apollo was born '...all Delos blossomed with gold, as when a hill-top is heavy with woodland flowers, beholding the child of Zeus and Leto...' He was wrapped in swaddling clothes (like Jesus) which were edged with gold and (unlike Jesus) was fed nectar and ambrosia, the food of the gods. But (unlike Jesus again) the swaddling clothes could not contain Apollo and he burst forth from them crying, 'May the harp and the bending bow be my delight, and I shall prophesy to men the unerring will of Zeus.'

There was no time to visit the Stadium and Gymnasium in the far north-east of the island. There the Delian Games had been held, said to have been founded by Theseus. On his way back to Athens, after he'd abandoned Ariadne on Naxos, it is said that he'd sailed to Delos to offer up sacrifice to Apollo, bringing with him a small wooden statue of Aphrodite, goddess of love, a statue which Ariadne had given him, it is said. This statue Theseus dedicated to Apollo, either because he no longer cared for Ariadne or, as the kindly second century A.D. travel-writer, Pausanius, wrote, because he couldn't bear to be reminded constantly of his love for her. In all events he finally married an Amazon queen by whom he had a son, then married Ariadne's sister, Phaedra, who fell in love with her step-son, and everybody died unhappily in typical Greek-tragedy fashion. Whether Ariadne ever had the satisfaction of knowing of the disastrous consequence of her lover's marriage to her sister is not known.

I hurried to find Harry at the museum and together we set off through the archaeological ruins. Apparently here on Delos Theseus and his companions had also invented what was to become known as the Crane dance, a sort of serpentining movement representing the winding passages of the Labyrinth. We now seemed to be performing the same desperate winding action to get out of the maze of ruined houses, shops, temples as we headed south-east towards Mt. Cynthos, the highest point on Delos.

On our way we passed less ruined looking sanctuaries which were in honour of gods imported from Egypt during the days of the

Macedonian kings in the fourth century B.C., a temple of Isis, for example, and a temple of Serapis. Surprisingly there was a temple of Hera. After all she had done to obstruct the birth of Apollo I was surprised she was honoured on this island. Perhaps, though, the inhabitants felt it prudent to appease her wrathful, jealous nature.

We began to climb the stepped path up the steep slope of Mt. Cynthos. The *meltemi* blew relentlessly, cooling the air but battering the senses. Every now and then the full force of it howled around a boulder and threatened to lift us bodily from the mountain.

Near the summit we managed with care, despite the force of the wind, to sit down on a rock. We were now in the location of a temple of Zeus and another of Athena. Whatever had once been up there was by now mostly blown away with only the odd drum of marble remaining.

It was again the light that most struck me about Delos – a wonderful pure, bright lustre over the mushroom-grey of the island with its marble ruins, domed by the blue sky and 'sea-girt' in shades of turquoise and sapphire. The sea was flecked with white crested waves. Here and there a white cruise liner could be seen sailing in, bringing more visitors and fulfilling the oath sworn by Leto that the island's former rocky barrenness would turn to riches as a result of the birth of Apollo.

"You remember Theseus?" I asked

"Do I?" Several years had passed since visiting Crete.

"Well, you know the story of the Minotaur?"

"Oh, that, yes."

"Well, when Theseus set off to Crete to kill the monster, the Athenians vowed that if he was successful they would annually send a sacred embassy to Delos to give thanks to Apollo. Athens kept the vow but whilst the ship was gone, no execution of Athenian prisoners was allowed until its return." And I told Harry how Socrates, who'd been condemned to death for corrupting the minds of young men regarding the gods, had had his execution delayed for this reason.

Whilst waiting, Socrates had remained cheerful and had passed the time in philosophical debate. On hearing that the ship (a *trireme*, a galley rowed with three tiers of oars one above the other) had just docked, the companions of Socrates had been filled with gloom knowing that his death was imminent. They'd visited him in gaol for the last time. Socrates, however, had no fear of death and was almost Christ-like as he prepared to sacrifice his life according to the law of the land. Unlike Christ, however, he spent his last hours in philosophical debate, arguing the case for the immortality of the soul. He believed that all things had their opposite – wet and dry, large and small, happiness and sorrow, life and death; and as all opposites were generated from each other, so there could be no life without death or death without life again.

Rather strangely in a pagan world he'd spoken of God (not the gods) and of the will of God. Man, Socrates claimed, was able to know God because each had in himself something akin to the eternal and immortal. The soul, as distinct from the body, was always scolding, ordering, disciplining the body. It was as well to keep the body as pure as possible for the sake of the soul whose life after death would suffer if during its lifetime the body had indulged its whims and desires.

Socrates believed he was, in death, being cured of the tribulations of life and entering into the purity of immortality. Good metaphysical stuff – the soul could perceive and appreciate goodness and beauty and was eternal. In Socrates' view this was not the complete truth but something close to it and as near to truth as humans could get. When I told Harry this he remarked: "Well, there you are! It's impossible for human minds to grasp the truth so if you're way beyond being able to, don't even try."

Such a dismissal raised my blood pressure. "It'd be really interesting to know what Socrates would have thought of Christianity had it been around in his day," I remarked.

"Hum."

"It's known what the early Christian Fathers thought of him. They said that God was using Socrates to prepare the Greek people for Christianity. Hindsight's an incredibly useful tool to prove a point."

Harry held his peace and purposefully looked at his watch. I saw that time was getting on.

With the *meltemi* relentlessly buffeting us we came cautiously down Mt. Cynthos until we were once again amongst the lower ruins. It was difficult to be sensible whilst blundering around and weaving in and out of marble ruins with one eye on a site-plan blowing in the *meltemi* and the other on my watch.

We wound our way between the remains of ancient houses, the House of the Masks and the House of Dolphins with their wonderful mosaic floors, and then found ourselves at the top of the great amphitheatre. It was impressive with stone-slabbed seats which were not now to be sat on as they had been shaken loose by centuries of natural disasters. A colourful character, a young man in patched baggy trousers, black jacket and straw hat with a long feather sticking out of it, was playing a pipe which was hauntingly beautiful in this setting and the only entertainment to be enjoyed at this theatre. He looked like a shepherd but had no sheep and, in fact, every now and then blew a police whistle to warn visitors to keep away from the tiers of unsecured seats.

He stopped his piping as we firmly sat down on a solid block nearby. I asked him in Greek to continue playing and he went through the usual routine of saying he was only an amateur. But soon he began again and I was enchanted by this attractive character who had been so courteous and who, I suspected, was a student from Athens earning his keep during the vacation.

From the seat looking west we could see the ruins of the Asclepeion (centre of healing on the island) and beyond it the Bay of Fourni and the Delos Straits. Seated at the top of this amphitheatre on Delos it was easy to imagine the *trireme* arriving on its annual mission and sailing into the ancient port. The original games as instituted by Theseus had in time died out until they'd been reintroduced by the Athenians in 426 B.C. The *Delia* (the main festival and games had been held every four years and the *Lesser Delia* every year).

On the arrival of the sacred ship those sent on the embassy from Athens would have gone in procession to the temple of Apollo singing a hymn recounting the story of Leto and the birth of Apollo and his divine sister, Artemis, the virgin goddess of hunting. They intoned chants in honour of Apollo whilst making a solemn tour of the sanctuary of the god. Afterwards they would have sacrificed to Apollo and then the games would have begun consisting of athletics, horse-racing as well as musical contests. The *Geranos*, or sacred Crane dance, was also performed before the altar of Apollo.

"Three hours on Delos just isn't long enough," I pronounced. "I'd really like to come back one day. Or we could miss the boat back?" I suggested.

"And have to pay for new tickets? And probably be fined as well? No fear!" came the voice of wisdom.

I could see there was no chance of persuading him. We showed absolutely no initiative when travelling and kept to whatever rules there were. It was a great bore being so law-abiding.

"Well, we'd better get weaving again," I remarked. "We've still a lot to see."

We continued the Crane dance downwards and north-westwards and came to the House of Dionysos with its wonderful mosaic floor depicting Dionysos seated on a panther. We were in the theatre quarter with houses and shops set back from a street which led from the theatre to the temple of Apollo. Three well-worn marble steps were all that remained of its great marble gateway with Doric columns. We mounted them and stood briefly on the site of the ancient temple of Apollo. It had been here in this temple that the Greek city states, who'd formed what had become known as the Delian League in 478 B.C., had met for discussions. The Delian League had been founded under the leadership of Athens to fight off the Persians and, because of the peculiar sacredness of Delos, the League had chosen the island for its meetings and its treasury.

We just had time to enquire after and find the ruins of a Christian basilica, a fifth century A.D. three-aisled building with two remaining tiered steps of a *synthronon* (semi-circular marble seats behind the altar for the bishop and his elders).

"Isn't it odd that the Christian basilica has gone the same way as the pagan temples?" I remarked. Apparently there had once been a large Christian community under a bishop living on Delos. I supposed they'd wanted to cock a snook at the Olympian gods and throw pagans into a state of religious confusion. For a small island it was surprising that they'd had several churches and even a monastery.

"You'd have thought some wealthy person would have paid for the upkeep of this basilica," I went on.

"You can't expect Christians to set sail in a flotilla of boats every Sunday in order to come to church here," said Harry reasonably. "Once Christianity was established on the mainland they could let these go."

I could see his point. I told him how, though, by the end of the fifth century A.D., route maps had Delos down-graded to A-delos (invisible) again. "Though it was visible enough to be ravaged by pirates," I added.

On the Greek island of Patmos where there is now the great monastery in honour of St. John who was the author of *Revelation,* the last book of the New Testament, it is said that many of the monks had first come as pirates but then had seen the light and become monks. It wasn't like that here on Delos, however; here the pirates looted the early churches and sailed away triumphantly as sinners. Pirates in the Aegean had been a perpetual danger as they knew that the treasures of the churches were worth risking their souls for.

There was no time for loitering, and no time for the museum. I picked a wild flower as we hurried back down to the boat. The captain of our motor launch was shading his eyes and watching out for his last two passengers who were by now running along the dusty track towards him.

I mumbled our apologies and stayed on deck to watch the boat draw away from the island. We had all the time in the world now we were sailing away from Delos. The lustre and sparkle of this solitaire gradually disappeared as the deep blue sea began to toss the boat on the white crested waves. The *meltemi* was relentless. Oooooh! Aaaaah! We staggered to the companionway and went down to the warmth of the cabin, ignoring several passengers who were already feeling seasick.

I took out my notebook and began to scribble. I wanted to get my thoughts down before memory faded and the miracle of recalling the few hours spent on Delos sank without trace and all became *A-delos*.

'It was the light that first struck me...' I wrote.

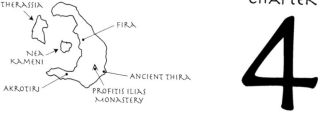

SANTORINI (THIRA)

It was mid-July and this was our first evening in Fira. We were sitting on the terrace watching the sunset. From the terrace – from our bed even – we looked over the sea to two volcanic islands, Therassia, a large one with a sprinkling of white houses along its northern ridge, the other small and round and uninhabited called Nea Kameni.

In the evening light the sea looked a silver-lead colour and as smooth as human skin. A gleaming broad sheen from the sun fanned itself out across the sea's surface. To the right and the left were white houses, and small domed churches linked together by narrow cobbled streets and steps. The higgledy piggledy buildings clung together, jostling for a view of the caldera, and forming an uneven line where they ceased at the point where the volcanic rockface plunged precipitously downwards.

"So where's the caldera?" Harry asked.

"You're looking at it," I replied. "Those islands there were once joined to Santorini by whatever's disappeared – sunk under the sea."

Far below was the small port over seven hundred steps down with its few buildings lining the quayside. Boats, and several two-masted schooners were moored up for the night. To our left an exotic white yacht lay at anchor near an outcrop of volcanic rocks; it had five masts and a line of portholes. Lying offshore was a majestic white luxury cruise liner.

Zigzagging up the cliff face we could see colourful mule trains still making their way up and down to the port carrying a few tourists. Beyond that six cable car capsules sailed through the air descending and ascending. A church bell chimed the hour. It was seven o'clock. Yes, it was hot, but the July heat was tempered by a cooling north-easterly wind, the *meltemi*.

The young man who'd met the mini-bus which had brought us

from the airport, and who'd carried our bags down twenty-seven steps to our hotel, now appeared with our supper laid on a tray. We had one dish between us because we knew from experience that one was more than enough for the two of us.

Trying hard to unravel a bit of Greek from my numbed-after-the-flight brain, I asked about the Profitis Ilias monastery feast-day on the 20th July. The young man looked blank but said he would ask his father in the morning.

"So what about this Atlantis story you were speaking about?" Harry asked, unwrapping his knife and fork from a large white paper napkin.

"Lost island of Atlantis – well – " I gathered my thoughts as I helped myself to chopped tomatoes, olives, onion rings, and barbecued chicken pieces cooked in oil with oregano. "Well, its disappearance was believed to have been the result of a violent volcanic eruption – due to divine displeasure," I added. "That's according to Plato, anyway."

"It just shows you you can't be too careful regarding divinity," said Harry, picking out as many pieces of barbecued chicken as he could find which I thought more than his fair share. "It's just as well to toe the line to deity," he said, looking at me briefly and rather severely over his spectacles which he'd put on to read the menu, and had forgotten to take off. "You never know when divine judgement mightn't pour molten lava on your head," he warned.

I told him how, according to Plato, when the Olympian gods had first come into existence, they'd portioned out their world amongst themselves, and Poseidon had been given the sea together with Atlantis (this island).

"So what caused the divine displeasure?" Harry asked.

"You mean why was Atlantis destroyed? It's the usual old story. When men are in paradise for too long then, like in the Garden of Eden, they become bored. Just think how dull life would be if everything was sweetness and light for ever and a day."

"So what happened?"

"What happened? Well, what first happened when Poseidon got Atlantis, he divided it among his set of five twin sons born of a mortal woman, and each ruled his share with great success – great success meaning that everyone became wealthy, generous and content. 'Truehearted' and 'greathearted' was how Plato put it. But endless comfort and luxury became monotonous, so over the centuries they became less and less 'truehearted' and 'greathearted', in fact they became hopelessly disgruntled and aggressive. Eventually, Poseidon could bear them no longer so, with a flick of the hand, he sank the island and them along with it – well, with a good deal of earth shaking – in fact, he was known as the earth shaker."

"To sink without trace! That makes you think!"

"And the weight of it collapsing into the sea caused a huge tsunami, and that's what is believed to have ended the Minoan civilization in Crete," I said.

"Harry lifted up a few tomato chunks hoping to find another chicken piece. "Ah!" He withdrew a small slither, then held it up. "You have it – the last piece?" His eyes were darting backwards and forwards from his plate to mine.

"No, you have it," I said. Years of married life had taught us both the art of giving and taking, even if taking was more one sided on occasions.

Reading that passage in Plato about Atlantis had almost given me a moment of enlightenment, when in a dialogue somebody described how the gods didn't coerce men like a shepherd or cattleman driving animals in a certain direction with sticks, but guided men like a rudder steers a boat. It was a nice thought that one was personally being steered through life, responding to an unseen hand.

It was getting darker and the sun was aflame as it neared the horizon. Lights were beginning to come on along the crescent curve of Santorini. The distant, spasmodic sparkle from a lighthouse could be seen to our left. The luxury cruise liner was now festooned with tiny fairy lights. A luminous half moon appeared over a roof top behind us. Before us a solitary star glittered above the sombre silhouetted outline of Therassia. It was magical.

This trip was a landmark wedding anniversary present to ourselves. The hotel was in a prime location and we had five whole days to live it up. Harry and I clinked glasses. "To this trip," I said. Harry nodded with a jaunty if slightly guilty air. Years of counting his pennies were difficult to throw off at the toss of a coin, but for once he was happy to let wild extravagance win over prudence.

He held his glass up and the last rays of sunlight shone through the wine sending a rosy glow over his features. "To us," he said. We clinked glasses again and he sank back into his basket chair with a contented sigh.

On the first morning Harry wanted only to bask on our hotel terrace, swim in the pool, read a little, cat-nap, and in general take it easy. His one 'must do' was to visit Akrotiri (known as the Pompeii of the Aegean). He'd become smitten with the thought of looking at the island's prehistoric culture which had been rediscovered after being lost for millennia under layers of volcanic ash and rubble. It had been a historical catastrophe – well, a prehistoric one.

Breakfast came on a tray to our terrace table. We sat out in our dressing-gowns, relishing this unaccustomed lifestyle. Harry buttered some rolls and filled them with cheese and salami – that could be our lunch and supper, he said. He hadn't quite broken with his careful-with-your-money habit.

"I think we should hire a car," I said. "If we're to get to Akrotiri, to ancient Thira, and up to the Profitis Ilias monastery for its feast-day, then a car's the only certain way of getting there and back."

"Organize whatever you like," came the unexpectedly reckless response.

A second cruise liner had anchored offshore during the night and as many as twelve small black and white motor launches were coming from all directions to take passengers off the liner to the port. They looked like voracious insects eager to be first to take the rich pickings from an unexpected washed-up carcass.

I was keen to get close to the action and told Harry I'd like to walk down to the port. I left him reading a book, and made my way to the numerous small shops and alleyways which were already busy and thronged with tourists. The air was full of the chatter of multi-lingual voices. Small shops cheek by jowl sold tourist knick-knacks, and such things as bright scarves, sun-hats, and attractive light-weight, loose garments, or chunky volcanic jewellery. I came to the zigzag pathway leading to the port. It consisted of shallow steps, each one inset with dark lava stones or ash coloured ones, and edged with white marble.

When passing each other the mule trains ascending and descending left little room for anyone on foot, and I often found myself having to shout 'oy!' to get the beasts to leave enough room for me. The farmers in charge of these animals were as strong as their mules and walked ahead or behind with their staffs, their weathered brown faces with fixed expressions of stick-with-it determination. They needed to keep up the tempo while the tourist season lasted. At five euros a go it was a good income. The mules with their colourful trappings, their bells tinkling, responded only to the commands of the strong peasants who owned them. There was a heady whiff and traces of mule dung which had been swept up, though the occasional deposit had to be stepped around. They were well fed beasts and, as far as I could tell, docile and willing.

The port, when I eventually got down, was a hive of activity with continual comings and goings of small craft and tall masted schooners (beautiful wooden vessels) docking to take on passengers to sail the caldera or along the coast to Oia in the far north of the island. They had such names as *Aphrodite* and *Hermes* which triggered visions of the Olympian gods.

Early Greek thought may well have been influenced by the prehistoric geological upheavals on Santorini. When the Olympian gods had begun to filter into the minds of the ancient Greeks, they conjured up the imaginative belief that at first there was only Chaos. In Greek mythology the earth and the heavens created themselves, and in due course Gaea (meaning earth) became personified as the daughter of Chaos and married Ouranos (the heavens) to give birth to the Titans and Cyclopes. One of the Titans, Kronos, (whose name means Time) became the father of Zeus, and Poseidon was another of his sons.

I bought a booklet about Santorini, picked up a brochure on boat trips then, sitting at a taverna on the quayside with a glass of orange juice, I began to read about the island's prehistoric past. It covered a period long before the idea of Chaos and her daughter Gaea and the Olympian gods.

Apparently, millions of years ago there had been no island, only sea and a couple of islets protruding, one of which was the mountain where the Profitis Ilias monastery now stands. About eighty thousand years ago, there'd been a monumental eruption, one so great that ash from it had been found as far away as North Africa and it had darkened the skies for a considerable time. The eruption had spewed out molten lava which had spread and gradually solidified to create the island.

Akrotiri, the newly opened archaeological site, had been a civilization at the height of its powers around two thousand B.C. when another colossal upheaval wiped it out. This was the disaster which became Plato's lost Atlantis story.

I found myself reading an eye-witness account of what must have been a fearful period during our own era, written by a Jesuit priest. He described how the island called Nea Kameni (the one we could see from our hotel) had first made its appearance in 1707; where there'd been only sea, a small protrusion had unexpectedly appeared. Thinking it to be a shipwreck a few men rowed out to investigate then, finding it was a tiny islet, they secured their boat and climbed onto it. Much to their alarm it began to move and tremble under their feet, so they hastily returned to their boat. Over the next days they watched it sink, then rise and swell. '...One day, a huge rock emerged from the very middle of the reef and rose to a height of fifteen metres...In the meantime the sea in the bay had been changing colour ceaselessly: from bright green to reddish and then to a light yellow. An oppressive odour rose from the depths of the water...'

The eye witness continued with his account month by month. Various small islands would appear, join and separate or sink. Smoke was seen rising from one of the new islets. Finally, in July (around the 20th July, the Profitis Ilias feast-day) '...flames were seen to spring from the midst of this smoke...'

As might be expected with the coming of these unexplained hair-raising events, people had turned to prayer. It was not till five years later that the disappearing then the reappearing islets had finally united and become the solid small island now known as Nea Kameni – *kameni* means furnace.

I glanced at the caldera brochure and saw that it was possible to take a boat to Nea Kameni and walk up the cone to the crater before being taken to a cove for a swim in the thermal springs. I left the taverna, and took the cable car back up to tell Harry about it. I found him doing a slow breast-stroke round the swimming-pool, his white legs behind working like a frog's. I told him about the boat trip.

"How much will it co..?" But his question ended in a splutter from a mouthful of water. He continued his slow swim, and then said: "How do you get ticke...?" His chin went under.

He got himself to the side of the pool and clung to the ladder. "I can get the tickets, if you like," I said. "I've also got to organize the car hire."

Harry climbed the ladder and stood dripping.

"Phew! That was good. I'll come with you," he said.

I'd hoped the boat, the Jason, would be a triple masted schooner, but at the quayside was a dull looking boat with an upper deck. It already had a number of passengers on board.

We climbed the ladder to the upper deck from where we enjoyed the view of blue sea, crested wavelets, dark volcanic islands, and the curve of Santorini with its densely packed snow-white buildings climbing the rockface. A few seagulls followed in our wake.

Fifteen minutes later we rounded Nea Kameni and made for a bay whose shores were astonishing. They were a jumbled conglomeration of huge shiny black rocks like coal. The sea here was shades of deep blue, turquoise and aquamarine. Several schooners were already moored up. I held my breath as two strong arms heaved me from the boat which was a yard lower than the quayside, and which was rocking and leaving a wide gap between it and them. I just managed the upward stretch of a leg.

It was midday, very hot with little or no breeze. We began the slow and steady trek, following a well worn pathway of trodden ash-covered black pebbles. We both had water and took frequent sips as we trudged on up passing several shallow craters on either side, on, and on, and on. Harry set the slow pace ahead of me. On, and on, and on, till after about half an hour I began to smell the slightest whiff of sulphur.

When at last we reached the crater, it was nothing more than a wide and deep depression covered with small black rocks, and ash-covered stones. The surprise was to see the blue sea beyond this ridge, and another small island known as Aspronisi, a dirty white lump of rock shaped like a scone, and beyond that the south-westerly crescent curve of Santorini.

In another earlier eye-witness account of an earthquake which had taken place on Santorini in 1650, the tremor had '…made the houses reel hither and thither like babies' cradles and shook them like reeds in the wind. After this tremor, we saw, four miles to the east, between Andros and Santorini, flames wrapped in dense clouds leaping from the sea. A pall of smoke rose on high from the blazing abyss. Then the fiery clouds lowered upon us with a fearsome stench as if the flames were coming from Hell itself…'

We walked around the circumference of the crater, and took another route down. We came across a bearded, stocky man with long, wispy grey hair who was busy with scientific instruments. From him we learned that he was one of several on the island taking continuous soundings and readings of volcanic activity; movements were taking place all the time, he told us, though it hadn't yet reached a level for the authorities to keep visitors away.

Our next port of call was an island called Palia Kameni. There, all who wanted to jumped overboard to swim in the warm thermal springs. Soon heads were bobbing around in the cove. Here the sea was different bands of colour: navy blue, emerald green, olive green, and dirty yellow close to the volcanic-strewn shore. Around the cove were strange deep greeny-brown rocks which appeared to be growing upwards like giant seaweed bushes. A schooner named *Odysseus* rounded the island majestically and moored up nearby. Her passengers also began diving overboard.

A small barrel-roofed chapel stood starkly white in sharp contrast to the seaweed coloured rock. Nearby was a shack where I spotted four tan-coloured goats delicately picking their way over the volcanic boulders. We'd been told there was no wild life on Nea Kameni where we'd just been, though a rat had been spotted there, believed to have come from a boat. And also a rabbit, which suggested there were more hiding out in burrows.

The swimmers came back on board, dripping but triumphant. One said it had been rather like swimming in mud. Soon our boat was plunging its way back through the choppy waves, and Fira came into sight with its white houses huddled together on the rockface in greeting like a welcoming party.

The first morning with our car we drove to ancient Thira, spiralling up the mountainside to the ruins of the fortified town perched some 369 metres above sea level. The ruins were mainly Hellenistic from the fourth to the mid-second century B.C. The Ptolemies of that period (rulers after Alexander the Great's conquest and death) chose this mountain top as a look-out post in order to control the Aegean. A more inconvenient site for controlling anything was difficult to imagine. Yes, it had amazing views over the Aegean to the east, to the south and west, but oh, the wind!

Turning to the north-west, and visible constantly from many parts of Santorini was the Monastery of the Profitis Ilias on the highest peak.

Fortunately we had a site-plan and, though my mind felt numb as we battled against the wind, I was drawn to a tiny double barrel-roofed rough stone building with a rope across its old wooden door.

Harry immediately said it was obviously locked, but I unhooked the rope and the door swung open. Inside was the sweetest simple two-aisled small church with its own *iconostasis*, and darkened apse which had an arrow slit of a window. The building was a third century Byzantine church dedicated to Agios Stefanos (St. Stephen, the first martyr).

We trudged on up to a sacred enclosure (*temenos*) dedicated to Artemidorus, an admiral during the time of the Ptolemies. On a long wall was a large eagle in high relief, sacred to Zeus, together with a lion said to be the symbol of Apollo, and a dolphin symbol of Poseidon. I actually thought the dolphin was the sacred symbol of Apollo, and the lion was identified with Hercules; I had never heard of Apollo and a lion, but who was I to argue with the written word?

We came to a small theatre cut out of the side of the slope, looking out over the Aegean; it had a capacity to seat fifteen hundred spectators and overlooked the sea to the east; a moonlight night and a performance of a drama or comedy written by one of the great fifth century dramatists would have been enchanting on a warm summer's evening.

Further down the mountainside were the unable-to-get-to ruins of the Church of the Annunciation. Continuing on along a stony slabbed pathway we eventually came to the remains of an important temple of Apollo. "Apollo Karneios," I told Harry, reading from the site-plan.

"Why Karneios?"

"Why? Good question. I've no idea." I found out later that there used to be a Spartan harvest festival called the Carnea held around August in honour of Apollo Carneus (protector of flocks) which, no doubt, answered his question as a 'c' in Greek can equally be a 'k'.

According to Herodotus in his *Histories*, in the fifth century B.C. a Spartan named Theras, dissatisfied with his life in Sparta, had sailed to this island and settled here. In Sparta he had held the all-important position of regent while his two nephews, destined to become monarchs, had been minors. Once they'd become old enough for their royal duties Theras, now no longer the ruler, couldn't stand being a subject, so sailed to this island because he'd heard that his forebear, the legendary King Cadmus, had visited it, and had liked it so much that he'd settled some of his kinsmen on it (at the time the island had been known as Kalliste, 'most beautiful'). As soon as Theras arrived he'd been spellbound by its beauty and pronounced himself king, hence the island had been re-named Thira in his honour.

Another Spartan festival had been celebrated up here, the Gymnopaediae, a great July festival with gymnastics, dancing, and hymns sung in honour of Spartan heroes and their gods. Beyond the temple of Apollo Karneios were the Terrace of the Festivals and the Terrace of the Gymnopaediae.

Back-tracking a little we climbed a stony pathway in amongst the ruined houses of the town and reached what little remained of the temple of Apollo Pythios.

"Pythios because of the Python at Delphi?" Harry asked.

"I suppose so," I replied. "Can you imagine living up here? All these narrow streets with the wind hurtling round each corner. What would it have been like in winter?"

"Spartan." was the positive response.

From our high vantage point we could see the Monastery of Profitis Ilias on its even higher level. A dot appeared on the ridge not far from the monastery which then separated to two dots, and then four. They were clearly humans who were slowly heading towards the island's major landmark. Maybe we could do that same walk along the ridge from the Profitis Ilias when we went up there for the celebrations?

We began the slow walk down. "So why is it now called Santorini?" Harry demanded.

"Because of St. Irene," I said promptly. I'd read somewhere that St. Irene, who'd been martyred 303 A.D. in Thessaloniki, had been buried here in Santorini. There were the ruins of a fifth century church, the Basilica of Agia Irini at a place called Perissa on the coast not far from here, but I had no inclination to look for it. It was also thought that it was renamed Santorini because the eleventh century Byzantine Church of Panagia Episcopi had been founded by the emperor of the day whose queen had been named Irene.

"Back to the hotel again?" Harry asked.

The thought was appealing. The following day we would be going to Akrotiri, the highlight of Harry's trip, and we needed to recharge our batteries.

The Akrotiri excavations were in the extreme south-west of the island, about six miles inland. Around 1550 B.C. the people of Akrotiri had attained a highly advanced life style. It was late Minoan and bore signs of Cretan influence, even Egyptian. Some say that it was Crete and Egypt which were influenced by the Akrotirians of Strangyle as it was then called, meaning 'round' – a round island.

Then, at the peak of its sophistication, when the inhabitants had acquired comfort, economic security and remarkable artistic ability (around 1450 B.C.) came the great catastrophe. There'd been a monumental eruption, and the expulsion of lava from the depths of the volcano had been so great that it had created a colossal subterranean void causing a huge area of this round island to collapse in on itself, and the sea to rush in.

At the excavations at Akrotiri we were advised to have a guide because there were no helpful notices to explain things. At ten euros a head I thought it a wild extravagance, but Harry was in spending mode and thought we needed the help of an expert.

We were put in the care of an attractive young woman in flowery cotton trousers. She had long blonde hair and hid her store of knowledge behind a serene countenance. She strolled ahead of us, expecting the half dozen in her group to follow. We entered a vast covered building designed to protect the archaeological site. The temperature, we were told, was kept constant in order to preserve the findings. It was certainly comfortably cool under its vast roof.

We walked above the ruins along decking which surrounded the excavations. There were no human remains found, our blonde beauty told us, which suggested that the inhabitants had managed to flee the island before the disaster. We were shown how this advanced civilization had built two- even three-storey houses, and how they had decorated their walls with frescoes (now to be found only in museums). She showed us photographs of them: two fishermen holding up their catch – boy boxers – a convoy of ships putting out to sea with houses and people on the shore – a young priestess – blue monkeys cavorting – I later learned that blue monkeys had religious symbolism, and were regarded as intermediaries between the world of men and divinity. At Akrotiri one fresco depicted a blue monkey gathering saffron from crocuses and giving it to a seated goddess, though little is known about the Akrotirian religion and no temples have been found there. It is thought, however, that the people were governed by priests, and certainly there had been traces found of animals sacrificed to the gods such as pigs, sheep and goats which only the wealthy could have afforded.

She showed us a fresco of a god with wings – no, it was not a depiction of the Greek Nike, goddess of victory (my suggestion). The winged deity (fresco) had been much earlier than any Nike belief, she said. The image, however, might well have influenced later minds with the idea of wings for the goddess Nike.

We continued on around the site, and she pointed out tall

earthenware jars, some decorated with designs, which stood in an area thought to have been the *agora,* the old market place. On, then, to the ruins of a building which showed their advanced drainage system. The wealthier area was where the frescoes had been found, and where they'd discovered marble stairways.

I was beginning to wilt mentally. Too much information all at once always left me bewildered – I did better with a book to read in my own time, when I could scribble notes and make margin references. Our guide pointed out some large volcanic boulders which had been spewed out of the eruption and still lay where they'd fallen. Tragically the archaeologist who'd masterminded these excavations had been killed in an on-site accident. His grave was to be seen near the ticket office, marked by a large volcanic rock with a white cross painted on it, she told us. To die whilst working on a project seemed to me the ultimate of misfortunes. Ordained by the Fates? Or a chance blow on the head, and just bad luck?

Our guide kept a last photograph for us to look at, it was of a gold ibex which had been abandoned by the fleeing inhabitants. It had been carefully wrapped and put in a box, and was thought to have been left behind in order to appease the gods. The original ibex was now in the Prehistoric Museum in Fira, she told us.

"We'll go to that," Harry said afterwards. "What a site! What a place! That was money well spent!"

We drove down to Akrotiri bay where we sat at a taverna beside the blue, blue sea under the blue, blue sky and had a plate of grilled sardines which Harry declared were vastly preferable to the tinned sardines in oil we got at home. Large motorized vessels were touting for passengers to take them to the white, red and black coves further along the coast. Such things were not on our agenda. We were happy to get back to our hotel, to have a siesta and, if we could bestir ourselves again, wander out to a taverna for supper.

On the other hand, we could just stay on our terrace, order another plate of food, and watch another sunset.

The road was steep up to the Profitis Ilias monastery perched on its mountain top. There was what looked like a half-mile line of cars parked along the roadside leading to the monastery. Clearly there were many people attending the prophet's feast-day. Harry continued driving and was lucky to find a vacant space quite near.

The monastery looked fortress-like, and only a multiple bell-tower betrayed the fact it was a religious institution. It had been founded in 1711 following the 1707 eruptions which had caused the Nea Kameni island to rise up from the sea. Such a visible religious landmark would surely in the future be a reassuring focal point in times of peril when unseen forces filled the islanders with terror.

On many high mountain peaks in Greece, where once were shrines to Zeus, there are now chapels dedicated to the Profitis Ilias (the Prophet Elijah, whose Hebrew name means 'the Lord is my God'). The chapels (in this case monastery), are a reminder to the faithful that it is no longer the supreme god of ancient times but the God of Elijah who is all powerful. High mountain peaks are where the early morning light from the sun first strikes and rain first falls. The fact that Elijah brought a three year drought to an end by his great faith, must also have played a part in his being chosen for mountain peaks in place of Zeus 'the cloud gatherer'.

We entered the monastery through an archway under the bell-tower, and found ourselves in a large courtyard where a throng of people were gathered. From there the monastery looked less forbidding with its several small windows, and arched entranceway to the *katholikon*. Chanting could be heard from the church.

Leaving Harry seated on a stone ledge which ran around the courtyard, I joined the crowds and began slowly to ease my way through till I was inside. The *katholikon* had a certain beauty with its simple architectural features, its frescoes and icons. Incense hung in the air. In the dome high above was a worn fresco of Christ Pantocrator (Christ with his hand raised in blessing). Suspended from the dome was a large twelve-sided perforated brass hanging which portrayed the images of what must have been the twelve disciples. Curiously, each side had an ornamental egg suspended from it and from that a red tassle dangling – did this represent the hatching of Christianity? Within this twelve-sided decorative hanging was an elaborate brass chandelier with lighted candles.

At the Royal Doors (the central doors to the gilded *iconostasis*) a priest was spooning the sacraments to the communicants from a rather beautiful gilded chalice studded with crystals, a gift from one of the tsars of Russia, I was to learn later.

I wanted to scribble down some details of the interior of this church and carefully withdrew my notebook from the central zip compartment of my shoulder-bag. When the liturgy was over, an elderly, long white-bearded bishop appeared at the Royal Doors. He was wearing the Orthodox dome-shaped gold and jewel encrusted mitre, and a white robe with a blue design of flowers and crosses. He stood for a moment with a near-to-death look about him. His crozier with its two long-necked griffin heads turned back on themselves and snarling at each other was, no doubt, a useful prop for this frail looking bishop. He was accompanied by two young black bearded priests in similar white robes, though one had a design of dark red crosses on it. The procession was joined also by a number of black-clad, black-bearded priests in their tall black caps. They filed through the crowds which parted respectfully to make way for them. One priest held up an ornate gold covered Gospels, another a silver reliquary which I later discovered contained the finger of St. Basil the Great, a fourth century bishop who'd studied philosophy in Athens and recommended the art of sophistry. He'd had a great influence on the early church.

Rather unexpectedly, and somewhat strangely, one of the priests left the procession, put an arm up to the inner chandelier and swung it in a circular motion, before doing the same with the twelve-sided outer one. What the symbolism to this action was I never discovered.

I followed the crowds out to the courtyard where the procession headed for the bell-tower. At some stage the bells were rung with joyful multiple clashes. The procession of bishop and priests then returned, and on this occasion one of the priests was holding a wooden *semantron* (a long, flat piece of wood) and was solemnly beating it with a hammer. It is the sound of the *semantron* which summons the monks to prayer.

I joined Harry by the wall. Everyone now was coming away from where a table had been set with food. They carried small perspex boxes of food and small mugs of white wine. This, after all, was the prophet's feast-day and that meant feasting. Harry and I joined in the celebrations and received a hunk of brown bread, a chunk of cheese and three tomatoes each – not forgetting the white wine.

From our seat beside the parapet wall we could see steps near the bell-tower going down to a lower terrace to a small goldfish pond with a wooden trellis where there were seats for silent contemplation. Along the terrace was a paved pathway lined with shrubs, maybe lemon or orange trees. On a lower level beyond this terrace a cock began to crow repeatedly.

We watched a young, black-bearded priest come from the church leading a small child by the hand. There was no conversation between them, just a slow, quiet walk along the courtyard, and down the steps to the goldfish pond, then back again. Was the child an orphan being cared for by the monks?

"I must buy a book about this monastery," I said to Harry.

I looked for my purse which I kept with my notebook and couldn't find it. I examined the other compartments of my bag. It wasn't there. Maybe I'd dropped it when I'd taken out my notebook in the church? But no, it was nowhere to be found.

We reported its loss to a shop assistant, and Harry bought me a book with his money, and said little more on the matter despite my having lost thirty euros. What was money on this our wedding anniversary trip? Somebody would be happy with those euros!

On our way out, near the bell-tower, a nice, honest faced young Greek was selling monastery produce – honey, candles, wine and food. He spoke good English and told us he'd studied for two years in London at the Camberwell School of Art. It turned out that his subject was paper conservation, and he worked on ancient manuscripts in monastery libraries. He had spent some time on Mt Athos, the Holy Mountain, he told us. It is extraordinary learning from strangers what their occupations are; it had never occurred to me that paper needed conserving, or that parchment or vellum might need experts to keep it from disintegrating. I just thought they needed to be kept from mice who could be caught in traps and that was that.

In due course this personable young man watched us sampling three bottles of monastery wine.

"Which wine do you like best?" he asked.

"Oh, I like all three," I said. "Unfortunately, I've just had my purse stolen, so – " I expressed my sorrow at not being able to buy any wine.

His eyes widened in dismay. "Stolen? Here in the monastery?"

In an instant he had disappeared and a moment later he returned with a carrier bag. "You must not leave here with bad thoughts about us," he said. "Please! take this!"

I looked in the carrier bag and saw it contained all three of the bottles of the wine we'd been sampling.

Harry took out his wallet and did the noble thing by offering to pay. But the young man would have none of it. No, he insisted, it was his gift to us and we were to go away feeling happy and with good thoughts.

"I have very good thoughts," I said. "Thank you." And I kissed each bearded cheek to show it.

We left our heavy carrier bag in the car, and found the track on which I'd seen the four dots when at ancient Thira. We began the walk along the precipitous narrow ridge, but only did about thirty yards of it as the steep incline on my left filled me with alarm. The view from it was magnificent, and we watched an aeroplane take off from the airport and curve away to its destination (way below us). Was it on its way to Gatwick? It wasn't long now before we would also be winging our way home.

"Back to the hotel again?" Harry asked, as we got back to the car. "Tonight we can open a bottle of monastery wine and watch another sunset."

What more could I possibly want?

Our last night, and here we are sitting on our terrace. Harry wants to stay where we are and finish off the scraps of food we've accumulated in our fridge over the past few days. I'm trying to resign myself to Harry's wish, but I'm beginning to understand those men in antiquity who became bored with Utopia, and finally stopped being 'true-' and 'great-hearted'. I can see the mule trains still wending their way up and down in the evening light, and I long to ride on one. I am badly out of tune with 'paradise' and inactivity.

I tell Harry I'm off for a walk. I intend to see the view again from another vantage point. There the crescent shape of Santorini can be seen curving around towards the islands, making it clear how once it had been round.

All too soon I've seen this view and retrace my steps. As I return I meet three mules with their muleteer, and two happy tourists being taken to their night's accommodation.

I get back to the hotel where Harry is still watching his sunset. The sun appears to be poised endlesly above the horizon, and not setting at all. I tell him about the mules I've just seen, and am hopelessly ungrown-up about not getting a mule ride. After a little while Harry can stand me no longer in my unrequited state and says: "God! If you won't be satisfied till you've ridden a bloody mule, we'd better get on with it!"

I quickly put on suitable mule-riding trousers and we set off. I hurry ahead of him, fearful that we might already be too late, and! AND! we meet a train of unmounted mules three-quarters of the way up the zigzag path making their way back to their fields or their stables, or wherever mules go to when they're not working.

I manage enough Greek to tell the muleteer that I want to be taken further up Fira. There is a convenient sloping ledge rising from the alleyway which I am able to use as a mounting block; I walk its rising length till I find the right height for getting on my animal. With a lot of shouting between the muleteers and a heave-ho, I'm helped astride the beast. A twang around the rib-cage warns me that the muleteer might have cracked one of my ribs, or else I've pulled a ligament. I hear Harry behind me also getting on his animal. The muleteer then takes the rope attached to my beast and away we go. Oh, how worthwhile this is! How much better to be doing this than sitting stagnantly in paradise!

I have no reins but grip the arched metal piece on the front of the saddle designed for novice riders to hold on to. I'm relishing the rhythmic motion of my mule as it carries me up the shallow steps, sure-footed and docile. The sun is still poised above the horizon, but now I'm appreciating its beauty as it casts its sheen along the silver-grey caldera, the eye of my mule glints as it reflects the light. Pedestrians hold their digital cameras up and flash, flash, flash. I feel like a celebrity.

"This is fantastic!" I call back to Harry. *"Einai polú kalá!"* I tell my muleteer in Greek.

After a hundred yards or so, the flight of steps end and I can see we are approaching an alleyway which will take us away from the town into the countryside. I don't want a long walk back, and say to my muleteer *'arketa tora'* ('enough now'). And somehow I manage to dismount without too much discomfort in the rib area. Harry looks relieved that I have called a halt, and does an expert scissor action to dismount, grimacing as he lands heavily on the cobblestones. But his muleteer holds his arm and prevents him falling. I ask in Greek the name of my mule. "Christos," I am told. "Christos? Hello, Christos!" I ask if they are now going home and am told they are going to their house close by. I stroke the furry forehead of Christos and thank him for the ride. The animal's eyes give nothing away; it is neither pleased nor displeased at fulfilling my dream.

We say our farewells, and the mule train continues on its way with tinkling bells and the muffled sound of numerous hooves.

"That cost ten euros," Harry grumbles. "Five euros each." Having been wildly extravagant over the past few days, he is back to counting his pennies – well, euros.

"Well worth it," I say with elation. My mouth is suddenly very dry, either from riding, fear, or general excitement. I spot a taverna which looks inviting with small round colourful mosaic tables on cast-iron legs, and alabaster lamps shaped like ducks with wrought-iron duck heads. It overlooks the caldera where the sun has at last dipped below the horizon leaving the sea a pewter colour, and the islands as black silhouettes against an amber sky.

"I'm absolutely parched," I say. "I must have something to drink before I pass out," and I lead the way to a table. No one else is at this taverna as yet, and a young, attractive waitress (maybe she's the manageress?) appears with a menu which she hands to me but, fortunately not to Harry. At a glance I see that the cheapest dish is twenty euros. I daren't ask only for a glass of water, so ask if she has tropical fruit juice. She says 'Of course!' (as if I could doubt it in such an establishment). To my surprise Harry is all smiles and tells me he would like a glass of vin rosé. The young woman departs taking with her the menu which is encased in fine leather.

Greek music rises to us from a lower terrace. Below are dimly lit tavernas on various terraces descending the rockface.

"An adventure!" I say to Harry. "This is better than eating scraps from our fridge. Let's have a grand finalé meal here – well, a small finalé," I say, not wanting to overdo this unexpected extravagance.

Our drinks are brought, and Harry raises his glass to me with a silent toast. I suck up my drink through a straw and ask for another – no, I too will have a glass of rosé as well as another tropical fruit juice.

"So what was it like for you on your donkey?" Harry asks.

"Mule," I correct.

"Mule, then."

"His name was Christos, and I enjoyed every minute of it."

"No ill consequences?"

"Not much. A bit of a twinge – I may have cracked a rib, but I wouldn't have missed it for anything."

"A cracked rib? I knew I shouldn't have let you do it!"

"Forget it," I say. "This is a fantastic way to end this trip!"

Our waitress/manageress asks pleasantly if we would like anything to eat. I would love something to eat, I say rashly. Harry doesn't object. From his half-smile I see that he too would like to stay.

Bravely I say to our charming waitress/manageress that we hadn't planned to eat here, but we find it so pleasant and lovely, could we have the smallest something, please – a *tzatziki*, I suggest.

"Of course," she replies with an understanding smile. No doubt she can distinguish between customers who are stinking rich and those who watch their pennies. She goes away, her smiling countenance masking any despairing thoughts regarding our penny-pinching. To have a couple seated at a table is surely better than having nobody, I think. I notice that we are off the tourist beat, much higher up from the many cheap tavernas which are, no doubt, filled to capacity. But, oh, how nice it is up here!

"What photographs did you take in the museum?" Harry now asks, referring to our time spent in the Prehistoric Museum. "I hope you took some of the frescoes?"

"Of course. And the large pots, and the small pots, and the marble bowls, the straining jug, clay oven, bath-tub – you name it, I've taken it."

"And the gold ibex?"

"Yes. That caused a flash so I was chastised by that guide fellow." The guide had been giving a running commentary about each exhibit to a woman just ahead of us. But, as usual, my concentration, as with all museums, had flagged, making me feel dim-witted. One of the first exhibits which had interested me most had been a large lump of grey-black rock displaying fossilized leaves, plants and fish.

Our small dish is brought by a dapper waiter. But it isn't just one small dish, there is a plate of *haloumi* (a flat round goat's cheese which has been fried or grilled and cut into neat triangular pieces). With a flourish the waitress/manageress squeezes a segment of lemon juice over it. She also places on the table a basket of warm crusty bread, and a small container of soft buttery something which has in it a dash of cinnamon or some other spice.

It is all so delicious that in no time, Harry and I have devoured every morsel of food, and have wiped the dishes clean with our crusts of bread. We toast the past, the present and the future. It is a fitting end to this trip.

Other couples begin to drift in and sit down. Their elegant dresses and tailored light-weight suits betray a certain affluence.

"We'd better get our bill, I suppose," Harry says eventually.

It is brought discreetly concealed in a folded leather case, and I retrieve it. What I see makes me gasp. But I put on an air of nonchalance.

"How much?" asks Harry suspiciously.

"Enough," I reply. He grabs the bill, puts on his spectacles, reads it at every angle and hisses: "That's monstrous! Ten euros a glass of wine? It can't possibly be!"

The waitress/manageress comes over quickly, and most charmingly explains each item and how the bill tots up. Harry never likes to argue – well, he never speaks to foreigners – so he now acts the part of one used to such extravagance, and tries to look sophisticated. He takes a wodge of paper money from his wallet, counts them under the table, and places a stack of twenty euros on the table.

The waiter – no doubt, taking his cue from the man at the monastery who'd been shocked that we'd been robbed – hurries over with small glasses of some red concoction in small Y-shaped glasses with a lot of crushed ice on top. It is a gift, he tells us.

"He wants a massive tip, the brute," Harry mutters.

"Something small," I venture. "It's not as if we'll come again."

Harry grudgingly scrounges around in his pockets and finds a few coins. "At least you didn't give that man anything who had his hand out hoping for money yesterday," he remarks, looking at me as though everything at this restaurant is my fault, which it is.

"Oh, him. He wasn't begging, he was holding out his hand to help me down a step," I say.

"He wasn't, he was begging," Harry insists.

"Well, weren't you lucky I thought he wasn't and took his hand to steady myself," I reply.

"Hm."

We say our goodbyes to the waitress/manageress and the waiter, and tell them how lovely, beautiful, etc. everything has been. We smile apologetically because Harry's tip is a disgrace, then quickly slip away into the shadows.

On our walk back to the hotel we see a Japanese bride in a voluptuous bridal gown with her husband of a few hours holding her train clear of the cobblestones and mule dung. I'd seen the bride earlier that morning and at the time she'd been striking a pose against the backdrop of the caldera for a professional photographer who'd arranged her long train in a swoosh around her. Now here she is again with her husband (having seen their first sunset as man and wife). Speaking strictly for myself, after decades of marriage and many sunsets, all I hope for now is to live through the night and wake up in the morning to see the sun rise. That is important if I am to visit other islands.

Samos has a charm all its own. At Vathy where we were staying in the north-east of the island, the whitewashed houses with their terra-cotta roofs climbed the hillside around the crescent bay like spectators in an auditorium. Groups of pine trees broke any monotony, and here and there cypresses were evident in slim shafts of bottle green.

Our hotel was superb with a view to the sea through pine trees. Dotted around the grounds were gigantic terra-cotta pots cascading with geraniums. It was early May and we arrived towards the end of Holy Week – that is the Holy Week of the Greek Orthodox Easter. The sun shone and the weather was balmy, though it was excessively hot by midday.

I'd come to Samos for the great temple of Hera – Hera, goddess of marriage, and of women and fertility. She was the wife of Zeus and, as such, understood the troubles of those who petitioned her with marital problems, having herself suffered from her husband's many infidelities. In those distant years of her worship on Samos the goddess had had a spring festival known as the *hieros gamos* (sacred wedding). It was celebrated annually to commemorate her marriage, and it was believed to be a continuation of an even earlier Mother Goddess spring festival of rejuvenation and fertility that had existed at her sanctuary site.

Because we were told buses were uncertain and infrequent over Easter we hired a car. That first afternoon we explored the east end of the island. The scenery there was of high hills and spring flowers – splashes of yellow broom, and scarlet poppies amongst tall sun-drenched wild grasses. Occasional houses and small churches were dotted about the hills. The blue Aegean and the looming mountains of Turkey in the distance were repeatedly to be seen as part of the scenery.

We visited the Zoodochou Pigis Monastery in its elevated peaceful setting where it stood isolated and invitingly cool with its whitewashed arched cloisters. Inside, the church was dark and ornate, with a decorated *epitaphios* (a representation of the tomb of Christ) placed ready for the Good Friday evening procession. A solitary black-clad nun was seated on a chair before the gilded *iconostasis* keeping silent vigil. From the monastery grounds was a view to the Aegean, and again the looming grey mountains of Turkey.

We drove on and came across an isolated small attractive church where yellow and pink rose bushes were in full bloom before its entrance. We saw the door open and entered. Inside, an overweight, florid-faced priest greeted us. He had long grey hair drawn back in a knot and a thick grey beard and was perspiring profusely.

He knew no English but I understood enough Greek to learn from him that he came annually to the church from Mt. Athos. There he'd been a monk for forty years. That he spoke to me, a woman, was amazing as on Mt. Athos, known as the Holy Mountain, no female presences are allowed – not even cats.

The priest/monk, breathing heavily, went on to tell me that the little church was dedicated to Agios Raphael who, he said, had been seen on the island of Lesbos but had suddenly flown with his great angelic wings to Samos, to the spot where the church now stood.

"Raphael, the archangel?" Harry queried, as we got back into the car.

"That's the one," I said. "He's sometimes called upon for healing."

"That priest looked as though he could do with some healing from the archangel. I was afraid I might have to give him mouth to mouth. I wouldn't want to do that, not with all that beard."

I wagged a cautionary finger at him. I didn't like the thought of making fun of an archangel, nor a priest from the Holy Mountain, for that matter.

That evening we drove down into Vathy for the Good Friday procession of the *epitaphios*. We found a church, parked the car, and joined the waiting throng. We could hear chanting from within. It was a while before the procession emerged, not with pomp and ceremony, but in driblets, little by little. First came men carrying banners, then one holding a tall black cross with three lighted candles perched precariously at either end of the cross-bar and one on top. A minute later there followed a brass processional cross, then young robed acolytes carrying candles. There was no formality as the boys turned to look for relatives or to see the decorated *epitaphios*. The *epitaphios* looked rather like a huge rectangular arched-from-its-four-corners Christmas table-decoration raised over a base scattered with rose petals. It was on two horizontal poles, and carried by four men.

The church bell tolled in mourning. Everyone fell in behind the procession, and followed the *epitaphios* which swayed above the heads of the crowds as it was taken down narrow streets, then along a shopping precinct, till it reached the sea. Here other church bells could be heard tolling and a second *epitaphios* came from another church, this one flanked by soldiers, their rifles in reverse as a sign of mourning.

Chanting was heard from the cathedral close by, and soon yet another *epitaphios* emerged, this one grander than the others. It was accompanied by the bishop of Samos in glistening gold robes and jewel-encrusted mitre. He carried a crozier, and had an impressive long white beard.

"Even better than your Raphael priest," Harry remarked.

After a formal address, prayers and more chanting, the crowds pressed back to allow the bishop and his retinue to walk through. Bells tolled and the three *epitaphioi* together with the bishop moved off down a side street.

"Well, that's that," said Harry. "Now we can go back to bed."

It was easier said than done. We'd been so caught up with the procession that we never noted where we'd left the car. To find the church we'd started from took a lot of calling on saints and archangels, head-scratchings, and enquiries from helpful passers-by who directed us to every church but the right one. When we found ourselves back at the cathedral again, I hailed a taxi and asked the driver to take us to a church somewhere at the top of Vathy where a white car was parked. The driver was very amenable. "A white car beside a church, yes, yes!"

I flopped onto the seat beside him, glad to be sitting. Harry perched on the edge of the seat behind in a state of high anxiety. I didn't regard the problem as serious, just annoying; after all, we knew we'd left the car beside a church, and churches didn't move.

I thought a little Greek conversation would ease the tension, so enquired about tourism on Samos, and whether the island was having the same difficulties as mainland Greece.

"Last year it was bad," said the driver. "This year we hope things will be better." I hoped that by distracting Harry, he would 'lighten up' as they say, so translated what the driver had told me.

"Get better? He's doing all right with us! Keep an eye out for our car, for God's sake!"

"So do you think Greece should get out of Europe?" I asked tentatively.

"I do not think we should get out," the driver said, and he listed all the industrial and technological advantages Germany and France had compared to Greece.

"Of course they want to stay in, they're not fools!" came Harry's retort when I told him.

"So what do you think is the solution?" I enquired.

"We in Greece have things to offer, but what we need is more money to develop what we have to create jobs for the people," came the reply.

I turned to Harry whose eyes were whipping from side to side scanning the streets. "They would like more money," I told him.

"More money? Don't we all? Why else would they want to stay in bloody Europe! Talk of pouring water into a bottomless bu – STOP! STOP!" he yelled.

The driver put his foot on the brake, and the taxi squealed to a standstill. Perhaps he spoke English? There, at any rate, was the church on the right, and our white car parked beside it.

"Let it be a lesson to you," said Harry, as we drove back to our hotel. "Never park the car without noting exactly where you leave it."

I seemed to be the one at fault. But I didn't mind taking the blame. The rejoicings at having found the car had almost made the stress of losing it worth while. "Like feeling well after a high fever," I told Harry.

"Like finding life after death," Harry added.

It was Easter Saturday, the day for the *Heraion,* the first of my three imperatives while we were on Samos.

We walked along the paved and weedy Sacred Way. This Processional Way to the goddess' temple had formerly come from the small and ancient port of Pythagorio, on the south-east of the island. It had been a seven mile walk for her devotees following the coastline. Today the *Heraion* is a vast, overgrown area with a large number of difficult-to-identify ruins amongst wild flowers and tall dried-by-the-sun grasses. The river Imbrasus had once been an important feature of the locality but it had, the caretaker told us, now gone underground.

The worship of the divine Hera had come to Samos when a wave of settlers had arrived around 1050 B.C. They'd come from Argos on the Greek mainland bringing their goddess with them.

The story didn't quite equate with the local belief that Hera had been born here under a chaste tree (*vitex agnus-castus*) whose properties were considered to be a cure for gynaecological problems. And what better tree than that for a goddess concerned with women's welfare and fertility?

"I thought she'd been spewed out by old whoever-it-was who'd swallowed all his children," Harry remarked when I told him about the chaste tree birth.

"Oh, that was another story."

"Which just shows you you can't take the pagan gods seriously."

I wasn't going to argue the matter, such as saying there were conflicting stories about Jesus in the Gospels too. I only knew that once the pagan stories had presumably been taken seriously.

In the earliest days of antiquity it was thought that an image of Hera in the form of a rough wooden board had fallen from heaven to her sanctuary. Her earliest altar had been of limestone and, when sacrifices had been offered up to the goddess, then the wooden image of her had been placed on a stone plinth by her chaste tree. Every year her effigy, or wooden image, would be carried to the sea for purificiation which was believed to restore her youth and virginity.

I told Harry about this.

"Another nonsense story," Harry said, seating himself on a low wall.

"She did the same thing at Argos, do you remember?"

"She did what same thing?"

"Bathed in a spring every year to renew her virginity," I said. "You didn't want to come, so I left you at the hotel and I went off to a convent where the spring is still in operation."

"Did you find it?"

"Yes. A nun showed me where it was. They, of course, don't say anything about goddesses, only the Virgin Mary."

"Did the Virgin Mary have to renew her virginity?" Harry asked.

"No, of course not. But it's interesting that the word virgin is used – Virgin Mary and all that," I said. And I told Harry how it was that here on Samos tradition had it Hera and Zeus had had their wedding, though tradition also had it that he'd first set eyes on her in Argos. "And their honeymoon lasted three hundred years!" I said.

"Three hundred years! No wonder Zoos began looking at other women!"

I regarded him for a moment, but thought better of asking him how many years he thought he'd put up with me without boredom setting in.

Hera, as patroness of women and marriage, hadn't managed her own so well. She'd had only two children: the lame god, Hephaestus, a brilliant metal-worker, and Ares, god of war. The stories of Hera and her family were endless, but they were mostly of her bitter rages when Zeus was having a fling with some new mortal beauty he fancied. But even Zeus on occasion had to defend his wife's virtue. When Hera told him she was being pestered by a certain King Ixion, Zeus, in order to catch the culprit red-handed, turned a cloud into the image of his wife, whereupon King Ixion tried to rape it/her. For punishment Zeus condemned him for eternity by binding him to an ever-revolving wheel.

The last temple of Hera to be built here was on the orders of Polycrates, the sixth century B.C. ruler of Samos. It was to be the largest ever, a wonder of the world. The plan was for double colonnades along the sides and triple ones at each end. All earlier structures were demolished and the river diverted in order to make room for this new temple. The all important chaste tree was kept within the temple precincts beside the altar. This final temple, begun with such hope by Polycrates in the sixth century B.C., was never to be finished. By the third century B.C. it had all but been completed but by then money was running out as the fortunes of the island waned. Nevertheless, pilgrims flocked to the sanctuary, following the Sacred Way which was by then flanked by marble statues and other votive offerings.

Polycrates, known as the 'tyrant' of Samos, was responsible for many astonishing achievements on the island. Hera's temple was one of them, his harbour built at Pythagorio (at that time known as Tigani) was another, and the tunnel of Eupalinus bringing water to the port was a third. We had visited the latter on our way here, an amazing underground arched stone tunnel through which we'd been able to walk for about a hundred metres. It had been dug by two teams of workers each starting at either side of a mountain, digging and shoring up till they'd at last met in the middle – well, they more or less met but were about seven metres out of sinct which had then to be corrected. It had taken ten years. Outside the mouth of this engineering feat I'd read a notice drawing attention to the many oak trees on this south side of the island. It said that the oak trees had been greatly respected as they'd been associated with Zeus and had healing powers. Somewhere in the locality there'd been a sanctuary and altar in honour of Zeus, nothing as spectacular as his wife's but a sanctuary nevertheless – a token one in order not to enflame the jealousy of his wife whose island this was.

I wanted my photograph taken by Hera's chaste tree, a rather modest tree which the word 'chaste' suited. I asked Harry to include the temple's one remaining column if possible. Apparently, that single column was only half the height of the original. Harry obliged and, with the photo opportunity accomplished, I went in search of the ruins of the first Christian basilica which had been deliberately built there in order to extinguish paganism – that wicked false religion!

I homed in on what looked like the wall of an apse; it was all that remained of a rectangular shaped ruin. I supposed it was the early church as it was aligned to the east.

Harry thought otherwise. "That's the Roman baths you're looking at." He pointed to a site-plan he was holding.

"It has to be the apse to the early Byzantine church," I said.

"Look at the plan. See here? It's the Roman baths."

"Oh." What did it matter anyway? It was either the one or the other – or neither.

"If you want to see a Christian ruin there's the remains of a fifth century Christian basilica called Tria Dontia, meaning 'three teeth' because all that remains of it are three projecting buttresses," he said, reading from the leaflet.

But by this time I was feeling numb-headed and didn't care where or what anything was any more. I cast a couldn't-care-less eye around the ruins knowing that I should make an effort to identify two smaller temples which I'd read had been built nearby, a temple of Aphrodite and another of Hermes, the messenger of the gods. But enough was enough, and anyway the caretaker was summoning us as the site was about to close.

We drove to Pythagorio. Soon we were seated at one of the many tavernas beside the port looking at the line of moored up yachts, each one competing with the other as to whose owner was the greater millionnaire.

I was conscious we were in the ancient port of Polycrates. He had built a great breakwater two hundred and sixty metres long and twenty fathoms in depth (which, if the dictionary is right in saying a fathom is six feet, must have been a hundred and twenty feet deep). This mole, or breakwater, was like a long arm stretched out to give protection to ships and million pound yachts from the violent gales. It was due to Polycrates that Samos had become a wealthy and important island, conveniently placed as it was for trade between mainland Greece, Turkey, Italy and Egypt.

The reason for changing the town's name from Tigani to Pythagorio was a comparatively recent idea due to the island's pride in having had the mathematician and mystic, Pythagoras, born on Samos. He'd lived at the time of Polycrates and had, in fact, had to flee the tyrant's wrath, living for a while in a cave high up Mt. Kerkis in the far west of Samos. Some say he'd been accused of corrupting the young with his teachings, others that he'd dared to object to the tyrant's political strategies. I hoped to visit the cave but, because of our calamitous visit to the Idaion Cave in Crete, and our hopeless attempt at Zeus' cave on Naxos, I hadn't yet mentioned it to Harry.

We drove back to Vathy. It was Easter Saturday, and we intended to see the bishop in action at the cathedral on this the night of the Resurrection. It would be another late night. This time we would note well where we left the car.

A well-built young waitress took time off from her work and, still in her apron, had one of the guests out on the flagged floor of the taverna where a young man was playing a bazooki, accompanied by another on a guitar. I always found Greek music exhilerating. Keeping her elbow bent the waitress held the smaller woman's hand up and danced in the Greek manner – foot to the front, to the side and on. She looked as though there were springs under her feet as she danced, passing by the small square tables where diners sat smiling, then back down past an extended table laid with red eggs placed on white plates at each setting, with several vases of roses along its centre. Nobody had yet arrived for what was clearly to be a private party. The foreign looking woman did her fancy footwork falteringly, and tried to keep up with the waitress as she bounded like a rubber ball and moved on with each step.

More diners were arriving when we finally left for the cathedral. There, people were converging from all directions, and Harry and I were lucky to find chairs on the aisle where we could sit and watch. The bishop was seated on a magnificent throne. The interior of the cathedral had multiple shadowed vaults and darkened frescoes lit mysteriously by many heavy multi-bulbed electric chandeliers. The building was full and the *psaltoi* (the men who chanted at revolving lecterns near the *iconostasis*) were in full voice.

At eleven forty-five the bishop appeared at the central Royal Doors. Tonight he wore a red and gold damask robe and a jewel encrusted mitre to match with a small cross on the crown. He chanted for a while, and soon I saw him with the new 'light of the world' consisting of three candles in one hand and two in the other. The congregation surged forward to light their own candles, and with a lot of censing and chanting, he came down the aisle with his crozier and I was able to admire the heavy jowls, hooded eyes and long white beard. He made his way to a platform erected outside and stood facing us where we stood on the steps of the cathedral. *"Christos anestei!"* (Christ is risen!) *"Aleithos anestei!"* (He is risen indeed!) The words were proclaimed and the answers given. Thunder flashes exploded in all directions, fireworks lit the sky, and the church bells peeled clashingly. It was the climax to the Easter celebrations.

Every year the Christian tragedy of the crucifixion is remembered, and the same triumphant words of the Resurrection are repeated. No one attending shouts a denial to what the bishop declares with such conviction. I too shout this customary response: *"Aleithos anestei!"* – It is easy to say. It's the believing that is difficult.

We were on our way to Votsalakia in the far south-west of Samos. We drove first along the northern coast road to Potami. I particularly wanted to go there (it was the second of my three imperatives) because there they had a small eleventh century Byzantine church which was still in its original state. We parked the car in a layby, and walked inland following a shallow, narrow river; it was midday and the numerous trees flanking it cast welcome shade.

A hundred yards or so, and there stood the church tucked in against the rugged rockface at the beginning of a canyon. It was a tiny Byzantine grey-stone building with a grey winkle-shaped roof above a slit window, then below that a small arched window, and below that again an arched entranceway. It was said to have been built on the foundations of an old pagan temple, though in honour of which god or goddess is unknown. Some pastoral deity maybe? Perhaps Aphrodite again? The beauty of the location seemed to suggest her.

We could only admire the simplicity of the interior of this small church: its stone dome and pillars, the whitewashed walls and icons, the marble-topped altar with a gold and silver cross placed centrally on it. Harry then left me in order to climb up steps behind the church to an old castle above.

I sat on a low wall outside the little church in its Arcadian setting. The great god Pan with his Pan-pipes might have passed this way. It was pleasantly warm with the sun casting splashes of light through the branches of the trees from which birds sang. A family arrived. The parents were good-looking and their three teenage daughters were beautiful – the three Graces? The three Graces were the daughters of Zeus and were the personification of beauty, charm, and many other virtues. They were attendants on Aphrodite and had been popular subjects for sculptors in antiquity.

The family climbed the steps up through the trees to seek out the castle. One beauty lagged behind; she wore a short, above-the-knee red dress which hung in folds like a Greek *peplos* gathered in at the waist by a belt. She wore flipflops which looked unsuitable for climbing anywhere, and I could see her reluctance to follow her family. After mounting a dozen steps, she turned and came down again. I didn't speak to her but her presence has stayed with me whenever I think of that rustic setting and the ancient small church.

When Harry returned we walked on along the canyon under tall, shady trees. The canyon widened, and we had to cross several bridges made from pine logs of different dimensions nailed together along which you had to balance. The canyon curved away out of sight, and we saw an intrepid young man in swimming trunks wading through the ice-cold water till he'd disappeared around the bend for what to many was an all important swim in the rock-pool at the base of a cascading waterfall. We were happy to rest on a boulder and let others swim.

The family I'd seen earlier arrived and stood conversing at the bottom of a narrow pine-wood stairway which spiralled almost vertically up to a taverna glimpsed through shrubs and trees clinging to the rockface. The father waited near us while his daughters and wife discussed whether they would climb the ladder-like steps or not.

"You have three beautiful daughters," I told him. "I think of them as the three Graces from classical times," I said.

"Ah, we call them the three Horae," he said with a paternal smile.

"The Horae? Why is that?"

"The three Greek goddesses of the seasons," he said. It is because my daughters are each one born at a different time of the year, one in the winter, one in the spring, and the other in the summer."

It turned out that they were Scandinavian. The decision was taken that they would go up to this taverna, after which two of the daughters would swim. The one in the short red frock had already swum in the rock-pool, the father said, and the water had been very cold. The girl heard her father tell us this and gave us a shy but proud smile which lit up her face, wiping away any of the sullen reluctance I'd seen earlier when she'd refused to climb up to the castle.

We watched them slowly mount the stairway and disappear from view. We stayed there in the cool a little longer, then returned the way we had come. We had the drive to do across the mountains to the coast in the far south-west.

We are seated at a beach taverna which is part of a hotel complex at Votsalakia. From our table we look out over the sea and the wide bay fringed by its pale sandy shore, backed by low, grey mountains. The sun has gone down and it is now twilight. In this darkening scene lights begin to twinkle around the bay. There is a strong wind and, though the sea looks calm, it is ruffled by the wind which causes strange shimmering movements across the surface in constantly changing patterns. I see a fish jump and do a skimming, circular movement before diving back into the deep. I draw Harry's attention to it, but it isn't repeated. There is a stationary boat with two fishermen in it, a silent, peaceful scene. Soon, though, they start the outboard motor and chug away. A pinpoint of a red light winks spasmodically where they've been. We suppose it's a marker for where they've left a net, or maybe a lobster-pot.

The place is very busy with people who have stopped for a break along the southern coastal road. It is a well placed taverna to catch casual visitors, and is also convenient for the hotel guests like us.

After a bottle of Samos wine Harry is relaxed enough for me to tell him about the Cave of Pythagoras which I hope to see.

"The fellow who did the sum of two circles on a whatever?" he asked.

"Not circles. Something to do with a right-angled triangle and something to do with a hypotenuse, whatever that is."

"Oh, yes, I remember. The square of the hypotenuse is equal to the sum of the squares of the other two sides."

I am impressed, and Harry sees I am. "I learned that at school. Everybody learns that!"

"So what's a hypotenuse?" I ask. I am playing for time, waiting for Harry to finish his wine when he will be at his most relaxed.

"Um." He is playing for time too while he casts his mind back to his school days. "I ought to be able to remember. Something to do with an angle – maybe a circle – perhaps an oval. By the way, did I tell you that before we left home I found an egg in a hayrack? The bantams have started laying!" He finished his glass of wine.

"Going back to Pythagoras," I said cautiously, "there's a cave not far from here I'd like to visit where he lived."

"A cave? Another cave?"

"We saw it signposted as we came along. It's not far."

"Why on earth do you want to visit a cave lived in by Pythagoras? You hate mathematics."

"He must have worshipped Hera," I said. "To think that he wasn't a Christian and achieved all the things he did," I went on.

"A hypotenuse! I remember now! It's the long side opposite the right-angle of a triangle!"

"And they thought he was the son of Apollo."

"Son of Apollo? What nonsense!"

"Apollo's priestess at Delphi was known as the Pythia. Pythagoras' mother's name was Pythaïs because Apollo apparently made her pregnant."

"What rot!"

"There's more, if you'd like to hear."

Harry said nothing, and I went on anyway.

"The Oracle then told the chap married to his mother that the child to be born would be noble, full of wisdom and of great benefit to mankind – much like the Angel Gabriel told Mary."

"Do you like this wine? I'd quite like to take a bottle back with me," Harry said.

"Or two bottles," I added, buttering him up. "So you're happy to come to the cave with me tomorrow?" I enquired hopefully.

"Well, it's something to do, I suppose," came the uncertain answer.

The third imperative for this trip was about to be fulfilled.

We were advised to start early and to take plenty of water with us as it would be a long, demanding uphill climb to the cave. This was said to me in Greek and I only translated to Harry the 'take plenty of water' part.

We set out soon after breakfast. The day was fine and warm and Harry was driving which was alarming as he hadn't quite mastered whatever it was that needed mastering, so the car frequently stalled whenever he changed down a gear going uphill. I tried to remain unflappable and said that he needed to give it more revs perhaps. It was only when we were taking a steep hairpin bend beside a precipice and the car stalled causing it to roll backwards, that I yelped and asked to be allowed to walk. Harry said that as the car would be lighter it would make it easier for him. He started the engine, reversed towards the precipice, then turned the wheel hard round to negotiate the bend. This had to be done twice before he got around. I got in again, and we drove on up the mountain road till it became a rough track when we parked the car and had to walk. It was already hot.

There was little shade, only the odd carob tree or fir which cast inadequate short shadows. In this sparse shade we stopped to drink from our water bottles.

There was nobody about, and Harry went ahead, turning occasionally to see I hadn't dehydrated and was still following. I suddenly saw him stop dead in his tracks and look down, pointing with his trekking stick.

"Snake!" he said. I caught up with him and saw the snake lying gracefully like an 'S' in the middle of the track. It was about one and a half feet long, and had attractive zig-zag markings along its back; it was rather beautiful as it lay sunning itself.

We gave it a wide birth and continued on, passing a wooden stall on the way where notices announced honey, oregano and other herbs for sale. We didn't want to buy, but had we wanted to there was nobody to buy from.

The mountain track was airless with not a breath of wind, no light breeze, just heat getting hotter. There was no point in stopping (except to drink), so we just kept walking uphill and on to the next bend; then on up to the next, and the next. Ahead of us the upper slopes of Mt. Kerkis were smothered in the now familiar pillow-sized scrub covered with tiny yellow flowers, making a decorative pattern over its slopes. On our left were stunted trees before they petered out as the grey rocky mountain rose higher against a deep blue sky.

We came at last to a cleft in the mountain where a cool breeze came up from the sea. Here there was a wooden building, a place for refreshments though it was locked up with nobody about.

"So where's this wretched cave?" Harry asked. He scanned the rugged mountainside and then spotted a long whitewashed wall and a small chapel high up the rockface. A second white chapel also clung to the mountainside.

We gave ourselves ten minutes respite before following an arrow indicating a narrow uphill track. I didn't look up, and I didn't look down as we began the climb. We had only one aim, to reach the cave by way of this spiralling rocky pathway.

Pythagoras must have been very fearful of the tyrant Polycrates to have made this mountain cave his hiding place. It wasn't surprising he had only remained there for a short while before taking himself to Croton on the toe of Italy. There he had set up a school and become the leader of a strictly disciplined and ascetic community. Croton was where there'd also been a great temple of Hera, and I wondered whether that was the reason he had chosen that particular location.

His connection with Apollo might have been another reason as it is said that Hera's temple had been founded there on the orders of the Delphic Oracle, in other words by command of Apollo.

We passed the first small whitewashed chapel but didn't stop. On up and around – up and around – "Are we nearly there?"

"Not far now. Another corner."

Plod, plod. Hesitation – trekking stick stuck firmly into a crevice and on up – up and around.

"How much further?"

"Quite near now. Sorry, not yet. Not this bend, it must be around the next."

And then quite suddenly we'd arrived. The long whitewashed wall had a flagged walkway alongside it which led to a small whitewashed chapel at the far end. But on our left were two caves, one with a wide arching mouth, the other smaller and rounder where Pythagoras had once lived and taught while hiding from the tyrant Polycrates.

His father's name had been Mnesarchos. He'd been said by some to have been a gem engraver, and by others a corn merchant. It is also said that it was while Mnesarchos was on business at Delphi that his wife had been impregnated by Apollo. Pythagoras was said to have a golden thigh which was a sure sign of divinity. He also habitually dressed in a white robe and wore a gold wreath on his head.

Fearing dehydration, I finished the last of my water, though I worried also at having no water left.

Pythagoras was described by those who knew him as having a noble air, great charm, and the sort of charisma which attracted people to him. Nearly all his pupils were academics or those from the higher strata of society. He was a stringent ascetic, a vegetarian, a mystic, an astronomer as well as a mathematician. It was Pythagoras who'd discovered that music had mathematical foundations, and that there were perfect intervals to be found in an octave. He detected music and its numerical relationship in the entire universe, hence the music of the spheres.

As a young man Pythagoras travelled widely and had spent many years in the Orient and in Egypt studying the religious beliefs of the countries he visited. I'd read that he'd been taken captive to Babylon where he'd remained for twelve years. There it is said he'd met up with the Old Testament prophets Ezekiel and Daniel and had been greatly influenced by them. The fact that Pythagoras was born around 570 B.C. which was the year of Ezekiel's last encounter with God, makes this claim rather dubious. Daniel, though, was his contemporary and I thought it exciting to think of the two men meeting. Apparently, the 'sum of two squares' discovery had been known to the Babylonians for centuries, and it had been Pythagoras who'd brought it to the west.

Pythagoras believed in reincarnation. He was convinced that in an earlier life he had been a Trojan warrior named Euphorbus (mentioned in Homer's *Iliad*). Euphorbus had been aided in battle by Apollo (another Apollo connection!) It had been due to Apollo's divine intervention that Euphorbus had managed to kill Patroclus, Achilles' greatest friend. Pythagoras' belief that he'd been Euphorbus in a previous life had been reinforced by a visit to the temple of Hera at Argos where he'd recognized his bronze shield when he'd been the Trojan warrior. It had been brought there with many artefacts by the victorious Greeks when they'd returned from Troy.

We entered the first cave with the rounded mouth. Its ceiling and walls were surprisingly black with whitish streaks. I thought it looked volcanic and streaked with white marble. Harry thought it was black from smoke. The cave itself was really quite unremarkable. Harry went in, gave one look around and said: "Is this all?"

On to the next one nearby. This had the wider arched entrance but was also quite unremarkable. It was, however, where Pythagoras had once taught, and it was sixty metres in depth. Fifteen metres into the cave it was blocked by a wire mesh fence with a warning sign not to attempt to go further. This cave had a natural supply of water which was considered to have miraculous healing qualities. Harry made no comment.

I took photos, hoping that I would get inspiration from them when I got home. All that sweat and effort to get up there! Yes, it had superb views from there over the lower slopes to the sea. And, yes, at night, there would be the advantage of gazing up at the heavens and studying the stars; from here the night sky would be stupendous. But, oh, what a slog to get here.

I heard the clang of a bell. Harry, somewhat abashed, came hurrying from the back of the chapel. "God! I didn't expect it to ring!" he said. "I hope people won't come running up." The bell was strung between two branches of an olive tree behind the building.

I didn't think anyone could possibly come running, and said that I thought they'd only come if it rang repeatedly. I got him to stand outside the mouth of the cave beside the chapel so I could take a photo from the mouth of the cave. I thought if I clambered onto a boulder I'd get Harry and a bit of the chapel into the picture. The next instant I was on my back with my legs in the air. It flashed through my mind as I did a slow tumble backwards that if I broke a bone Harry, who didn't speak to foreigners, would have a major calamity.

I picked myself up carefully and was relieved to find only a little finger was hurting. I offered up my usual prayer of gratitude to – to what? Well, to the powers that be.

I left the cave and entered the chapel. Inside it was cool and also unremarkable. I lit a candle and pushed it down into the sand amongst other stubs of candles. I then sat on a chair, glad to be able to rest and cool down. I stared around at the badly faded, smudgy blue, grey and white frescoed walls, and thought I detected the Virgin Mary seated on a donkey. Her head (so faint it was barely noticeable) had a halo, and her eyes were looking directly at me.

Had she then been watching over me? Was that why I'd only twisted a little finger and not compacted my vertebrae, or broken my back? What on earth triggered in the mind a picture of the Virgin Mary in smudges of blue, and smears of grey and white where nothing was really distinguishable?

Pythagoras disciplined his pupils to move gradually from material, tangible things, to the intangible existing beyond bodily things. It was something he believed needed a gradual transition with expert guidance in order to prevent a clash or jarring of the senses as the soul passed from the body and its existence in the material world to the eternal and the spiritual one. St. Paul's blinding flash on the road to Damascus, I supposed, had been just such a clash.

"Do you know," I said to Harry, "there was a St. Paul, a Christian saint from Turkey who came and lived here in Pythagoras' cave?

"When was that?"

"Ninth century. He was known as St. Paul Latrino because he came from Mt. Latrinos in Turkey where he'd lived as a hermit – well, he'd wanted to live as a hermit. But he was so admired for his self-denial and holy life that pilgrims kept flocking to see him. In the end he couldn't bear it any longer and, having heard that Pythagoras had lived in a cave here on Samos, came here."

And I told Harry how St. Paul Latrino had lived for a while below this cave, praying daily to God. One day a nobleman named Theophanis (God appears) was hunting when his dogs began to bark. Theophanis shot arrows into where he supposed there was a wild animal hiding and narrowly missed the saint. The bow then fell from his grasp and the saint was revealed to him on his knees in prayer. Horrified, the nobleman implored the saint's forgiveness. St. Paul Latrino then asked his help to get up to the cave of Pythagoras.

"The nobleman rushed home and brought a ladder," I said. "I can't think how a ladder helped. Anyway, that's the story – a somewhat exaggerated Christian one – quite unbelievable, like some of the pagan stories."

"He got his solitude all right," said Harry, peering over the wall down the rockface to the refreshment pavilion way below.

"And so he lived in peace and prayer," I went on. "But in time his followers discovered his whereabouts and implored him to return. This he did for a short while, but he was so badgered again by pilgrims that he set sail with a few students and returned to Samos. When he pointed out the rugged mountain where they would be living, his students quailed. They wanted to know how on earth they'd reach the cave. The saint told them there'd be a man on shore with horses to welcome them."

"And was there?"

"Of course. The man in question had a dream telling him to harness his horses and go and meet the new arrivals. The saint stayed again for a number of years till again his followers implored him to return to Turkey."

"He was probably quite pleased to get away by then."

"Somebody at some stage was bitten by a snake and the saint miraculously cured him with the water from the cave here. Anyway, he lived on till his death in 896 A.D., returning occasionally to Latros to give spiritual advice and consolation to his followers. And this little chapel here was built in his honour in the eleventh century."

Harry took my hand and looked at my finger. "How is it?" he asked. "Ow!" he said involuntarily when he saw it was swollen and turning a livid blue. "We'd better think about getting down before it gets worse."

It didn't particularly hurt, and it wasn't a part of the hand I used – well, it didn't have to be used. Harry took my elbow preparing to lift me up as though I were a cripple. I took a last look at the faint trace of the Virgin Mary on the smudgy frescoed wall, said a silent 'thank you' again, and went out into the glaring sun. Harry let go of my arm, and I couldn't resist going round to the back of the chapel to give the bell one triumphant ring.

On our way down we looked into the Chapel of St. John – another small and unremarkable building. Tradition has it that St. John the Evangelist also stayed a while on Samos and was the first to bring Christianity to the island. He came from Ephesus where, it is said, he'd taken the Virgin Mary after the crucifixion. He was exiled from Ephesus to nearby Patmos which was within easy reach of Samos. Inside St. John's chapel was a large bottle of water from which I refilled my half-litre bottle. I saw it as a gift from the Virgin Mary, or maybe St. John (I was in holy mode). If I was stealing it from the caretaker I was sorry, but I thought it miraculous.

Back at the wooden pavilion we found a man busily whitewashing the interior. Drinks were now for sale and also what were known as Pythagoras mugs. These were glazed goblets with a ring around the inside which marked the limit of wine recommended for the drinker – a sober amount which demanded discipline. If you filled it beyond the mark then all the wine poured out through a hole at the base of the stem, and you were left with nothing – your punishment for excess. It is said to have been invented by Pythagoras, and we were given printed details on how it worked, though neither of us could really understand it.

I have fulfilled my three imperatives and am now happy to fall in with whatever ideas Harry comes up with. He wants to return to Vathy by another route skirting the central Ampelos mountains. He has a road map open and with a finger points out the return route he intends to take – Marathokampos, Neochori, Pirgos, then out on a limb to Pandroso.

Pandroso turns out to be an attractive village in the foothills of Mt. Ampelos. We have come through valleys and plains of olive groves and vineyards. We are surprised at how few animals we've seen. A couple of goats, and three cows only. There is a dearth of farm stock. But Greece is going through hard times and people can't afford to keep animals that don't pay their way.

We explore the village, walking up through it and passing many houses in a state of dilapidation. It needs property speculators, an injection of money – but what a location with its extensive views!

We are invited to drink coffee with a family seated out on a terrace. The invitation comes when I want to take a photo of a toddler who, I'm told, is called Demetrios, and whose mother is holding him up by his small hands and helping him along with his first steps. The young woman's mother is there, as is her aunt and her grandparents. Four generations living in this house in the back of beyond. It transpires that the young mother is back in the family home because times are too difficult in Athens. Her husband works in Athens and has a reasonably good job, but is never certain he'll get paid. Any pay-packet comes months after it is due. The toddler's mother says they have to re-think their lives. She will grow vegetables, perhaps have a goat. They will live simply, get back to basics. Her husband will come to Samos at weekends when he can. It isn't ideal, but what else can they do?

In ancient times people would beseech the gods and offer sacrifice. In this day and age they pray and hope for a miracle. Things change, they always do. Nothing remains static. If you are a believer and things change for the better you will say God has heard your prayers. If you don't believe, and you don't pray, things change anyway – and if not for the better, then you see to it that you alter what you can till it is for the better.

God helps those who help themselves! I have argued this with Harry frequently. If God helps those who help themselves, I say, then since you've helped yourself why bring God into it? But Harry says I'm looking at it from the wrong end, from the human angle. I should, he says, start from the God end. It's then quite obvious God is there to help those who help themselves.

It is a conundrum. I am, though, aware that life has treated me kindly. And for many people that just isn't the case, whether believers or unbelievers; and whether pagans or Christians, or any other religion.

When we leave this family there are hugs and kisses all round.

Harry is greatly embarrassed by this 'foreign hugging nonsense', but bows stiffly forward, arms hanging down as he is embraced by daughter, mother, aunt and – no, not grandmother. She is sitting preparing vegetables for the family meal, and holds out a hand for him to shake. Unexpectedly, Harry breaks all rules and bends and gives her a quick kiss on her weathered cheek. He is surprised by himself. His gesture though has made all the women scream with pleasure. "See, how he kisses you! You are beautiful to him, my mother!" (All this in Greek so, fortunately, Harry doesn't know what they're saying). "Truly he is an English gentleman! The Mr. Darcy in your English book. We see him on the television!"

And Harry breaks the rules again and speaks to these 'foreigners'. He backs away saying 'thank you' repeatedly as he bows his way out of what has become a horribly embarrassing situation for him.

Soon we are gone.

Goodbye to the family. Goodbye to Samos.

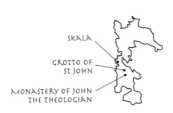

CHAPTER

6

PATMOS

As the hydrofoil shuddered and skimmed the waves heading for several small islands, we at last saw the one crowned by the great crenellated fortress of the Monastery of St. John the Theologian. Surrounding it was a cluster of whitewashed houses known as Chora. Below the hill was the port of Skala.

At one point the sun's rays threw a rainbow ring onto the glass of our hydrofoil which gave the illusion of a halo around the island. A halo was appropriate as it was on Patmos that the Word of God had come to John the Theologian in a cave and *Revelation,* the last book of the New Testament, was written. In it was predicted the imminent end of the world and the coming of Christ to gather up the faithful at the final Day of Judgement. To read *Revelation* is to be caught up in poetic imagery; to comprehend it is another matter.

At the quayside a number of women stood waiting to catch travellers.

"You want room?" We were approached by a well dressed young girl in jacket and jeans and high-heeled shoes; she had dark curly hair swept sideways and wore white-rimmed sun-glasses. Yes, we wanted a room. She was very ingratiating. To all our questions she answered 'Of course!' and 'No problem!'

She pointed to a smart looking hotel at the far end of Skala. How to get to it? "No problem! I have the car, of course!" The price for her room was so low that we felt there had to be some problem. We were driven to her hotel where we were taken along gleaming corridors and shown into a room with every convenience including a balcony from which was a view of the monastery.

"You can walk after dark, no problem! It is safe here on Patmos," she told us. "You take the path there and you find the sea. Food? No problem! There by the sea is a taverna."

That evening we followed the track to the sea. On the way we came to a small whitewashed chapel which stood peacefully with its doors open in the twilight inviting passers-by to enter. In the dark at the back sat a young couple hand-in-hand communing silently with the powers that be. These small chapels are a common sight in Greece; families who have the money build them in gratitude for some good fortune or in memory of a loved one.

We walked down to a bay and stood on the sand and shingle shore watching the wavelets gently caressing it. To one side a long finger of black rock groped its way far into the sea's depth. Patmos was beautiful, a sort of jewel in the Aegean sea, wrought with creeks and coves with the monastery like a precious stone, a dark gleaming pearl, dominating it.

We found the taverna and sat at a table on the terrace under a woven canopy of vines. We were the focal point for cats and kittens who disconcertingly sat mewing around us. It was getting dark and a huge luminous ball appeared low on the horizon from behind a cloud. As it was twilight we were for a moment uncertain whether it was the sun setting or the moon rising. In time we saw it was a full harvest moon. As it rose higher, and we fought with the many cats and kittens as to who would first get the fish off our plates, we watched this moon. At one moment it was hidden behind a volcanic streak of cloud but then slowly, slowly the cloud thinned and it reappeared. I said that I thought it looked like an ancient fresco of the Day of Judgement, with the devils of black cloud being scattered as the light triumphed.

Harry was much less imaginative and said it looked more as if we were in for a spell of bad weather.

"I don't like the thought of coming before God to be judged," I said gloomily. "The idea's alarming."

"Nothing alarming about it if you've nothing to feel guilty about," came the reply.

"And you, I suppose, have nothing you wish you'd never done?"

"That's where repentance comes in," said Harry with a certain smugness.

"I've never heard you repent about anything," I said, rising to the occasion.

"I don't go around baring my soul out loud."

"I'm sure," I said, "you'll go straight to heaven, no problem."

But I was less interested in Harry's welfare after death than the historical facts of where we were now whilst alive.

According to archaeological finds and modern scholarship the island had once had on it many pagan temples. The most predominant had been that of the goddess Artemis (twin sister to Apollo and goddess of hunting, sometimes equated with the moon). Her temple had stood spectacularly where the Monastery of John the Theologian now stands. Coincidently, Ephesus, the city from which St. John had been banished, had also been a centre for the worship of Artemis.

Legend has it that the prayers of John on Patmos brought the columns of a pagan temple – it was said to be a temple of Apollo – tumbling down, killing the priests of Apollo. Such pious tales were useful for helping to win pagans over to the Christian faith. Another claimed that at the time of John's exile to Patmos there had been a magician whose name was Kynops. His forté had been the ability to bring back as apparitions to the bereaved those who had drowned at sea. St. John, however, had gone one better and had brought a newly drowned child back to life. That was powerful stuff. As powerful and persuasive had been the occasion when this same magician went wading out to sea to retrieve yet another apparition but St. John's prayers to the Almighty had caused the poor man to be sucked down and drowned.

It was the limit! a kitten had leapt onto my plate, scattering my food. The waiter apologized and the proprietor's wife came to remove our entourage. She was last seen walking out into the night making high-pitched kitten noises. In an instant our feline friends, recognizing the sound as of a dinner gong, leapt and scampered into the dark after her departing figure.

The next morning we followed an ancient mule track up to the Grotto of St. John, to the cave where the voice of God had been heard. The cave is now incorporated within a monastery halfway up the hill between Skala and Chora. I was as ever pursuing my search for an understanding of the Christian faith and hoping for final enlightenment.

Because we were two lone travellers we were able to ease our way past the crowds of visitors awaiting their turn, each group seemingly surrounded by an invisible chain securing it to a tour-guide. There was room only for one conducted tour at a time inside the Grotto.

Squeezing our way in at the back we heard the guide point to where St. John had laid his head, his pen, his hands in prayer; we saw the arm indicate the triple fissure in the rock from which the voice of God had boomed; the three fissures were symbolic of the Trinity, said the voice.

I had come prepared to feel awe and reverence but my only vision was of human heads, each neck stretched, each ear strained to receive words to fill the mind with credulity.

"Yah-boo?" said Harry when I told him afterwards what I'd thought. "That's really condemning yourself to everlasting hell." But he didn't seem too concerned about it. When later I got indigestion I thought at once it was the wrath of God teaching me a lesson; but it had gone quite quickly and I tried to compose my mind more suitably to the holiness of the island.

A chance second visit to the Grotto found us there when a service was just over and visitors were pouring out of the cave. As the place emptied we made our way in. Only a few monks and a couple of priests were inside conversing quietly in the Grotto. Candles were lit before the icons and wall-paintings and the polished brass glinted.

We sat in the adjoining chapel of St. Anne. The smell of incense hung on the air. From there we could see the spot where St. John had been with his scribe, the faithful Prochoros, who had written *Revelation* at his dictation. I was able to ponder over the Word of God which had poured forth through the triple fissure less than two metres away.

St. John's warning in *Revelation* against 'the Beast' (the emperor) and 'the Harlot' (the Roman Empire) and 'the great Distress' (God's impending judgement) must have alarmed pagans who had at the time been faithful to their 'lifeless idols', If I'd been around then I'd have been scared.

Any such pagan refusing to follow Christ would have been threatened with 'the lake that burns with fire and brimstone, which is the second death.' Before death, though, they could expect to suffer horribly because after the blowing of trumpets, from 'the shaft of the bottomless pit' would come smoke 'Then from the smoke... locusts'. To cut a long story short, those who didn't turn to Christ would be tortured with pain and would regret it for all eternity; those who worshipped the Beast, those who remained pagan would at the time of Judgement be reaped with a great sickle and thrown into the 'great wine-press of the wrath of God...'

Harry said 'not to worry', all such writings were only poetic imagery and shouldn't be taken too seriously. But why was it there in the New Testament if not to be taken seriously? And, if one needn't believe it, was there any reason why one should believe any of it?

We were nearly two thousand years on from when *Revelation* was first written. At the time Christ had been imminently expected to come on clouds of glory to gather up the faithful at the end of the world. But the end of the world hadn't come, neither had Christ. So why was it that people were still in awe and wonder at it? It was all very odd.

My musings in the Grotto were suddenly interrupted by a short but magnificent chant sung by the few monks and priests present. When it was over one of them took from a silver reliquary a human skull bound with silver bands. With great reverence it was passed around and each kissed it. I hoped very much that it wouldn't be handed to me as I'd no wish to kiss a skull. Harry looked studiously in the opposite direction. To the monks this skull was a holy relic of a saint and as such deserved the greatest honour. It was this extra perception which we clearly lacked. Where we saw only a skull they saw something infinitely wonderful and powerful.

We left the Grotto to go on up to the monastery. As Harry had predicted the sky was overcast and the sea was the colour of steel except for the crashing waves along the coastline sending up high fountains of white spume and spray. The weather forecast was terrible. Harry was agitating about getting away in order to be in time for our flight home from Athens. Since it was not for another five days I really thought he was stressing unnecessarily. "Have faith!" I said. But he wasn't convinced.

A bus took us up the coils of road, serpenting up to Chora, to the great Monastery of John the Theologian. As we went higher, the black volcanic looking island spread out below us. Chora was a maze of cobbled, vaulted alleyways and huddled whitewashed houses. The dark fortress walls of the monastery rose from these small prostrate buildings at its feet. It had been founded in 1088 by Osios Christodoulos, a deeply devout monk and ascetic. By diplomacy he'd managed to acquire Patmos in exchange for lands on the island of Kos (an island we had yet to see) and had set to work to create what he'd called a 'workshop of virtue'.

We entered this fortress monastery through a small door and found ourselves in a cobbled and whitewashed cloister with terra-cotta pots of bright flowers. We approached the main church but found that a number of monks were rehearsing some chant. As we didn't like to disturb them we took ourselves to the monastery museum where I found the one thing I particularly wanted to see; it was a marble plaque taken from the temple of Artemis.

The plaque described Patmos as the 'loveliest island of the daughter (Artemis) of Leto which came up from the depth as a resting place of her (Leto's) wanderings'. Patmos too, it seemed, had provided a respite for poor Leto in the days before she'd finally given birth to Apollo and Artemis.

The plaque also mentioned Orestes, son of King Agamemnon, who had sacrificed to Artemis here at her temple in thanks for being rescued from the Furies (winged women who tormented ceaselessly those who'd committed murder). Orestes had been guilty of matricide because he'd avenged his father's death after his mother, Clytemnestra, had murdered him on his return from the Trojan War. Orestes had been tried and acquitted in Athens and the Furies had become well disposed thanks to the wisdom of Athena. It was a nice thought that Orestes had come to the temple of Artemis on Patmos and had prayed and given thanks to the goddess.

The museum was about to close and we had to leave. The monks by now were gathered in the courtyard and we were introduced to a Father Bartholomew who was handing out blue plastic bags of mixed grain, the *kollyva*, the food of the dead. It is symbolic of burial and resurrection and is handed out at memorial services. In fact the custom can be traced back to the time of Homer.

The monk told us that as the next day was the feast-day of Osios Christodoulos there would be a Vigil in his honour that night and, if we liked, we could come. I said we'd be delighted to, though from the look of Harry's fixed and polite smile I could see I was speaking only for myself.

It was late afternoon and we found ourselves seated in Skala, the port of Patmos, with a young Greek who was very earnest. We had just met this young man in a shipping agency where he had come to our assistance over some misunderstanding with the clerk. Much to Harry's consternation it appeared we were marooned on the island because it had no airport, and no amount of Greek or English on my part could change the situation. I was enjoying the novelty of being stuck on this holy island; but Harry was thinking of money and felt quite unholy.

The young man asked us to join him for a drink. He was a personable and likeable character in his mid-thirties and soon we learned that his job was in insurance which took him frequently to London. He told us that he was spending a short time on Patmos to help him get over the death of his mother. He went on to say that over the years he had pondered the great religions of the world before finally returning to Christian Orthodoxy.

He began to speak about the extraordinary phenomenon of consciousness. It was consciousness which made people feel there was an even greater consciousness, an all-consciousness, which was God, he said. I was a believer at once.

This consciousness of each individual was unique; the individual was unique; no matter what nationality you were, no matter what happened to you in life (or when you died) you would never be anything other than the unique 'You'. That was an amazing thought. I had always been 'Me'? Yes, always and would remain 'Me' throughout eternity, he informed me.

He spoke with such earnestness and belief, it was as if the rest of the world ceased to exist as we sat at the quayside taverna in Skala. He was a thickset thirty year old with a lot of body language. Whilst making a point he would raise his shoulders to give emphasis to his words and bend his arms with clenched fists towards his innermost being.

He told us he hoped and prayed he would soon find a wife and have children; this was his dearest wish. No, he would never – could never – become an Orthodox priest (and he was slightly abashed at having to confess this, but he did so most charmingly) because he had not remained celibate and to become a priest he would have to admit to this. Then don't confess, I suggested glibly, and he regarded me with sorrow. He could never live with his conscience if he failed to admit to something of such importance.

He went on to tell us about the Orthodox belief of encircling oneself with the protection of Christ by repeating the words *'Kurios Ihsous Xristos eleison me'* (Christ Jesus have mercy on me). These words formed a spiritual ring of defence about a person in the centre of which was the essential 'You'. The words helped to ward off temptation and evil.

I told this young man that I had great admiration for the music in Orthodox churches and loved the Byzantine chant. How was it that all the priests had the ability to chant? Did they receive special training in this? He replied that some training was necessary but a firm believer would find that his voice came true from within. As he said this his shoulders rose and he bent his arms with his clenched hands towards his breast. What was truly felt within could not come out wrong, he explained.

So much to think about! So much to come to grips with!

Death? At death your soul was taken by St. Michael, he said. You were taken here and there and were shown the bad things and the good things you had done. What? Big panic! It was best to confess all before death because to confess all was to receive forgiveness and you then went to what was called the 'First Rising', which was one step nearer to God.

Fanciful stuff. I was beginning to lose faith again. Why was it that people talked wonderfully at one moment but then went 'over the top' with their ideas and beliefs? I asked him how he could explain that God had chosen the Jews but then seemed to have gone on to choose the Gentiles which rather brutally had confused the issue for the Jews. Without hesitation he said it was because the Jews had got it wrong and were awaiting the anti-Christ, not that he had anything against the Jews but that was the sad fact of the matter.

I wished people wouldn't go 'over the top'. Any faith I'd had was by now gone.

My earnest companion raised his shoulders and bent his arms with clenched fists to his breast once more declaring his conviction that a husband and wife were one body and, therefore, would be united in the next world. I looked at Harry who was smiling benignly. Was he happy at the prospect of having me into life everlasting – wasn't one life of me quite enough for him? 'Over the top stuff again', I suspected.

After an hour's discussion of these weighty matters in this all absorbing conversation, the outside world began to break in on us. Our consciousnesses had been briefly united, but now we looked around and saw other tables occupied by those relaxing over beers, teas, Coca Colas. Boats were bobbing at their moorings along the seafront. The sky was overcast, the sea choppy. A storm was brewing and I could see no ships in harbour. We couldn't get off the island but it was time to move on.

Harry had a 'who-dun-it' which he thought would be infinitely more exciting than any Vigil and was determined to finish it. I was on a spiritual plain and 'why-God-dun-it' was my constant enquiry, so I took myself off alone up to the monastery for the Vigil.

About twenty monks were gathered for the celebration with the Abbot seated on a high-backed throne. He was elderly, dignified, with a long white beard which hung down his chest. I was fascinated by the chanting which came as true from within as could be and was never monotonous; there was always contrast to it as though light and shadow were playing on each other.

I supposed that even if God didn't exist that all this beauty and music was very elevating, bringing one nearer to men's perception of what God should be. What I didn't like was God's anger and threats of vengeance in the Old Testament. Then for God to send a son into the world to have him crucified for us mortals seemed even worse. Why should I take God seriously? Why, actually, did I, come to that? God or no God I loved the poetic wonder of the Orthodox Church and was spiritually 'with it' if mentally 'without it'.

I tried to remain unobtrusive whilst, rather like the family dog wanting the best place before the hearth, crept slowly forward. The church was richly furnished and exquisite. The floor was of inlaid marble and there were several heavy silver multiple-branched candelabra and silver icon lamps. Its major feature was its magnificent carved and gilded ornate *iconostasis* with its seventeenth century icons.

I began to notice the key figures at this celebration. There was an extraordinarily handsome young monk with aristocratic features; tall and graceful in his movements as he passed backwards and forwards in a flowing black pleated gown and black cap with veil. His expression never for a moment revealed anything but total dedication to his many tasks. He kissed a gold stole and reverently placed it around the neck of the Abbot, arranging the long white beard over it.

At the left revolving lectern was another young monk with curly lashes, a good strong chin, small beard and determined rosy pink lips. He was the lead chorister of a group of three and used an index finger to keep time as he moved it from note to note on his open psalter.

I managed to sidle into a seat at the back, the arms of which were carved with griffin heads. From there I watched a monk stand patiently trying to light the many candles on one of the gigantic hanging silver candelabrum. The highest was many feet from the ground and the weight of the taper at the end of the extended holder trembled as he strained to hold it steady. The job completed and the numerous candles were a flickering blaze of light. I was looking forward to seeing all the candelabra lit but soon the one which had been so painstakingly done had all the candles extinguished and the monk again stood for many minutes lighting another. There must have been some symbolism to all this or else it was some penance he was having to endure.

A black bat of a monk approached me and it took only his eye to indicate 'out!'; not a word was needed to persuade me to vacate my seat promptly. He settled himself into it and chanted comfortably behind me.

A book-stand was placed nearby by 'handsome aristocrat' and an elderly monk began a reading. He read rapidly in a very precise high-toned flow, sentence by sentence, following the lines with a finger. I wondered how long it would go on. I still hadn't acquired the art of standing for long stretches at a time when attending an Orthodox service and felt my back was breaking.

An elderly bushy bearded monk on the right had his eyes shut and seemed to be sleeping on his feet like a horse. 'Rapid Reader' suddenly ended his half-hour endurance test but now, oh dear! the monk sleeping on his feet was awake and reading – on and on and on. Fortunately the one whose eye had ordered me from my seat was himself called away and I seized the opportunity to sit again.

I could see very little now except the backs of those standing before me. I could only glimpse between black gowns a small child running forward in dungarees and staring at the chanters.

I was quite pleased that a taxi was coming for me at midnight. Meanwhile, though, high above the altar, there was a small window and the moonlight was so bright it looked as though dawn was breaking. I remembered that the goddess Artemis, on whose temple site this monastery had been built, was identified with the moon. All seemed symbolic tonight.

It was time to leave and I sidled out. In this monastery where all was ordered and holy I sidled everywhere and was as unobtrusive as possible. As I came from the *katholikon* I found an array of solemn faces. These were men and women listening to the relayed service from seats in the arcaded and cobbled courtyard with its surrounding vaulted passageways and narrow stone stairways which led to other parts of this great complex.

I came down to the road and on the way saw fireflies darting about like miniature fireworks. Whilst I waited for the taxi I leaned on a parapet and looked down at the twinkling lights of Skala far below and the sombre density of several small islands out to sea. The moon was high in the sky, but from a bank of black cloud on the horizon I saw constant flashes of sheet lightning and occasional forked lightning and I could hear rumblings of thunder.

These forebodings and boomings served as a reminder of God Almighty whose warnings in *Revelation* were intended to frighten those who heard them into preparing themselves for the imminent end of the world and, if deserving of it, of life everlasting. Equally, on this island, it was a reminder of Zeus, father of Artemis, who reigned supreme over the heavens and punished erring humanity with thunderbolts. In the one men went to heaven or to hell, in the other to the Islands of the Blest or to Tartarus. Was there so much difference?

A few days later we were still marooned. Harry was fretting almost to the point of apoplexy. At the various shipping agencies we were witnessing other unfortunates who had been unable to get out having left it too late.

I tried to soothe Harry's anxieties whilst not betraying my secret enjoyment of being unable to get off this island with which I'd fallen in love.

Marooned as we were we wandered the narrow, vaulted alleyways of Chora and found small concealed whitewashed churches. We sat in the small *plateia* and fortified ourselves with food and exchanged words with other marooned foreigners. Sudden torrential rain caused the alleyways to become small streams, and prompted artists to run for cover clutching their canvases. Athens was having terrible problems with flooding and mud slides, we learned. Nine people had died.

The next day the weather forecast was good. It was almost certain we would be able to leave the next morning. That evening we took a stroll up the hill past the chapel which had been open our first night. We turned right and walked along a promontory and came suddenly to a stupendous view of the bay and the port of Skala.

The port was a cheerful scene now that the storms had passed. Fishing boats set out and there were several motor-launches full of people chugging out of harbour on their way to some celebration, a barbecue perhaps. A rowing-boat set off on some solitary mission; a couple of sailing-boats tacked gently, their sails filled by a light breeze. A speedboat suddenly and noisily scored the water, leaving a white frothy wake; in contrast black ravens quietly flapped by overhead.

Beyond the landmass, shaped like a slim waist, we could see

another bay and stretch of sea. The sun was setting over there. A dark cloud hung midway between the sea and the heavens. As the sun went down it hid behind the cloud sending shafts of light seawards. It looked like a vision of paradise. When I told Harry this he said that in his opinion the sooner I got home to normality and away from this fanciful nonsense the better. "'Red sky at night, shepherd's delight', and thank God for it!" he remarked.

The sun sank below the horizon leaving the bay beyond the slim waist of land an inky blue and the black hills suffused in a golden light. The dark veil of cloud above became a fiery red streak – more 'shepherd's delight', I told Harry who said he very much hoped so.

We walked down to the cove where we'd dined our first night. Tonight the sea was tranquil as it lapped the sand and shingle shore. As we walked back up the track, tall craggy rocks were starkly black against the sky. They were like Indian ink silhouettes painted on the finest pale gold silk.

It grew dark quickly as we strolled back. Beside the track a number of goats had gathered under a solitary roadside light which shed a warm glow around them. A small owl flew down and perched precariously on the wire stretched taut to hold the telegraph pole. The owl gave a screech whereupon a goat snorted contemptuously. A cat came mewing down the track to join us and immediately we had the owl and the pussy-cat scenario.

I realized suddenly that they were all a part of present day consciousness. We were all heading towards the end of our mortal world and everything we said and did had consequences, setting the example to those following on. It was a sobering thought.

PAROS & TINOS

We arrived at Paros on the 14th August, the eve of the festival of the Virgin Mary. As Paros was the proud owner of a miracle-working icon, the island tended to be over-crowded for the occasion and it was important to book accommodation well in advance. I had expected the weather in August to be unbearably hot but, in fact, the *meltemi* helped to cool things down.

Paros is famed for its Church of Ekatondapiliani, dating from the fourth century. The name means either that the church has a hundred doors or, as some have suggested, there are a hundred different ways leading to salvation. The church is one of the most important and best preserved of the earliest churches.

The story is that St. Helena, mother of Constantine the Great, had been on her way to Jerusalem to find the True Cross when a violent storm had forced her boat to seek shelter at Paros. Whilst there Helena had gone into a small chapel to pray. Today the chapel is the Chapel of St. Nicholas on the north side of the large basilica; it is an ancient and beautiful domed building constructed in multi-coloured stone with Doric columns from an earlier pagan temple.

While on the island Helena vowed that if she successfully completed her mission to the Holy Land she would build a large and majestic church here on Paros. As she was to die two years later it had been left to Constantine to fulfill his mother's promise.

I asked a plump adolescent at our hotel reception what he could tell me about the celebrations which would begin that evening. He replied loftily that he knew nothing and with some pride said he took no interest in the church and never went. His indifference startled me, but who was I to pass judgement on sceptics?

When we arrived for the Vigil that evening a beggar woman dressed in black was lying against the outside whitewashed and windowed wall which surrounded the church complex, a shaking arm outstretched for alms. On the orders of a young policeman she got unsteadily to her feet and crept slowly away, a bent black figure against the whitewashed facade to the great church.

Once through the entrance we found ourselves in a large cloistered courtyard with the domed basilica before us. Scattered around the cloisters were marble blocks and column drums, remnants from its pagan past. A tall pine tree was the venue for five church bells whose ropes were being held by a young man who pealed them in bursts of deafening clashes for the Vigil.

Five bearded priests in their black chimney-pot headgear and black robes appeared from an office and with aloof dignity walked with long silver-topped canes to the church entrance. The evening star glittered in the twilight above the terra-cotta tiled dome of the Baptistry.

Many people were present both filling the church as well as the courtyard for the Vigil of the Theotokos. In Greece the Virgin Mary is called Theotokos which, translated, means either 'Mother of God' or 'God-bearer'.

It is interesting how veneration for the Virgin Mary gradually developed. When building his Christian city of Constantinople, the Emperor Constantine had also appeased the pagans by giving prominence to the great goddess Rhea (mother of many of the Olympian gods including Zeus) and Tyche (Fortune). At the same time he instituted Christian ritual and bound it into traditional pagan civic ceremonies which, though not entirely acceptable to Christians, was an advance after three hundred years of struggle to get their faith recognized. Because Constantine honoured Rhea, and gave great honour also to his own mother, Helena, devotion to the Virgin Mary as Theotokos in this city had been a natural development. Unlike Christians pagans had always been very tolerant of new deities in their midst.

What the bishops of the early Church had become wary of, however, was a growing sect called the Collyridians who, in the fourth century, began to worship the Virgin Mary as they would a pagan goddess, and offer up sacrifice to her. This the Church quickly had to stamp out.

It seemed that all of Paros, even my plump adolescent (briefly glimpsed) came that night to the Church of Ekatondapiliani during the hours of the Vigil: believers, non-believers, non-thinkers and the indifferent crowded into the church, whilst many sat in the cloistered courtyard in the cool of the night. The scent of jasmine filled the air.

Harry seated himself outside on a marble block and propped himself against a wall where he proceeded to catnap through the night.

Stone steps outside the church gave access to the gallery inside. People went up and came down in a continuous flow. In the gallery I found several families settling down for the night in the hope of a miraculous cure. Most conspicuous amongst them was a young girl in her twenties who had a complexion like white candle grease, who sat cross-legged with her eyes shut in a state of deep meditation. Beside her was another young woman with dark curly hair who was prostrate on her bed-roll for as long as I was up there. A woman with a club-foot came up to the gallery and shook a mound under a coverlet until it emerged. I expected to see someone chronically ill but instead a burly man sat up with his hair on end. Blue plastic supermarket bags containing food and bottles of mineral water were arrayed beside the invalids or on window-sills.

From the gallery I was able to look down through a haze of incense, past a multiple-armed brass chandelier to where three majestic bishops in glittering Orthodox mitres and several richly clad priests officiated. Everything possible was being done to help bring about a cure for these invalids. I was hoping to see something miraculous take place that night, but didn't like to remain in the gallery for too long for fear of appearing too inquisitive.

Before belief in the Virgin Mary as a divine and compassionate healer the people of Paros had been accustomed to taking themselves to a nearby Asclepeion sanctuary for divine healing. All that remains of the sanctuary today is one small shrine to remind the inhabitants that miracles were once presided over by a pagan god, by Asclepius, son of Apollo.

"Do you know there was a man with no eyes who suddenly had them after spending a night in the great Asclepeion sanctuary at Epidaurus?" I remarked, when Harry was awake from a catnap.

"You don't really believe that?"

"Why not? If you believe Christian miracles why not believe miracles that were done before?"

"Christian miracles were witnessed, that's why," said Harry confidently.

"And you suppose the eye miracle and others weren't witnessed?

"Yes. No. Well, they weren't written about."

"You mean because a pagan miracle was never spread around in a Gospel, that makes it suspect?" I demanded. "Or do you just not want to believe that pagan gods were able to work miracles? In fact there were even raisings-from-the-dead done by the pagan gods. If you give me a moment I might remember who was raised –" But by the time I'd conjured up Alcestis, who'd given her life for her husband, and who'd been led back from Hades by Hercules; and Euridice, the adored wife of Orpheus who was so grief-stricken at her death that the gods arranged for her return except that Orpheus made an irredeemable blunder and she died again; and had remembered Hippolytus who'd been raised from the dead by Asclepius himself, I turned to my beloved spouse and saw he'd fallen victim to another catnap and I was merely talking to myself and those seated nearby were smiling at me.

What time would the procession begin, I enquired on several occasions as the evening wore on? Confidently the reply came: nine-thirty – ten-thirty – midnight – . I had little faith in Greek information; experience was teaching me to be cautious. If someone said such-and-such a time it invariably meant some other time. If somebody tried to be helpful by writing down the name of the ferry-boat we were to travel on then we should put our trust in the time not the name or, alternatively, in the name not the time. Such things were there for the inconvenience of the traveller but were well meant. If you missed the boat or failed to see the purpose of your visit, well, what did it really matter? Northern Europeans took life too seriously. Promptness was a harassment and not to be encouraged in Greece. Trying to find out the time of the procession I discovered to be a hopeless agitation. It would happen when it happened was all I needed to know.

In fact it was eleven-thirty when the miraculous icon, overlaid with ornate silver and revealing only the face of the Virgin and Child, was eventually carried from the church. Everyone stood up and crossed himself and stopped munching the bread of Christian fellowship which had been distributed earlier. The majestically clad bishops and priests followed behind this flower-bedecked icon which was carried with solemn pomp around the cloisters. I had imagined invalids would be waiting for this moment and that the icon would be bowed over them with miraculous results. But there were no spontaneous happenings.

I had quite forgotten Harry and suddenly saw him still comatose on his marble block. I couldn't reach him in time before the bishops passed and several ecclesiastical eyes dropped their gaze to the sleeping figure. I expected a Pastoral Staff to stretch out and hook him to his feet but, apart from it being noted that he was way beyond praying for the sick, no more attention was paid him.

It was past midnight when we left the Vigil. The queue of people waiting to get into the church to kiss the icon was as wide and as long as ever. It was extraordinary to witness this column of humanity patiently advancing over the course of several hours. The good side of me thought 'what faith!' the bad side thought 'what superstition!' Harry said that it was surely better to have some sort of faith even if a little superstition was picked up on the way. He was a fine one to speak as he was the first to jump on me when I began touching wood, bowing to the new moon or saluting magpies.

On the feast-day itself the miraculous icon was carried from the Church of Ekatondapiliani to the sea where prayers were said for those who had died at sea and general blessings sought for the islanders and mariners in particular.

For the occasion no less than five bishops accompanied the icon on its mission. A marine band, smartly turned out in white uniform with gold braiding, together with white uniformed sailors bearing rifles, led the procession with a throng of people following after it.

But Paros is not the only island with a miraculous icon. On Tinos there is thought to be an even more miraculous one, certainly it is a much older one, and the following day we were on our way to it.

The sea was very rough and I sat down below and chewed crystallized ginger which I hoped would ward off any seasickness. Seated nearby were two Greek women who chattered incessantly, occasionally studding their conversation with 'Ooooooh!' as the boat rose high on a wave and 'Aaaaaah!' as it sank down.

It was when these women fell silent that I eyed them with misgivings. A moment later one of them left hurriedly and after five minutes the other looked frantic and waved to a young steward collecting rubbish in a black plastic sack who ignored her. Suddenly she seized a sick-bag and began to retch horribly beside me. I felt I should help by holding her head or the bag but I was no Florence Nightingale. Instead I put a handkerchief over my nose and turned my back. I noticed a vacant seat some way off and, fearful of hearing the woman retch again, I made for it. It wasn't so easy to get along as many young backpackers lay full length in the gangway unaware that

I was lurching my way past grabbing at any solid object, and narrowly missing an outstretched arm or treading heavily on an upturned sleeping face.

Not long afterwards it was announced that Tinos was imminent and Harry came down from pacing the decks to join me. He gave me a wan smile and said nothing but nodded when I asked if he was all right. I made no further comment fearing the worst. I knew if he was sick I'd be immediately sick also. Early that morning he'd shown symptoms of having the dreaded foreign bug. The hotel on Paros was fully booked and he thought he could make it to Tinos.

Up till now we'd found island-hopping fun. We were learning, though, that you have to be strong; to be in peak condition in order to hold your own in the scrum; to survive being punched in the face by a bulging haversack as a sturdy backpacker turns suddenly to his companion; or keep up the pace as you're forced along by a piece of luggage which hits you in the small of the back. Harry looked as though the smallest haversack would knock him down. We had our own bags to heave about and began using them as weapons.

We went down into the hold to get ready to disembark. It was oppressively hot down there and smelled of engine oil, exhaust fumes and ship's paint. It wasn't a place for anybody already feeling queasy. The boat shuddered as it went hard astern. Harsh light poured in as the ramp was lowered on hydraulics amidst a noisy rattle of chains. As it descended the heat and brightness of the day flooded in.

The ferry-boat disgorged its passengers like a lava-flow from a volcano. Lorries and cars rumbled off with motorbikes weaving their way forward. Harry disappeared in a hurry and when he returned found me waiting with a taxi which took us the short distance to our hotel. On the way I caught a fleeting glimpse of the renowned Church of Panagia Evangelistria on the hill behind the port; it was quite different to the domed Byzantine basilica church on Paros.

I had been torn between Paros and Tinos for the 15th August festival; despite all modern wizardry and technology, it is still impossible to be in two places at once. Harry had no idea which island and I'd settled finally for Paros because there the church was much older. Here on Tinos, however, even greater multitudes of the sick and disabled come hoping for a miracle. Maybe, in the deep recesses of my mind, I'd chosen not to be amongst too many invalids, fearing I might catch some disease and fall ill alongside them. Harry had got a germ anyway but that, we hoped, would soon pass.

Later that afternoon I left Harry with bottled water and pills and went off up the wide road to the famous church. It was an imposing pale yellow and white edifice with two arcaded levels to which wide balustraded stairways ascended either side. Below its ornate cornice was a row of arched windows. Before Christianity a temple of Dionysos had stood on the hill with an amphitheatre below it.

In the tenth century Saracen pirates had destroyed the earlier church and the icon had been lost. It had been rediscovered in 1823 after a nun had had repeated visions of the Virgin Mary who'd commanded her to dig for the lost icon. The nun, Agia Pelagia, had at first said nothing fearing that she might be hallucinating or it was a visit from the devil. It was not until the third vision when the Virgin Mary had begun to be angry that she'd found herself fearing the Virgin more than being thought a fool and had reported the matter. When the bishop heard he'd immediately ordered digging to begin, and the whole island had joined in with enthusiasm. After some months of this and finding no icon, the islanders began to lose interest and the work stopped. But immediately there was an epidemic and hundreds died. So the Archbishop ordered the islanders to start digging again, and as soon as they began then the epidemic stopped.

The search had started in the autumn of 1822. At the end of January 1823, one of the islanders had felt his spade strike wood. He discovered that he'd split a piece of wood in half and the first piece he took from the ground depicted the Angel Gabriel presenting a lily to a missing figure. He had then taken out the other portion and had found it portrayed the Virgin Mary. The Virgin was in a room kneeling in front of a *prie-dieu* on which was an open book with the words of the Annunciation. A dove, representing the Holy Spirit, was included in the scene. Amazingly, after being in the ground for over eight hundred years it was in an excellent state of preservation.

Because the nun had had her vision at the start of the War of Independence and the icon had been recovered a few months later, the icon became identified with Greek freedom and liberation from Turkish rule. Money had poured in from all quarters of Greece and the Orthodox world to help build the new church. No expense had been spared and whenever money had run short more had miraculously been donated to replenish the coffers.

The custom for those who have had their prayers answered by the Virgin Mary is to make a pilgrimage to Tinos to honour her icon. On their arrival such people show their gratitude and humility by crawling up on hands and knees from the port to the church until they reach the icon inside. Several narrow strips of carpet are laid up the road for the greater comfort of these pilgrims. As I walked up I passed several of them on hands and knees slowly and resolutely approaching their goal in the afternoon sun.

Inside the church was magnificent. The miraculous icon was to the left near the entrance. It was only about eighteen inches high but, like a diminutive monarch, was made to look imposing and majestic by its large and exquisite arched frame, and the strings of pearls and precious stones which overlaid it allowing only the face of the Virgin to be visible. It stood on a marble pillared stand adorned with Madonna lilies. Every now and then an attendant wiped the glass protecting the icon, polishing away the many kisses which threatened to smear the glass and obscure this treasure.

Those in the know about icon paintings believe it to be one of several painted by St. Luke. I was suddenly struck by a thought: St. Luke the physician! Could he also be working miraculous cures through this icon?

Heavy silver chandeliers hung down amidst dozens of icon lamps, each with a silver or gold attachment depicting either a leg, a ship, a house, a child, a cow, a mule, each representing the gratitude of some pilgrim whose prayers had been answered. Hundreds of candles of supplication cast their muted light and reflected off marble, silver, gold and brass.

I watched a pilgrim come crawling through the entrance, the grey head down, a handbag an added encumbrance which had to be swung forward in the right hand. Those standing in the church made way for her. When she finally reached the icon she stood up without any particular show of emotion, made the sign of the cross and kissed the glass covering the icon three times. This done she brushed the dust from her hands, tidied her black dress and went off to light a candle.

A stout young man also came crawling on his last lap to the church. He was the only man I saw doing this. The piety of these people and their humility filled me with curiosity and I began to regret not being on Tinos for the great 15th August festival. Here was the Mecca, so to speak, for pilgrims, the sick and the disabled.

Remembering a Greek woman's insistence that icons should be honoured, I too crossed myself in the correct Orthodox manner and kissed the glass over this treasure, expecting at the same time a sudden rush of blood to the head but, feeling no different, I moved on to make way for the next pilgrim.

Before coming out to the Cyclades I had written to the Abbess of the convent where the nun, Agia Pelagia, had had her vision, to ask if they took overnight visitors. In due course I'd received a reply inviting me to telephone when I arrived on the island. Harry had no intention of spending a night anywhere that didn't have its own private bathroom. I left him lying prone on his bed with a hand over his eyes as I continued my bid for holy understanding.

It was late afternoon when I set off by bus for the Kechrovouni Convent. On the way I passed several of the famous Tinian dovecotes, unusual whitewashed buildings whose upper half are intricately decorated like smocking. After twenty minutes climbing steadily into the hills I was put down at the convent set amongst trees. The change in temperature was astonishing; down by the sea the *meltemi* had been welcomingly cool, up there it was quite cold and I was glad of a jersey.

The nun at the entrance was expecting me and I was directed up stone steps to the Abbess' quarters. There I was shown into a reception room where holy pictures adorned the walls. A young Greek couple was waiting also and I learned from the girl that they had come up for a blessing as they were soon to be married.

The Abbess came in to greet us all. She was plump with a round face and merry brown eyes. She led us through to another room where she presided at the head of a long table. Cakes and glasses of iced water were passed around and the Abbess warned that the cakes were very light and beware, but too late; I had already bitten into one and had blown clouds of glucose onto the table. This the Abbess thought hilarious. She was so youthful and merry that I couldn't believe she was really in charge of this convent.

In my letter I had said I was interested in Orthodoxy and because of this the Abbess now invited me to ask questions about it. I could hardly say that I was fascinated by the pagan gods and how Christianity had triumphed, so racked my brains for some suitable question feeling something of a fraud.

I asked her how she had come to convent life and was told that young girls were brought there if for some reason their families were unable to support them. She herself had come at the age of ten and had remained there all her life – she was now forty-six. When such children were taken in they went to the local school and when they grew up they could leave the convent and have careers; they were quite free to choose for themselves and no pressure was put on them to become nuns.

The Abbess said that she had recently been to England for a conference and I asked her what she thought of women priests in the Church of England. She replied that if it was God's will then the Holy Spirit would move the Orthodox Church to have them too. I nearly said that I thought it more the will of women that had got them there, just as the will of men had tried to keep them out, or gay wills brought gay marriages and gay offspring, and so on. But I forbore which was probably more sensible as I doubt my Greek would have been up to it anyway.

After a while the couple left and the Abbess saw them out. I was now at a decided disadvantage as I had no one to consult and with their heads and chins covered I found all round-faced nuns looked identical. When the Abbess returned and took me off to my guest quarters I didn't recognize her but thought her to be another nun allocated the job of conducting me there. I enquired about the Abbess and asked what her name was. She must have thought she was dealing with a mentally deficient English woman trying to speak Greek and getting her verbs and nouns seriously muddled.

The guest quarters consisted of several rooms and I was told that supper would be at eight. Because by now the Abbess thought me a complete imbecile she repeated this many times to make sure I understood. In fact I knew the Greek for 'supper at eight' but we stood facing each other, repeating the words over and over again, the Abbess with a merry look in her eye, and I trying to reassure her that I knew it wasn't seven or nine or any other hour but eight.

The meal was taken alone in a small anti-room (for fear, perhaps, of what the lunatic might say in front of the other nuns). Before I was allowed to eat I first had to pause for grace said by the Abbess (I was beginning to recognize her). This took several minutes, but was not so long as the prayers that were to follow. Then I was taken to the reception room where all the lights were switched off leaving only the dim glow of a single icon lamp. I could just make out the silhouette of the Abbess and a tiny nun about four feet tall standing beside her.

For what seemed like hours I stood with head bowed whilst the two of them alternately recited by heart screeds of prayers and passages from the Gospels, occasionally crossing themselves. Minute followed minute as I stood with my mind slipping from holiness to the positive fear that I was about to collapse in a dead-faint. The beginning of discipline was being taught; I was being given a lesson in obedience and serve me right for asking if I might stay due to my interest in the Greek Orthodox Church. If I was so interested then I could learn to stand for ever as a mark of respect.

When the ordeal was over I was kissed on both cheeks and told to say my prayers before I went to sleep. The morning Liturgy would begin at five a.m., I was told. I knew it would be a long service and courageously I asked if I might come at six. Certainly, was the reply. And could I be allowed to sit, I asked? Of course, was the answer. I felt I should have been chastised, but love was everywhere; no criticism, no judgement, just an apparent joy.

I was shown to my guest quarters by a long faced nun who lit the way with a torch to make sure the lunatic didn't fall down a steep unguarded flight of stone steps into a cellar. I said goodnight, tried to remember my prayers but got distracted by a telegraph pole outside my bedroom window which had a transformer on it which every now and then crackled and showered out sparks. I worried it might run along the wires and set fire to the building. In contrast on the wall of my sitting-room was a small oil lamp whose tiny flame sometimes flared uncannily. I could see it through the open bedroom door. I was prepared for it to burst into a vision and wondered what it would be like to be picked out by the Virgin Mary to carry a message to the people. A devastating blow to the equilibrium of one's life, no doubt. Harry would take to the hills if he was suddenly faced with a wife who had been selected by the Virgin Mary for a mission. But whatever his reaction I felt I would be a very unwilling deliverer of news from the spiritual world, and could quite understand Pelagia's first instinct not to do it as she feared being thought a fool. Another flare up and fortunately I fell asleep.

The next morning I was dressed and ready when a nun fetched me at six o'clock and took me to the *katholikon*. Candles and a chandelier of crystal drops shed mysterious light on the *iconostasis* with its ancient icons in arched recesses, each separated by gilded twisted pillars. Above it a tall crucifix reached to the blue barrel-roof which was painted with gold stars. Frescoes from the New and Old Testament covered the side walls.

I was shown to a seat near the Abbess who sat on a high backed, highly polished wooden throne. Nuns who came in kissed her hand. A young priest officiated and whenever he came from the sanctuary he was led by a nun bearing a candle.

As usual my mind raced around the circuit of whys and why nots. Why had the Virgin Mary revealed her icon's presence to the nun from this convent only comparatively recently, and not centuries earlier to someone else? Why had she made the islanders dig without a precise idea of its whereabouts instead of illuminating the exact location with a glow as had happened with other icons elsewhere, as she had on Cyprus, for example? Why, when she responded to the prayers of some people, did she not respond to the prayers of others? Why couldn't she make it clear to me that it was she and she alone, and not some other inexplicable source of energy, working wonders? I realized that it was useless to ask such questions that were unanswerable. As Harry would say, there were some things that couldn't be understood and, therefore, there was no point in asking questions about them.

Several times the young priest censed the church and gave me, the visitor, a prolonged censing as though I was an insect to be flitted. I was quite ready to die to this world and keel over into the faith, but nothing remarkable happened. My efforts to understand Christianity was making no progress at all. I found it really strange that some people believed implicitly in God and Christ, even believed themselves called by God to serve him, whilst others blundered blindly through a fog of incomprehension and doubts as to God's very existence. There was no way of forcing belief, you either had it or you hadn't.

Before leaving the convent I asked the Abbess if she could show me an icon which I knew the convent possessed. She led me to a glass-fronted cabinet and pointed out a small silver-plated icon in which only the faces of the Virgin and Child were visible. This had formerly been in the possession of a man called Kaniaris, captain of a fire-ship, and hero of the War of Independence. Fire-ships during that war had been very effective against the more cumbersome ships-of-the-line of the Turkish fleet. As ever, a Virgin Mary icon had been a focal point for prayer in those days of war, just as she had been when, in the early days of the Byzantine empire, her icon had been placed on the walls of Constantinople to protect the city; or just as the goddess Athena had defended Athens against the invading barbarians, or had appeared miraculously beside those whom she favoured in times of trouble.

On my way back to the port I shed my jersey as I left the cold of the north wind in the hills and entered the heat down below. I shared a taxi with the tiny nun who had been at prayers with me the night before. She told me she was going down to the dentist because she had toothache. It is odd that one supposes that those who dedicate their lives to God will never suffer from anything so mundane.

Back at the hotel I found Harry standing before a mirror examining the whites of his eyes, pulling down the bottom lids and staring at them. He thought he might have overdone the pills and was now bunged up. Did I think he looked jaundiced, he asked? I said I thought he looked nicely sun-tanned.

As Harry was still feeling groggy I left him nibbling dry biscuits and drinking Lucozade with a tot of brandy – he was a great believer in brandy being a kill or cure remedy, and if he wasn't cured he might as well be killed. I knew this mood of fatalism in him but sympathy, I knew also, made him wallow with the pleasure of being ill; too much attention only complicated matters, so I said I'd leave him to sleep it off as I had more exploring to do.

The sun was hot but the wind cooled me as I walked along the coast road to the sanctuary of Poseidon and his wife Amphitrite, a Nereid (a beautiful sea-maiden). Rather strangely on Tinos in the years of paganism it had been Poseidon who'd been accredited with healing powers. He had been known as the 'Doctor of Tinos' whilst his wife, Amphitrite, had been invoked for fertility problems.

At their sanctuary I found a helpful young attendant who identified the various temple ruins for me. He had an odd eye which swivelled around before fixing itself on its object. With his eye at last focused on the foundations of Poseidon's temple he began to tell me how he hoped tourism wouldn't cause this archaeological site to have hotels built on it. With such a prime location beside the sea he feared one day this might happen. I agreed that that would be a tragedy and found myself saying in an extraordinarily authoritative manner that if he ever thought there was a real danger of this occurring then he must let me know and I would raise the matter with the British Museum. I gave him my address and this pleased him so much, and his swivel eye had such a look of happiness in it, that it was worth playing the part, if briefly, of someone with influence.

From this ancient sacred site I returned up to the church again. I still found the switch from pagan gods to Christian worship strange. Why had it been necessary, and if not necessary why had it come about?

At the time of Plato the Greeks believed in a higher, immutable and changeless being they called God who was the supreme deity in the hierarchy of the spiritual world. What had altered? What hadn't was the human need to have a god out there to call upon.

On my way to the church I passed more penitents on hands and knees making their slow progress up. In a shady area with trees and seats I paused for a while to admire a large bronze sculpture representing a gaunt pilgrim on her knees with an arm outstretched towards the church.

On this occasion I found doors open to a mausoleum in which a torpedo was exhibited. The torpedo had been responsible for the sinking in 1940 of the Greek cruise ship the Elli. This calamity had happened on August 15th, of all days. That such an outrage could occur on this the Virgin Mary's feast-day and not a miracle must have been a challenge to belief. But such disasters often urge the faithful to ever more devotion supposing that it came about from lack of adequate faith in the first instance.

Around the terrace sat several family groups with neatly folded blankets and plastic bags of refreshment.

I wondered if they were invalids about to spend the night in the church, but I didn't like to ask. There was a fine line between good health and happiness and ill health with all its consequences. We were fortunate to be without pains in the body, without recurring digestive problems, kidney failure, diabetes – I didn't know how I'd handle a major personal disaster if it did happen. Would I be dignified in misfortune or would I howl miserably? A few months back Harry had discovered a lump at the top of his leg and I'd immediately jumped to the conclusion he had terminal cancer. I'd foreseen the amputation of his leg, the pushing him about in a wheel-chair, last painful farewells and his funeral. But at no time whilst imagining these death-bed scenes had I for a moment supposed that he would rise from the dead and go and live with God. We'd been lucky as the problem had finally been diagnosed as a benign lump of tissue which he'd thumped off when using a heavy metal bar for banging in fencing stakes.

I visited the grotto where the miraculous icon had been unearthed and found it lit by many tall red candles, some as high as two metres, bought from the many booths which sold them on the way up. I then went down into the crypt where a marble plaque depicting the Virgin and Child above a marble basin marked the spot where the spring which had dried up had suddenly begun to flow again after the icon's discovery. Nearby were several large and gleaming copper baptismal fonts fitted with taps and plumbed to the ground.

I was told that a baptism was imminent and I asked if I could stay to watch. Noddings and gestures to sit on a stone ledge a few feet from a font had me at once at the centre of proceedings. Could I take photographs? Yes, of course. In Greece a stranger is an honoured guest, a tradition from ancient times.

A bent and elderly nanny-like woman with her grey hair in a black hair-net, and wearing a large white apron, stood by to help with the baptismal duties. She had unusually bright blue-green eyes. I later spoke to her and she told me she'd been attending at baptisms there for over thirty years.

A man came in with a white suitcase containing the christening garments which were laid out on a ledge in a corner with a large white bath towel. I was told that it was customary for a child to be baptized between the age of six months and a year as it required complete immersion. To do this earlier ran the risk of an infant catching cold, or presumably drowning.

In pagan times children had never had to be baptized to be accepted in the worship of the gods. The gods were freely available to everybody and were part of temple tradition regarding ritual and festivals. Only certain mystery cults demanded initiation.

A little girl of a year old was carried in on the arm of her godfather who whispered and cooed words of encouragement to her. She was entranced by the candles, icons and the attention of her elders. The child's name was Irene (meaning 'peace') which for the time being suited her.

Two priests arrived and now the godfather was asked questions and made his responses. When these were wrong he was corrected which did not disconcert him at all. He was then given a Bible to kiss and Irene was taken to the corner where she was undressed. She was then wrapped in the bath towel and brought back to the font.

Now began strange incantations from the older of the two priests who rolled up his sleeves and exuded great energy and put his hand into the font and flung the water into the air three times and then appeared to blow and whistle over it, presumably to drive away all evil spirits.

A small bottle of oil was blessed and a little put into the water. Irene, who was by now starkers, was annointed with oil on different parts of the body. This was her Chrismation (the receiving of the child fully into the Church, the equivalent of confirmation in the west). She was then plunged three times into the water, and then re-annointed before being wrapped in the towel and held by her godfather whilst she had a lock of hair cut by the priest who chanted loudly into her face. By now the poor child was yelling with rage and shock. She did not stop until she was taken back to Nanny who helped dress her in her new white satin bonnet and frock. After that she was carried three times around the font. This was followed by the mother kissing the floor three times and the hand of the priest three times.

In this vaulted, whitewashed crypt I sat close to an ancient column which I thought must be part of the old temple of Dionysos which had once stood on the site. I wondered how much pagan ritual had filtered down from the past. In antiquity there had been nymphs of springs, rivers and lakes known as Naiads. The malignant ones had to be exorcised as they sometimes took possession of people forcing them into evil ways. Holy water had always been used as a purifying element and oil, of course, had been a gift to the people of Athens from the goddess Athena. It was used as a salve for healing and the olive branch had been an emblem of hers, a symbol of victory and peace.

With the baptism over I was given a baptismal cake wrapped in gold paper and was asked if I would take a photograph of the family group. I was not the best person for the job as photography is not one of my most polished accomplishments. But I did what they asked and, using their camera, hoped that I had all of Irene in the picture and not just her bonnet or her feet.

That evening Harry was feeling decidedly better, even hungry, so we went out to a taverna for supper. Seated nearby was a large overweight woman with her back to us. She looked like a tramp with lanky unkempt greyish-blonde hair. After we had pored over the menu to decide on a dish which would be the least likely to give us high cholestral, salmonella poisoning, lysteria or any other horror and the waiter had gone with our orders, she turned and asked us if we were English. I was surprised to see that this 'tramp' had an amiable plump face and very intelligent eyes.

She was Greek but spoke impeccable English and shifted her chair around to talk and we learned that she came from Athens and had once lived in New York where she had taught English to foreigners.

She told us how she herself suffered from arthritis of the shoulders and knees and hoped one day to be cured by 'Our Lady'. She then went on to explain how her daughter some years back had developed eczema which had spread all over her body. As the doctors had been unable to cure her she had finally brought her to Tinos for the feast-day of the Virgin Mary's Assumption.

First she had attended the Vigil with her daughter who had received holy unction from the priest who had spread oil on her hands. They had then spent the night sleeping in the gallery of the church. The next day the girl had had her hands wiped with the holy water from the spring in the crypt. Finally they had stood in a long column amongst the many other invalids in the middle of the wide road ascending to the church and the icon had been carried on its gold and silver ciborium and passed over their heads. At lunch that same day she had noticed that her daughter's hands were clear of eczema as was the rest of her body.

"I cannot explain it, I only know that with the help of Our Lady this is what happened in my own experience," said the woman. "My daughter is now thirty and she has never had a recurrence of the problem." We smiled and nodded and I was completely won over by her faith and belief in miracles.

After we had left all the old hesitations and questions regarding faith or lack of it began to rear their heads again. I seemed to be a sort of chameleon, endlessly taking on the colour of whatever setting it was in.

Probably it was time to settle down into a background of faith – not belief as that was impossible – but faith. But then what was the point of faith if you did not really believe? Harry was no help when I asked him.

"Don't ask me! It's like having faith in pills believing that they'll do you good."

"All in the mind?" I suggested.

"All in the gut's more like it," he replied instantly, unable to think beyond his recent predicament.

"Taking what's on offer and trusting in its benefits?" I went on, hoping to get some positive feedback from what promised to be a mystical discussion.

But Harry was only interested in the fact that he was feeling better and not in the minor miracle of it. He wanted to know if we had any chocolate in our room.

Miracles or no miracles I knew I could never settle for faith – at least, not whilst I was in good health, not whilst there were more spiritual explorations to be made.

It is nine days since the 15th of August festival of the Virgin Mary, and we are now back on Paros, this time at the small fishing village of Naoussa in the north-east of the island. We are seated at a taverna, and are about to see the re-enactment of a pirate raid which I am sure Harry will enjoy after our recent church-goings.

I am struggling with an extraordinarily tough pork chop which is quite unchewable, and am becoming increasingly unhappy about things as crowds flock into the village lining the quayside with their backs to us. I'd been told we'd be able to see everything from this taverna but I can't see how.

I can stand it no longer. We are so obviously well away from the scene of action. I abandon my chop, leave Harry who is determined to finish his food, and join the throng.

Gradually, I ease my way forward through the crowds till I find myself up against a lamp-post at the water's edge. It is a useful object to lean against to prevent being pitched into the sea by the crush behind. By now it is quite dark and lights shimmer on the black water which moves gently, causing the small boats to creak and strain at their moorings.

Excitement rises as the lights of six *caiques* are seen sailing out to sea beyond a mole some hundred metres away. The pirate raid will soon begin; it is a re-enactment of an attack led by the notorious Barbarossa (Red Beard) in the sixteenth century. Once ashore Barbarossa had commanded the girls of the village to dance before him and, selecting the most beautiful, made off with her, leaving the others to the mercy of his fellow brigands.

The incident today is commemorated annually at this small fishing village. This morning we attended the church at Naoussa and watched a parade of school children come down from the church led by the village band. Incense was burning in small pots before the front-door of houses either side of the street – an aid to warding off evil spirits, I was told.

And now it is beginning! Out of the darkness the pirate boats sail into harbour, the first one rounding the mole in a blaze of glaring orange flares. A pirate stands at the mast-head of the lead boat with arms outstretched as though crucified. He is lit up against the night sky as his fellow pirates swing their garish orange flares which send smoke and lurid light over the boats and reflect along the dark ripples of the sea. More *caiques* ablaze with orange smoky light follow the first into harbour. The pirates look appropriately threatening and brandish cutlasses.

The raid is swift and exciting with battle cries and guns booming. As the pirates gain the shore the gunfire from a nearby boat gives way to a firework display. Rockets are let off and soar into the night sky, higher and higher until they whoooosh into a myriad sparks and arch seawards, each reflecting brilliantly in the sea.

In the *plateia* close by is a brightly lit stage festooned with light-bulbs where two men play bazookis, another a fiddle and the fourth a drum. The pirates jump from their boats, seize their girls and carry them over their shoulders up onto the stage where they perform a wild pirate dance with their victims. The girls seem willing enough; this, after all, is only a reconstruction of the tragic event which took place several centuries ago. It is a joyful reminder that life can be fun when not a traumatic affair.

The pirate dancing ends and they disappear, running barefoot up the maze of alleyways behind the harbour. They wear red or black kerchiefs tied about their heads and white full-sleeved shirts and black, baggy knickerbockers. The maze of alleyways is a feature of such fishing villages, designed originally to confuse pirates, so giving the fleeing inhabitants a chance to escape.

While at Parikia, we'd explored behind the port. We ourselves had become immediately lost in its twisting, narrow, marble-flagged alleyways flanked by small whitewashed houses, vaulted archways, and steep steps going up to low doorways or down into cellars. At the time the sun was casting both glaring white light and welcome dark shadow. While lost we came across a tiny church, then discovered the *kastro*, an old Venetian tower built with many incorporated temple blocks and column drums. We continued past it and on up further till we arrived at the Church of Sts. Constantine and Helena which, according to a plaque, was built on the site of a temple of Athena. The church there was poised on the edge of the high point of the town overlooking the sea.

Now here at Naoussa the amplified bazookis, fiddle and drum start up again for the village dancing. People join hands as a dignitary in a light coloured suit steps out with a certain formality. But soon it is a lively middle-aged man who leads the dancing, a white handkerchief waves energetically from his free hand. There are beads of perspiration on his brow and he looks a little drunk but he doesn't lack rhythm, and draws his equally dynamic wife after him. Her bent elbows and raised hands keep him from losing his balance, whilst the man on her other side keeps her from losing hers.

Seeing me she suddenly hauls me out from the onlookers and I find myself bobbing along after her, elbows bent and hands held, a few steps to the side, foot across, then a hop and onwards. The circle grows larger and larger and a second circle is made beyond. All ages participate, children and grandparents, husbands and wives, teenagers, lovers – it is only necessary to unclasp loosely held hands to join in. As the circle slowly revolves and I get nearer to Harry standing amongst the onlookers, I grab his hand. He is reluctant at first but I hold on, and others push him forward. Soon he is doing a sort of side-stepping fox-trot and moves in time to the beat with the best of them.

Fifteen minutes of this and the music ends. It starts again for a slow erotic dance which only four couples perform and is compulsive watching. First the woman squats down on her haunches before her man whilst he performs slow sensuous movements in front of her. They do it unselfconsciously and with passion. A grey-haired, wild looking fisherman dances with surprising grace before his portly wife who watches him as she squats within the circle of onlookers. The wild fisherman is lost in his world of music and love, and rotates seductively before his wife. After some minutes he suddenly puts out a hand and pulls her to her feet, and he himself crouches down. She in her own portly way abandons herself to the music and the gaze of her husband, and dances seductively, as seductively as a portly sixty year old can which, in fact, is surprisingly attractively done – grey hair, large bust, large bum, arms extended in a flowing movement. The wild fisherman has eyes only for her.

I wonder how Harry would react if I attempted any such seductive dancing before him; I suspect he would look anywhere but at me. Perhaps someone else's attention could be drawn? Perhaps I could lure the wild fisherman? But, for everybody's sake, I forbear.

The sensual dance ends and another, also only for the enlightened, begins. It is performed by couples who dance side by side – foot forward, behind, across, a few fancy steps before advancing.

Young children are fully in the spirit of the evening and several are on the stage near the bazooki players doing small-legged movements with little jerky steps. One of the small boys is brandishing a cutlass as he tries to mimic the steps of his elders. His time will come when he will be able to carry off one of the girls. The music of the bazookis is already in his blood.

We join in another dance where all take part before we finally leave. It is already past midnight and it is today that we are flying home.

We are now waiting for our flight to Athens at the small Paros airfield. To pass the time I speak to my neighbour about the Naoussa pirate raid, and am told that the worst pirates used to be the Portuguese prior to World War I whose sole purpose had been to steal valuable icons from the churches. They would sail into port having run down their Jolly Roger pirate flag and were, therefore, welcomed ashore before going on the rampage. The islanders had been devastated by the loss of their precious icons.

We are told our plane is ready and we cross the tarmac to a very diminutive aircraft. The pilot gives one of the propellers a turn and it revolves sluggishly.

We each find a bucket seat beside a window (there are nine of these either side) and I watch as the first propeller is started. It revolves slowly at first and then revs up. The same occurs with the second propeller. We cruise down the runway, turn and poise ready for take-off. The plane shudders and hops along as the engines get the adrenalin going and we accelerate down the runway and take to the air.

In the plane there are no luggage racks, no air hostess, no toilet facilities, just a sick-bag and a worn-with-age notice informing each passenger there is a life-jacket under the seat; I do not feel around to see if it is there, and I doubt it would inflate and keep me from sinking without trace if I'm lucky enough to find it.

We fly noisily above the stretch of flat sea flecked with crested waves. The door is open to the pilot and his navigator who sit confidently at the controls, and I suppose all will be well. If it is not then that will be that. But I continue to make plans and to think about the future.

We are buffeted severely as we enter bouffon white clouds, and become wrapped up as though in a cocoon. Ten minutes of this and we begin to descend – lots of swallowing to break the pressure on the ear-drums. We emerge from the bouffon cloud, and I can see a ferry-boat leaving a long wake as it makes for Piraeus. We pass over an island and I can see bathers – the mainland – tennis courts – basketball – houses – roads – Phew! something seems to be falling out of the plane. Ah, it is the undercarriage and I can see a tiny wheel, so be it! The runway comes up to meet us – suddenly lots of small bump-bumps and we have landed. All those on board applaud the pilot with prolonged clapping.

At the airport I ask a girl, who is arranging magazines on a stand, if she has any with photos of the festival of the Virgin Mary which would have been celebrated throughout Greece. She replies in the negative. Surely they have some printed matter concerning their greatest annual festival? No, she is sorry but she has nothing. Why not, I ask? Because, she says, the Greek people are a very proud and private people, and have no need to publicise their traditions and religious customs for strangers. She begins to warm to her subject, explaining that every household has its own shrine just as in the past families had a shrine to Hestia, goddess of the hearth and home. In fact, she tells me, the Greek Church and traditions are so important to the Greek people it is why they have a cross on their national flag. They are brought up to their religion which is taught in schools so that it is imbued in them from an early age.

I want to continue talking to this young girl who is pouring out information, but her superior is calling her to task; she must get back to her duties. With many apologies she continues to stack up magazines.

We have a long wait. The only information I can glean is that there has been a 'bad landing' at Gatwick. That surely is a euphemism for 'crash'? I comfort myself that if crash there has been, then there is unlikely to be another so soon after. Anyway, for the time being, I for one have complete faith in my destiny. I can not believe that our trip to Paros and Tinos, and my intention to write about them will be wasted. All that is needed is patience

It was late October and the sun was shining, the sky was blue, and the sea was a sparkling sapphire as we walked from our hotel along the curve of Kos harbour. The island was quite different from any other we'd visited as it had tall, slender palm trees along the sea-front. A picturesque assortment of high-masted schooners, their gangways down, lined the quayside, together with yachts and fishing boats.

We passed several fishermen with metal stands on which their catch of the day was displayed for sale. One fisherman in yellow oilskin trousers stood bludgeoning an octopus beneath three or four hefty white pebbles tied to the end of a rope; he ceaselessly banged the weights down on the creature, making circular movements with his hand as he held the rope so the numerous legs twisted this way and then that – tenderizing it, I was to learn later, not killing it as I thought at the time.

We stopped to watch a large grey boat sail slowly into harbour with half a dozen crew on deck. When one of them looked in our direction I couldn't resist asking him what sort of boat it was. A patrol boat, came the reply. The landmass of Turkey with its high mountain ranges loomed menacingly only a few kilometres offshore. A patrol boat? Turkey was, I supposed, an ever present threat to the islanders; four hundred years of Turkish occupation could not easily be forgotten.

A number of cyclists shot past perilously near using the cycle path alongside the water's edge; it seemed the islanders were bursting with energy and good health, which was as it should be here on the island of Hippocrates – Hippocrates, the renowned doctor of antiquity remembered for his Hippocratic Oath. We were on our way to see his ancient plane tree claimed to be (rather dubiously) the very one beneath which he himself had expounded words of medical wisdom to his devoted followers.

Following signposts, we came to a cobbled pedestrianised area in the centre of which was the famous tree. Its massive girth was disfigured by a wide hollow gash in its trunk as though it had been blasted by lightning. Metal poles supported the weight of its branches, and it was surrounded by protective railings. We sat down on a nearby seat to enjoy the moment, and imagine the father of medicine instructing his students seated at his feet.

All around were reminders of the island's historic past. Nearby was a single column with a Corinthian capital from the period when Kos had been under Rome. To our left beyond some trees was the fourteenth century castle of the Knights of St. John, built when the Crusaders had for two centuries occupied the island. To our right a minaret soared up from amongst trees which hid an old mosque from the period of Turkish occupation. The Italians had also invaded the island in 1912, leaving in their wake attractive tall houses with arched windows and arcades.

I rummaged in my bag and found some printed-out pages of the Hippocratic Oath I'd brought with me. I read aloud from the first sheet: *I swear by Apollo, the Physician, by Asclepius, by Hygiea and Panacea and by all the gods and goddesses, making them my witnesses, that I will carry out, according to my ability and judgement, this oath and this covenant...* "The Hippocratic Oath," I told Harry.

"Asclee, who's that? And Hygee whoever?" Harry demanded.

"Asclepius, god of healing and medicine – son of Apollo," I said.

"Oh, him! And the other?"

"Hygiea? Asclepius' daughter. Hygiene and all that – a very suitable name for the daughter of a god of healing," I replied. "As is Panacea whose name means universal remedy, or something of the sort. Shall I go on with it?" I asked.

Harry nodded, and I continued reading: *...I will, according to my ability and judgment, prescribe such treatment for my patients as may be most beneficial to them, seeking to keep from them anything that may prove to be wrong or injurious...*

"Presumably doctors today don't swear by Apollo and the Ascleep-god?" Harry asked.

I turned to another sheet of paper: *Praise be Allah, the Teacher...* "Oh, no – sorry, that's the Moslem version." I found the page I wanted which was the Oath as sworn by Christians: *With gratitude to God, faith in Christ Jesus, and dependence on the Holy Spirit, I publicly profess my intent to practice medicine for the glory of God...*

"And atheists?" Harry asked. "What do atheists swear?"

"Oh, I'm sure there's one for atheists. I suppose they just cut out the God and Allah bits and swear to do their best," I said.

"So, are we going up to this Ascleep place?" Harry had had enough of oaths.

The occasional bronzed autumn leaf fluttered down to the cobblestones. This ancient tree, despite its hollow trunk and the props that kept it upright, still had dignity.

"It's why we've come to Kos," I said.

We left the shade of the plane tree, and found a taxi to take us to the Asclepeion some four kilometres away. It was there that in antiquity the sick and disabled had flocked for treatment – there that Hippocrates had practised his medicine.

There was something gently therapeutic and almost poetic about the Asclepeion; you could feel the peace and harmony of the place as soon as you entered the site and saw before you the hill with its three vast landscaped terraces. The whole site was fringed by conifers with numerous cypresses rising up through them.

In the fifth century B.C. it had been Apollo who'd been first worshipped here. His sanctuary had been surrounded by a Holy Grove of cypresses, considered sacred to him. He'd been known as Apollo Kyparissios (an epithet denoting 'cypress tree') and it was forbidden to cut down any one of them within his sacred boundaries.

In the fourth century worship had shifted from Apollo to Asclepius, his son by a mortal woman, who'd given birth to him at Epidaurus in the Peloponnese. There she'd exposed the baby on a mountainside. The infant had been found by a shepherd who, recognizing the child's divinity from the light that shone about him, took him home where he was protected by the his dog and suckled by his goat.

In another story Coronis, the mortal beauty whom Apollo had loved, had been unfaithful to him while pregnant with Asclepius. Apollo had been informed of her infidelity by a white crow (at the time all crows were white), and he'd been so outraged that he'd killed Coronis (some say Artemis his sister killed her) but had rescued his child and had then entrusted him to Chiron, a centaur (half man, half horse) who was renowned throughout the ancient world for his medical knowledge, his music and his justice. Afterwards, Apollo had been so filled with remorse at having killed his beloved Coronis, and so furious with the crow for informing against her, that he turned all crows black.

It was thought by many that the worship of Asclepius, this god of healing, had been brought here by the Dorians who'd come to Kos from Epidaurus. And maybe it was the myth of the birth of Asclepius and the death of his mother, that caused it to become the rule that no one was allowed entry to an Asclepeion who was on the point of giving birth or dying.

Hippocrates was descended from a long line of priest physicians known as Asclepiads. His father had been one, and Hippocrates had learned the art of medicine from him. What distinguished Hippocrates, however, was his focus on medicine as a science. He believed there was a natural cause to all disease, and he opposed the Asclepiad priest-physicians who held on to the traditional idea that it was the gods who inflicted accidents or diseases on people. 'It is not the god who is to blame' was something Hippocrates had repeatedly insisted. What was required, Hippocrates said, was proper diagnosis, painstaking research into curative medicine, and treatment appropriately given in each individual case.

Where the priest-physicians might have made an incision to let out what they regarded as an evil demon that had gained access to the patient showing mental stress and instability, Hippocrates looked for the causes to mood swings or depression. He could be said to be the first ever psychologist.

His essay, *On Airs, Waters, Places,* was full of fatherly advice and concern, describing how climate and the changing seasons, environment, and diet, all played a part in the good or bad health and well being of an individual. 'Excess of any kind is an enemy of nature' was one of his maxims.

Hippocrates was a great believer in nature. Nature was untaught and unfailing in itself. 'Nothing arises without its natural cause', was something he wrote.

He recognized that in every human being there was a vital force and energy at work which kept that person healthy. Being only aware of the outer appearance of a person, I'd never given any thought to the workings of their interiors.

"Revolting!" Harry said when I mentioned the 'vital forces' busily at work in every human being.

"But have you ever thought about it?" I persisted.

"No fear!" Harry wasn't one to speculate.

"Think of your digestion. Think of all the things which go into action as soon as you've swallowed your breakfast."

"Oooof!"

I ignored his squeamishness. "As soon as you've swallowed, say, a bowl of cornflakes," I said, "something gets to work on what you've eaten, sorting out the good from the bad, and seeing to it that what gives energy passes to the right department. When you think about the myriad things that are ceaselessly at work which could as easily stop functioning, it's remarkable that anybody feels well."

"Doesn't bear thinking about!"

"People don't think about it, that's what's remarkable. It all goes on silently and secretly. People only think about it when they're ill. Meanwhile, everything goes on quietly. Your red and white blood cells divide or don't divide but do whatever they're supposed to, while your heart keeps beating, and your lungs keep breathing. Nature untaught and unfailing in itself. It's a brilliant thought from Hippocrates."

"Good for him," said Harry who refused to contemplate the miracle of good health.

We climbed the twenty-three steps to the first terrace where a gentle breeze cooled us. Apparently there had originally been a colonnade on three sides of this terrace. A massive retaining wall flanked the stairway to the second terrace. In this wall were large arched recesses, which had once contained statues. At the far left of the wall two giant-sized headless statues rested on the turf propped against the wall. One was of Asclepius, the other of his daughter Hygiea.

"You know Hippocrates' ancestry could be traced to Asclepius?" I said. "And, therefore, to Apollo. In fact to Zeus, if you think about it, since Zeus was Apollo's father," I added.

"Says who?" Harry was sceptical.

"Say those in the know – though how they know is another matter."

"They don't," said Harry positively. "Those Greeks just gave god ancestry to anyone of note."

"Like the early Christians saying Jesus was the son of God?"

"That's quite different," Harry said.

"In what way?" I asked.

But Harry didn't answer. I didn't pursue the subject. The sanctuary was not a place for controversy. Calm acceptance of mysteries was what this therapeutic site demanded of its visitors.

We left the first terrace and climbed the thirty steps to the one above where we were faced with a third century B.C. altar with sculptural decorations on it. To our right were the remains of a small temple of Asclepius.

After wandering around that, we walked to the east of the great altar, to tall Corinthian columns which were part of another temple of Apollo, this one built in the Christian era, second century A.D. to be exact. Beyond it we found great chunks of marble from its pediment which lay pell-mell on the ground. The marble had sculptured decorations and grooved gutters with lions' heads through whose open mouths rain-water could escape. How such weighty pieces could be hoisted up to roof level was a mystery.

Water had been a necessary commodity in temple worship, and up here there had been a sacred spring to the west of the Asclepius temple. Animals being brought up for sacrifice had been driven up the gentler slope beyond that temple. It had been important to appease the gods with sacrifice.

Before an invalid could enter the temple he'd had to go through certain strict procedures. First, he had to fast, then undergo purification, then offer up a sacrifice. Those who could afford nothing greater offered up a cock, others would sacrifice a sheep or goat.

Having done all these preliminaries, the patient was expected to take part in a 'temple sleep'. This took place in a long portico where invalids lay side by side. During the night they hoped for a miraculous cure, or to be sent a dream by the god informing them what cure was needed to help their recovery. Temple snakes, sacred to Asclepius, were also used; they'd slither up and lick the festering wound or skin complaint and so effect a cure. If no cure took place then it was from lack of some essential detail in appeasing the gods.

I supposed all those who'd been cured in the past regarded their recovery as a miracle. Miracles have occurred down the millennia. Without such miracles people would not have continued going to Asclepeions for treatment or undergone a 'temple sleep'.

Now, of course, such human faith continues but an invalid spends the night in a church that has a miracle-working icon. Sometimes there is an unexplained recovery (a miracle), sometimes there's not.

"If I have a pain the first thing I think is that I've pushed my luck too far with the Almighty," I remarked.

"You don't really think that," came the comment. "Not in this day and age anyway. Do you?" Harry was alarmed at such a possibility. "You're far too sensible!" he pronounced.

Was I too sensible?

We mounted the sixty steps to the third terrace beyond which conifers grew up the remainder of the hill. Turning to face the view, we stood gazing out over the lower terraces to the tree-covered flat terrain, the sea and the ominous Turkish landmass where the town of Bodrum (ancient Halicarnassus) was spreadeagled.

Because we were mentally cast back into antiquity we spotted what looked to us like two *triremes* slowly making their way from west to east on the calm blue sea. I thought I could see the rows of oars dipping into the water and forcing the boats forward. There seemed to be what I took to be square sails also.

I drew the attention of a young man who was on duty there. Were they two *triremes,* I asked? He looked at me as though I'd lost my wits. Those were container ships he told me. Container ships? Surely not! Oh, how mundane life is when the wings of the imagination are clipped and you are grounded back in reality!

I dragged my mind back to the Asclepeion. Hippocrates had been in demand throughout the known world. Pericles, the great Athenian statesman of the fifth century B.C., had sought his help when Athens had been suffering from the plague. When it subsided he had rewarded the great physician by crowning him with a golden wreath at the time of the great Panathenaea in Athens, as well as giving him Athenian citizenship which meant free meals for life. Not long afterwards an Asclepeion sanctuary was founded in Athens below the Acropolis on its south side.

The Persian king, Artaxerxes, had also appealed to Hippocrates because of plague infesting his army. He promised him untold wealth and luxury if he came – he had a nerve, considering the long term enmity between Persia and Greece. But Hippocrates was not one to be tempted by riches or comfort, and had refused.

We sat down under a tree and I read another couple of paragraphs of the Hippocratic Oath: *Into whatever houses I enter, I will go there for the benefit of the sick; I will abstain from intentional wrongdoing and harm, especially from abusing the body of man or woman, bond or free.*

If in the practice of my profession – or in social life outside of it – I chance to see or hear anything that should not be told abroad, I will hold it a secret and maintain on that subject a religious silence...

I looked up and noticed a young woman listening. She was seated on a fallen column nearby, and had dark curly hair, and an open cheerful face. Somewhat strangely she was wearing a thick padded jacket with a fur collar.

"Where would we be without such a person!" she said, smiling in a friendly way.

I was curious about her jacket. "How can you wear a thick jacket when the sun is shining and it's so hot?" I asked.

"It's cold," she said cheerfully. "On Kos now it's winter!"

"Winter? The weather here is fantastic!"

"Where do you come from?" she asked.

"England."

"Ah, that explains it. There you are always cold and wet. It's good to work here in the summer. But now – brrrr- it's winter!" And she drew her neck down into her fur collar and pulled her jacket tightly around her. "So how do you like my island?" she asked.

"We've only just arrived. I love the Asclepeion here. It's so therapeutic," I said.

"Ah, you feel it too? We all feel it. It's as if the gods are still around," she laughed.

Soon she was telling us that she had a son of six, and a year and a half ago she'd had cancer of the pancreas and had undergone surgery and chemotherapy. I looked at her, amazed that anyone so vibrant and healthy looking had had to go through that sort of trauma.

"You must have been afraid for your son," I said.

"Afraid for him? No, I was never afraid for him. He has life and if I die he has his father, my sister, my mother, my aunt, they are all there for him. He will be all right. The important thing is to be happy because if you are happy you make others happy. If you are unhappy and let others see it, then they are unhappy." And she made a grimace of disapproval.

"Is that why you are working here in this centre of healing?" I asked her.

"No. I work here because they pay very well," she said lightly. "Though, as you say, you can feel the healing powers of the place. It's as if the ghosts of the Asclepeiads – the priest-physicians – are still here." She laughed. "So are the gods! They are all here. You think I am crazy? But I feel them all inside." She placed both hands on her heart. "The gods all had human characteristics – they were an extension of us humans! They had passion!" She regarded me critically, saw that I wasn't in opposition to her views, and continued in an unstoppable flow. "The Greeks have passion! Gods and humans, we are all the same!" she added with conviction. "The ancient Greeks were very intelligent, they were great thinkers. They brought philosophy and medicine and drama to the western world."

"And democracy," I added.

"Bravo!" she nodded. "And democracy. Nothing has changed from ancient times," she said decisively.

"What about the Orthodox Church?" I asked. "Surely that changed everything? The Church is very strong here in Greece, isn't it?" She looked at me with reproof and remained silent. "The churches are always full, aren't they?" I went on.

"Look, there are many people who have little education, and they have a narrow vision." She used her two hands holding them to her eyes like blinkers. "But others who have had more education, they ask questions, they are like the philosophers from the past." She paused a moment, then said: "You hear Greeks shouting at each other and you think they are angry. But they are not, they are just talking." She smiled at the follies of her people. "I don't believe that our old gods are gone. They are still here under cover of the Church. Maybe they are the saints," she laughed. She looked at her watch and quickly got to her feet. "Ah, I am late! I have to get back to my work," she said. "I will see you again, perhaps. It's been nice talking to you!" She waved a cheerful goodbye and went down the path alongside the terraces.

I put the Oath into my bag and turned my attention to the Asclepeion again. This third terrace, I'd read, had been landscaped in the early second century B.C. and had had on it a great Doric style temple of Asclepius which would have been visible to those approaching by sea. It had been necessary to build this terrace to house the increasing number of pilgrims and invalids coming to the island, especially for the Great Asclepeion Games when there'd been athletics and music contests.

When the fifth century emperor, Theodosius II, decreed the closure of all pagan sanctuaries, a Christian church had been built here on this terrace to put a lid on paganism. A massive earthquake in 554 A.D., however, had destroyed the site and for centuries the whole area had lain forgotten under layers of alluvium. In the first years of the fourteenth century the Knights of St. John had arrived on Kos and had again Christianised this historic pagan site with a church on this third terrace, dedicating it to Our Lady of the Grove. It wasn't till the early twentieth century that excavations had begun in earnest, and the lost buildings of this ancient Asclepeion were again revealed.

We were by now wilting. It was time to move on, to find food and relax a little before going on to the next thing on this our first day's agenda.

On this island of Hippocrates it seemed right to pursue the treatment of ailments by taking a bus to Embros Thermi where a hot spring was known to have medicinal qualities. It was said to alleviate rheumatism and arthritis, and to help in the relief of gynaecological problems. It was some twelve kilometres from Kos town on the south-east coast.

The bus rattled at speed past the usual paraphernalia of seaside houses, hotel complexes and suchlikes flanking the coastal road. The mountain range of the Turkish mainland appeared to run parallel. We rounded the end of the island and passed Agios Fokas where we glimpsed an array of bright coloured wind-breaks along the sandy beach; this end of the island caught the north wind.

A few miles further, on a deserted stretch of road, the bus drew up. We were told that we'd arrived. There was only one shack of a café, and a few listless donkeys sheltering nearby. A rough dusty track descended steeply to the dark blue, sparkling sea lapping at the black and grey sand-and-shingle beach. Some fifty metres away to the right a lofty honey-coloured craggy rock loomed with several liver-coloured boulders at its base. We could see a large round pool below the towering rock where people were paddling, and a few swimming. A strong smell of sulphur hung on the air. Several donkeys waited down here too, ready to transport anyone who might have difficulty in walking back up to the road again.

Along the beach to our left were wide ragged-looking sunshades made from reeds, and sun-loungers for those only wanting to laze and swim in the sea, though there were few people there.

We took off our sandals, and walked tentatively into the shallow water where small waves were breaking on the shore. Oh, how cold it was! We came out and approached the large pool around which people were gathered. As we stood beside it we noticed numerous small bubbles on the surface as though some huge hand had thrown food to a multitude of fish who were rising for it. We tried the water here, tentatively at first, then going in up to our knees. It was hot – very hot.

After a while Harry and I found a boulder to sit on. I heard a man's voice behind me on my left say in English: "I'm not into excitement."

The words amused me, and I looked around to see who was

speaking. I saw a scrawny, middle-aged man in swimming trunks and wearing a small straw hat. The woman beside him, whom I took to be his wife, was overweight, wearing a sleeveless dress and a flowery linen sun-hat. They were seated side by side on a rock.

I couldn't resist saying: "Is this the excitement you're not into?" I waved a hand towards the pool. The man had a fixed lugubrious look about him.

"Oh, he's never one for excitement, he's not," said his wife.

"They said it would be hot, but not bleeding scalding," the man complained. "Look at them!" He stretched out two red stick-legs.

"Hot enough to boil an egg!" Harry said. He didn't mind speaking to strangers from his own country.

"Boil a leg," prompted the man mournfully. Then, deciding we were friends not foes, he said: "Where you from, then?"

When we told him, the woman said: "When the kiddies were little we always took our holidays down there – Torquay was where we went. But now we come to Kos."

"So you know the island well?" I asked.

"Kardameina, that's where we stay – every year."

"What's Kardameina like?" I asked.

"Quiet in October," said the man.

"A lot of nightlife in the summer," said his wife.

"Too much excitement," put in the man.

"We like Kardameina 'cos it's convenient for Nisyros. The boat leaves from Kardameina for Nisyros," she explained. "We always like a day on Nisyros," she added.

"Bleeding Nisyros," the man complained.

"Nisyros?" I asked.

"Over there, love." The woman turned and pointed out a distant island.

The man said: "Them blessed Greeks, they liked their excitement. They said that their god, Possy something – "

"Poseidon," prompted his wife.

"Poseidon, then. He went chasing after a giant. And while the giant was legging it away, the god struck off a corner of Kos and flung it at him, and he got caught underneath."

"Which is why you can hear sighs and groans when you're there," put in his wife. "It's volcanic is Nisyros."

"I'd rather be in Torquay," said the man. "Every year we come to Kos, and I wish we was in Torquay."

"You don't get the sun in Torquay," said the wife.

"You do."

"Not like you get here, you don't. I like the heat. They say the hot springs here come from Nisyros," she went on.

"It's the volcano there what heats the water and comes on a current," the man added.

"It's why they won't build hotels along here in case it causes an environmental upset," said the woman.

Harry nudged me, and murmured that we ought to get going if we wanted to catch the last bus back.

"You don't want to miss that," said the man. "Can't do with waiting for a bus what never comes, nor a bus what's gone without you." He eyed me gloomily. "We rents a car. You get where you wants with a car. Costs, mind."

I said that I hoped we'd get a car for a day, but there seemed to be a good bus service. We dried our feet, scraped the sand out from between our toes and put on our sandals.

"Not taking a donkey up?" asked the woman.

"I think I'd rather walk," I said.

"Too much excitement on a donkey," said the man.

"No, you don't want excitement, not on a donkey you don't," agreed the woman.

We said our goodbyes, and wished them a happy rest of their holiday – with not too much excitement, I added, and the man gave a doleful smile, as he raised a listless arm in farewell.

It was a hot heave-ho of a walk back up the dusty track, and we were glad of cooling drinks when we reached the café. The bus-stop was only a stone's throw away.

"So what's the plan for tomorrow?" Harry asked.

"A trip up the mountain to a place called Palio Pyli," I said. "You'll like that."

"Not another cave?" Harry was suspicious.

For once I didn't have to use subtlety or cunning. "No, not another cave," I assured him.

"From here you must walk," our taxi driver said. "Palio Pyli is up there." He waved a hand towards the mountain.

"How far is it back to Pyli?" I asked.

He shrugged. "Four kilometres maybe."

We got out of the taxi into the cool mountain air. To my dismay I found I was still wearing my bedroom slippers, not my walking sandals. Well, too bad. On these trips my bedroom slippers were, in fact, *espadrilles* and fitted well, though the heels were trodden down and could only be pulled up with difficulty.

The taxi left and we were alone on the mountain. We walked on along the hard-packed sandy road, across a wet patch where a stream trickled, till we found ourselves at the base of a worn-with-age shiny stone-slabbed pathway disappearing up through pine trees. A wooden signpost pointed the way.

As we climbed up I mentioned to Harry that I'd read that Hippocrates had been descended from Heracles on his mother's side.

"Heracles? Who's he?"

"Hercules – the twelve labours of Hercules fellow – Heracles in Greek," I explained.

"I thought he was just a myth," Harry said.

"All myths are founded on a grain of truth," I said positively. "Shall I tell you the story?" I paused for breath, and Harry bent his head down which I took as a 'yes'. "According to the myth Heracles was washed up on Kos after being shipwrecked in a storm but, instead of being offered hospitality which was usual with the ancients, he was insulted by a shepherd who refused to sell him a sheep." And I told Harry how the then king of Kos wanted to capture or kill Heracles as he thought he was a pirate so he'd had to escape up into the mountains disguised as a woman. "Up here, I suppose," I added. "But when the locals discovered his true identity they were so furious with the king for his treatment of him, they killed the king, and Heracles married the king's daughter."

"Another of those mad Greek stories," Harry remarked.

"It's why they used to hold religious ceremonies in honour of Heracles here on Kos, and the chief priest dressed up in women's clothing."

The evening before we'd come across a large excavated area near the port. There we'd seen a sanctuary of Heracles, as well as two important sanctuaries of Aphrodite, one in her capacity as goddess of love, and the other as protectress of sailors at sea. The area had been carefully landscaped in the late third and early second centuries to impress those sailing in to port. Beyond, in the distance, on a higher elevation the Asclepeion too would have been visible in all its magnificence.

Our path was momentarily blocked by a flock of ragged sheep leaping across it, the occasional melodious sheep-bell sounded in the silence. Somewhere in the vicinity were once temples of Zeus, and also Demeter whose *Thalysia* festival (the offering of the first fruits to the goddess) was known to have been celebrated annually.

The mountain air was invigorating. Up we went, making good use of our trekking sticks. Up here there had once been an ancient settlement which had been abandoned when in 1830 there had been an outbreak of cholera. The inhabitants had then moved down the mountain to their new location they called Pyli.

It wasn't long before we came to a squat little ancient stone church in a clearing, but it was locked. Continuing on up we came to a second one. But my goal was the larger eleventh century church and monastery founded by the monk Osios Christodoulos who later founded the great Monastery of St. John the Theologian on Patmos.

What a fantastic setting! Although this church was locked also, we sat outside enjoying the mountain scenery and the views over the lower slopes to the sea. But there was a higher elevation still, atop which were the ruins of the ninth century Byzantine castle which had flourished till the eleventh century. I wasn't doing the climb in my 'slippers' and said I would wait where I was.

I watched Harry make the ascent, glimpsing him through the trees. When the Crusaders had come to Kos in the twelfth century they'd taken over the castle and reinforced it. I found it amazing that such isolated locations were chosen – so inconvenient! But then, I supposed, when you had enemies, inconvenience (to the enemy) was the best line of defence. It was always preferable to be above those wanting to kill you.

I wandered around the ruins of the monastery, and felt frustrated that the church dedicated to the Mother of God was locked and the windows sealed. I had read it had interesting frescoes, but there was no way of seeing them.

Osios Christodoulos (whose name means 'Christ worker') had fled from the Saracens in Asia Minor and come to Kos in 1085. Here he'd met the son of a wealthy landowner who, like himself, was an ascetic and devout Christian. Having founded this monastery Christodoulos dreamed of re-establishing a monastic life on Patmos. With the support of his companion (the son of the wealthy landowner) they presented a plan to the then emperor, who granted Osios Christodoulos the sovereignty of Patmos in exchange for his holdings here on Kos.

I caught sight of a small figure up on the battlements waving a trekking stick. Harry had arrived. From there he must surely have the most fantastic views. I waved back, then indicated that I would start making my way to an isolated *kafeneio* we'd spotted through the trees on a ridge behind.

It was a stiff climb, up widely spaced and very steep steps, some of which I could only reach with the use of my stick like a pole-vaulter. But how worthwhile the achievement when I finally arrived. I was met by an alsation dog, and a young man with a beard. The view over pine trees from this terrace was unbelievable – far off Pyli, the plateau spreading to the sea, and beyond that no, not Turkey, but the island of Kalymnos.

How extraordinary to build a monastery and live a life in such isolation dedicated to God – to live in isolation with your beliefs with your vision of an after life. Did such isolation addle the mind? Or did it concentrate it wonderfully? I supposed it concentrated it wonderfully and, if addled, became increasingly so. As someone who falls way behind in the realms of belief, I found such devotion and dedication bewildering. Such people couldn't help their convictions, just as I couldn't help my lack of them. It was like falling in love – you were either in love or not, it couldn't be forced – which surely told me something else also? That either God didn't exist, or he didn't want me to believe in him.

I sipped a long cooling drink and watched the slow progress of Harry picking his way along the cobbled path, pausing every now and again, then starting the long haul up the steps to the *kafeneio*. He was triumphant that he'd been to the castle. I should have come with him – the views! – the battlements! I waved a leg in the air and pointed to my *espadrilles*.

"And we still have to walk to Pyli," I said.

An hour later we were striding along the road downhill. There was little shade but a light breeze cooled us. Sometimes it's helpful to be ignorant because one remains hopeful. We walked and walked. In due course we came to a few straggling houses – but where was the town? Where was there a taverna where we could stop for a drink, and enquire about the bus back? We continued walking.

At last a bus appeared and we waved our sticks at it. But it was a school bus not one for the public. It was drawing away again when the driver of a white rented car asked us if we would like a lift.

What I had secretly hoped for had happened. We were taken several miles on and deposited where we were told the Kos bus could be picked up. We had time to sit and cool down at a nearby taverna.

I felt triumphant having completed what I'd set out to do, and Harry was also, having climbed up to his castle.

Tomorrow we would be hiring a car for the day to get to the far west of the island. Harry was happy about the arrangement because I'd told him of another isolated castle he could visit.

"Wait, and I show you." A middle-aged, Greek with impeccable manners and a small black beard stood beside me at the breakfast serving table. There were many hotel guests milling around, all helping themselves from numerous dishes laden with food to suit every foreign palate. The well-mannered Greek had profound patience. He took a small copper pot with a wooden handle and carefully embedded its base in a bowl of sand which stood on a gas-ring over a low flame. He had just made his own cup of Greek coffee, and I'd shown curiosity as to how he'd set about it.

"First you take this long spoon – and you fill it with this coffee as strong or as weak as you want it – Like this – You like it strong? So –" He heaped a little more coffee on the spoon. "Or not so strong?" He shook a little off. "Ah, a little more you like?" He scooped up more. "And you place it in this pot we call a *briki*," he explained, sprinkling in a small quantity at a time. "Now, If you want sugar, you add it next –"

"No, no sugar, thank you," I said.

He slowly emptied the spoonful of sugar back into its bowl. "No sugar. So now you add water like so –" And he carefully poured in the water as though he were an alchemist mixing a secret potion. "Now you raise the sand at the base –" He cautiously ridged up a layer of sand around the side of the pot. "And now you wait." He peered into the *briki* to see if the liquid was heating up. He reached out for a small Greek coffee-cup and held it out for my inspection. "When you see the coffee in this *briki* rising, then it is ready to pour into this small cup. But now you must wait."

"Thank you," I said.

"Please – enjoy it," he said and, with a little bow, he took his own cup and wended his way through the numerous tables to one in a corner where he sat alone.

I saw Harry seated at our table on the hotel terrace overlooking the harbour. He had sent me to get a couple of hard-boiled eggs which he thought we could spirit away in our pockets for lunch. He turned around to see what I was up to, saw me by the Greek coffee-making table and pointed to his watch. I pointed to my *briki*. The gentle bearded Greek saw me gesticulating and returned. He stood over my pot and peered at the contents. Very precisely he stirred up the sand around the base of the pot so it was more embedded.

"With Greek coffee you must be patient," he remarked. "Soon you will see the water rise. Another minute, perhaps two."

Patience! It wasn't my strongest point. I drummed with my fingers on the white table cloth. I stood on one leg, then the other. I watched, and watched, and watched. The gentle Greek came over yet again. "Ah!" he said as I looked at him with exasperation. "Look, it is beginning to rise! There! Your coffee is ready!" He poured it into the small white cup, and reached for its small white saucer. With another small bow he handed me my coffee, and we parted company never to meet again.

It's been a long day and, on this our last evening, we are seated at a fish taverna close by our hotel. By walking through the taverna we find ourselves on a terrace beside the sea looking out at the port. A great jetty stretches out into the sea. Smaller yachts and schooners are sailing beyond it into Kos harbour.

The evening is balmy and windless. Streaks of thin cloud hang in the air and turn a pale pink against an azure sky. In contrast the sea here is a molten metalic colour and appears to be in perpetual motion with numerous diminutive wavelets with no forward or backward movement. How odd that the sky is so still and the sea so restless. Today we hired the car and got ourselves to Kefalos at the far west end of Kos – well, not to the town itself but to Agios Stephanos, an ancient site situated on a small promontory a few kilometres from the town. It was very beautiful there with the ruins of a fifth century double basilica church dedicated to Agios Stephanos (St. Stephen, the first ever Christian martyr). It was built on a levelled area above volcanic rock which descended to a dark green sea. Pale sandy beaches extended either side from it and offshore, not far away, was a high rocky islet with a small whitewashed chapel at its base.

On this ancient site there were areas where a light-weight meshing could be detected half concealed in sand. By lifting the mesh and drawing it back, then gently scraping away the sand, we'd found perfectly preserved black and white mosaics and words in Greek, though what they said remained a mystery. Amongst the ruins was the clear outline of the old baptistry in the shape of a cross. This early

Christian basilica had been built over the site of an old pagan temple.

From there we had driven up into the mountainous region behind Kefalos, to the isolated Monastery of Agios Ioannis, only to find the place locked and apparently abandoned. On this island it seemed that many churches were either locked, or were in ruins.

Afterwards, we'd driven back, past the airport, and turned right at Antimachia. From there the landscape looked as though a child had been drawing swirls and whirls with a crayon, and there were round hills and scored valleys without any recognizable pattern to them. And there suddenly we'd seen the great and isolated Castle of Antimachia. That had been Harry's reward for not grumbling about the earlier long drive to find the abandoned monastery in the back of beyond. The castle had been more of a huge fortification within which the Crusaders had built small residential houses. There had been two churches within its massive defence walls, both still standing and undamaged, but both of them locked with sealed windows so nothing inside could be seen. The whole fortification had been magnificently left to nature, and was filled with wild flowers and tall dried grasses.

A ship's siren sounds and I look up from my meal. A large Blue Star ferry-boat is sailing into port. It appears to be heading at speed for the wide jetty which it is about to ram. If it doesn't stop it'll continue straight to our table. But a miracle occurs. Its bulk slowly reverses sideways, and a great splash of sea water flies up as the ship's anchor is dropped. The metallic coloured, perpetually-in-motion sea by our taverna turns into small tsunami waves which crash onto the large boulders set along the sandy beach alongside us.

We watch as a crowd of newcomers disembark. The island depends on tourism. What, though, if people stop coming? Already we've been told there are less this year than last. What did they do before tourism? We'd seen little agriculture – a few fields of barley, some acres of tomatoes, not many olive groves, a handful of cows, a few sheep and goats –

I turn my attention back to the evening tranquillity. The Turkish landmass reminds me of a zigzag cardiograph against the skyline before trailing gently downwards to the sea. Evening shadows enhance the folds of the mountains. The twinkling lights of Bodrum mass along the coast. There is a distinctive, pyramid-shaped smaller mountain to the fore, and I ask the waiter about it. That, he says, is a small Greek island. A Greek island? So close to Turkey?

Harry asks what the plan is for the next day. Our flight is not till the evening. I say that I would really, really like to return to the Asclepeion as it was relaxing and would be a tonic before our late evening flight. Has he anything else he wants to do, I enquire? Yes, we haven't seen the Crusader castle yet, he replies. And so our last day on the island is arranged as dusk falls and the moon rises above Kos.

"Hello! You're back!" It was the cheerful woman we'd met at the Asclepeion on our first visit. She had her padded jacket tied around her waist on this occasion.

"Oh, hello!" I said. "Yes, we're back!"

She was seated on a terrace wall, and we sat beside her. She waved an arm at the Turkish landmass, and said: "You know the Greeks colonized the Turkish coastline many centuries before Christ, taking with them their gods? There you'll find many ancient sites founded by them – Cnidus was one of them with a medical school which rivalled Hippocrates' school here on Kos."

"Wasn't Bodrum there the old Halicarnassus?" I asked.

"Where Mausolus built his great tomb, one of the wonders of the world. It is where the word 'mausoleum' comes from."

"How did you learn such good English?" I asked.

"Oh, my mother worked for a family who employed an English nanny," she said. "While my mother cooked I was cared for by the nanny along with the other children. Have you been to Turkey?" she asked.

"Yes. We visited Didyma, the ancient oracle of Apollo. And Ephesus, where St. Paul got worked up about the silver statues of Artemis."

"I don't know why," she said, "but I feel I belong more to the east than the west – to Anatolia," she explained, pointing to the Turkish coast. "My maternal grandmother came from there. Maybe that explains why I feel more eastern than western. She and her family were caught up in the Great Catastrophe of 1922," she went on.

"What happened?" I asked.

"It was terrible," she said. It was a crazy political decision when all the Greek Christians in Anatolia were forced to leave their homes in exchange for the Turkish Moslems living here in Greece. It was compulsory." She raised her hands in a gesture of despair. "An exchange of peoples because of their religious beliefs! Are humans crazy? My mother's parents were driven out of Smyrna and came here to Kos. It wasn't because of language or culture but because of their religion! Pah! Give me the old gods!"

She was so incensed by this episode of Greek history it was difficult to know what to say. "They came with nothing!" she went on. "And they were the lucky ones because they had relatives here on Kos so had somewhere to go. Smyrna was torched and people fled in terror to the sea. My grandparents were the lucky ones because there was a boat – the very last one to leave. They had life! If they had not survived I would not be here now. I have life! My son has life! We all of us are alive – NOW!" she emphasised. Her gesture of defiance reminded me of her cancer, and I wondered if she would be alive the following year.

"But I!" She pointed to herself. "I will never die!" It was an emphatic declaration said with a laugh, as though she'd read my thoughts. She put her sandwich wrappings away, dusted crumbs from her lap and said: "I must leave you again. It is time for me to collect my son from my mother. You must excuse me." She stood up, and tightened the arms of her jacket around her waist.

Spontaneously, I said: "Let me first take a photograph of you. Give me your address and I will send you a copy."

"But you must stand with me," she said.

I handed the camera to Harry. The job done, and with her address written down, she suddenly said: "Wait a moment!" She searched in the pocket of her jacket and pulled out two objects. "Do you know, yesterday I bought two of these, and I didn't know why. But now I know, it was because we would meet again." She presented us with two evil-eye talismans. "Everything is meant," she said.

When she was gone, I thought about her words: 'Everything is meant'. Sometimes it seemed to me that it was true.

"Everything is meant," I said to Harry. "Do you believe that?"

"I don't see what's meant about those things," came the answer. "She probably regretted buying them and just wanted to fob them off on us."

As on our first visit to the Asclepeion, I didn't think it was a place for argument. Fear of the unknown seized hold. The evil-eye talismans were not things to be treated with contempt. Both must be kept carefully for good luck, and kept for ever.

Our last few hours here on Kos. We've been to the Castle of the Knights of St. John, and are once more seated close to the ancient plane tree of Hippocrates. The spread of its great branches, and its bronze autumn leaves fluttering to the cobblestones, is a majestic sight despite its hollow trunk, and the props to keep it upright.

I feel I want to compose a paean to its magnificence. The word 'paean', which today means a song of praise, was once a chant of supplication to Asclepius for protection against disease, or of thanks for a cure.

"Do you know the Turks hanged a lot of Orthodox priests from that tree?" I say suddenly. "It's odd to have the Hippocratic Oath then, because of religious differences, wham! healthy people kill each other!"

"Hm."

"The ancients never killed one another because they felt fanatical about their gods. I wonder why today Jews, Christians, and Moslems get over excited and in such a rage they hang or shoot or blow each other up."

Harry feels too relaxed to get into a discussion on the matter.

A smallish, perfectly shaped leaf flutters down from the plane tree and I pick it up from the cobblestones. It is five-pointed, bronze, and has a slender purple stem. I put it carefully in my bag between my pages of the Hippocratic Oath. It will be my small but lasting memento of the island.

RHODES

Rhodes! An island of sea and sunshine! When Zeus was dividing up the earth amongst his family, the sun-god Helios was unwittingly left out. When he found he'd been overlooked Helios complained to Zeus who immediately awarded him an island which had just emerged out of the deep; this was the beautiful, flower-bedecked island of Rhodes.

In those ancient times Helios had been regarded as a charioteer with a team of fiery horses who drew him across the heavens from east to west heralded by Eos (the dawn). At night he disappeared to the other side of the earth in a golden bowl floating on Ocean who girdled the globe.

The story goes that Helios married Rhodos, the daughter of Poseidon and Amphitrite, hence the name of the island. The first cities, founded in the second millennium B.C., were named after three of Helios' grandsons: Lindos, Ialyssos and Kameiros. The city of Rhodes on the northern tip of the island was founded much later in 408 B.C., and became the island's major port with three natural harbours.

Helios was already starting his night's travels when we landed on his island, and it was dark by the time we reached the city of Rhodes with its monumental medieval gateways and massive defence walls.

A taxi took us to our hotel – well, as near as was permitted, as no cars are allowed into the city centre between certain hours. We were put down in a pebble-cobbled street close to a bazaar, brightly lit and colourful with stalls selling clothes, bags, sun-hats, trinkets, children's toys and anything to attract the tourist eye. The taxi-driver trundled our luggage some fifty yards to our hotel.

Where to begin with this island with so much history behind it? Well, I was there for its pagan past and its Byzantine churches. Harry and the Stoic (yes, the Stoic was to join us the next day) were there for the Crusader period, for the Knights of St. John of Jerusalem who'd been in control of the island from 1309 till the coming of the Turks in 1522.

So many religions! The worship of Helios first, then Apollo, and the goddess Athena and Lord Zeus himself. A settlement of Jews once occupied a corner of the city from as far back as the second century B.C.; then had come Christianity and finally Islam with the Ottomans, till they were ejected and Christianity returned.

It is a day to relax and take stock of our new surroundings. We expect the Stoic to arrive this afternoon, so this morning we are wandering, and finding our way around. We go through the bazaar and come to the Street of the Knights, dead straight and cobbled in black and white pebbles, leading up to the Palace of the Grand Masters. We do not pause to look, but know that on either side of this road there are the Inns of the Knights of the Order arranged in what are known as 'tongues', each Inn belonging to a nation speaking its own language. For me the Palace of the Grand Masters is only important because it is in the area where Helios once had a temple, or so it is believed.

We pass the Archaeological Museum housed in the Great Hospital built by the Knights in the 15th century. The Crusaders saw their role as the noble protectors of pilgrims to the Holy Land, and carers of those who fell sick. Known as the Hospitallers, it was they who opened this massive infirmary here in Rhodes.

The morning is already hot with little if any breeze. We wander down past the ruins of what our town map tells us was once a temple of Aphrodite. I cannot get excited about the blocks of stone and scattered column drums. More interesting is the nearby monumental Gate of Agios Pavlos (St. Paul's Gate) and Pyli Eleftherias (Freedom Gate), even more massive and impregnable.

We walk on to Mandraki Harbour where there is a welcome sea breeze. As we stroll along the quayside, we pass three solid stone windmills before coming to the Agios Nikolaos Fort. From there we can see the two famous columns flanking the entrance to the harbour; on top of one is a large bronze stag and on the other a doe. In photographs they appear to be much larger, and I am surprised how small they look.

"This is where the Colossus stood," I say to Harry.

"Where?"

"One foot astride the harbour entrance where that stag and doe are."

Harry mulls over the information as he gazes at the two columns. "What exactly was the Colossus anyway?" he asks

I've been reading up about it and am able to answer: "It was a bronze statue of Helios, one hundred and fourteen feet high, weighing twenty tons, and cast by a fellow called Chares from Lindos in two hundred and eighty something B.C. Apparently, each finger was the size of a man."

"The size of a man? Each finger?"

"Well, it was a Colossus," I reminded him. "In fact it's possible it didn't stand here at all, but up near the Palace of the Grand Masters. Anyway, at the time it was one of the wonders of the world. It was built to commemorate Rhodes' victory over some enemy who wanted to attack Egypt and get a foothold here first. Rhodes was besieged for a whole year with some gargantuan bronze siege-machine. Can you imagine being battered for a whole year by the enemy using some monstrous bronze thing?"

"Did the bronze thing succeed?"

"No. The Rhodians tunnelled under it till it eventually overturned. They used the bronze from it for the Colossus to show their gratitude to the gods for their help against the enemy, and also as a memorial to their victory. The Colossus took twelve years to cast!"

"Twelve years? Hum." Harry stares at the doe and stag columns, and swings his walking stick absently. Yachts line the quayside, and the sea is a fantastic blue.

"Actually, the poor chap whose brain-child the Colossus was, found he'd made some ghastly error while creating it, and committed suicide rather than face up to the disgrace of having made a bosh of it," I said. "It was finally finished by one of his pupils."

"So where is it now, the Colossus?"

"All that sweat and tears to get it cast and set up, and then, wham! Seventy years later there was a great earthquake and the Colossus cracked at the knees and crashed to the ground, which probably caused another earthquake. You'd have thought Helios, protector of the island, would have prevented it!"

We wander past the fabulous yachts, and I try to catch the eye of one of the skippers. It would be nice to be asked on board.

But it is too hot to stand around, and none of the wealthy yacht owners glance our way. We decide to return to our hotel where we can sit on one of the shady terraces and eat our lunch salvaged from breakfast. Breakfast is served outside under a tree, and this morning's was much more than we could eat – Greek yoghurt and hard-boiled eggs are enough at that time of the morning – so we'd buttered the rolls and filled them with cheese and ham, and had them ready to go back to.

"My dears, I've arrived! And you're here! What magic is at work to bring us all together once more – and in Rhodes!"

It was the Stoic at the wrought-iron gates. We greeted her with enthusiasm, and helped carry her luggage up a flight of external steps to her room on the first floor. We saw her settled in and, as it was siesta time, we left her to recover from her journey. We ourselves needed a siesta now Helios was at the highest point of his journey through the heavens.

With my feet up I set myself the task of studying Rhodes' ancient acropolis site. In the Hellenistic period, in the third or second century B.C., a temple of Apollo Pythias had been built on the higher acropolis west of the city. The following day, while Harry and the Stoic did the Crusader beat, I hoped to take a taxi to that ancient site.

The upper acropolis of ancient Rhodes is now most unromantically named Monte Smith after a British admiral, Sir Sidney Smith who, in the early nineteenth century, used the hill for spying out shipping movements during the Napoleonic wars.

The taxi-driver who dropped me off said there would be many taxis coming and going and I could easily pick one up when I was ready to return. It was the first piece of Greek misinformation I was to be told that day.

But what did I care! The sun shone, and the few columns remaining of Apollo Pythias' temple soared up to the deep blue sky. The ground had been levelled for the temple, then descended steeply to a lower area. Here and there on the rough terrain juniper trees gave welcome shade, and the whole site was fringed with them. Juniper was a slow growing tree and its timber was hard and used for shipbuilding.

Beyond this temple sanctuary site I could see the flat rooftops of the city's whitewashed buildings, and beyond that the sapphire blue sea. I'd got glimpses of the sea as my taxi passed through various parts of the city, climbing the hillside. Its shades of blue ranged from a sort of boiling white tinged with blue along the coastline, to stretches of turquoise, to sparkling sapphire. Helios drenched his island with his light, heightening the colours both of sea and land. Where I stood now by Apollo's temple I could see a white cruise liner; the passengers, no doubt on deck, would be looking this way at the island, glimpsing the few columns against the skyline which are all that are left of the temple now.

I wondered whether from this high point the Colossus when standing would have been seen straddling Mandraki harbour – or astride the lower acropolis where the Palace of the Grand Masters now stood. The Delphic oracle had been consulted by the Rhodians regarding what was to be done with the Collosus' shattered, prostrate pieces, and Apollo had advised against re-erecting it. It had consequently remained where it had fallen for nine hundred years causing, no doubt, considerable inconvenience to pedestrians having to walk around the lumps of bronze or, had it straddled the harbour, causing a major hazard to shipping.

I sat in the shade of a juniper, soaking up the atmosphere of the site. Apollo had at one time been equated with the sun, and he'd been known as Phoebos Apollo, Apollo the shining one. In this manner he had taken over from Helios. It is thought he took the epithet Phoebos from the Titaness, Phoebe, daughter of Ouranus (heaven) and Gaea (earth), who had been the original protectress of the Delphic oracle. Apollo's mother Leto was Phoebe's daughter, and the Python at Delphi, a monster female snake, had originally spoken with oracular powers on behalf of both Gaea and Phoebe. When Apollo'd killed the Python he'd named his priestess Pythia after it – hence the dedication of Apollo Pythias for his temple here.

I could see steps cut into the rock descending to where there'd been a well from which sacred water had been drawn. From inscriptions found it is believed there had once been oracular pronouncements from this part of the temple.

There had been another Doric temple in the vicinity in honour of Zeus Polieus and Athena Polias. I supposed I would come across it on my wanders, together with what were Nymphaia, subterranean chambers to do with nymphs, personifications of various natural objects such as water, trees, mountains, etc.

I came to the stadium on the lower levelled terrace. There I sat down, this time on the topmost tiered seat, again in the shade of a tall juniper tree stretching out its branches from behind me. Opposite, the front-row seats had upright backs to them for dignitaries and their guests come to watch the athletic events of the Alioi Games which were part of the major festival held in honour of Helios.

To one side of this stadium was the small theatre whose tiered seats were of white marble. It was thought to have been used not so much for drama as for classes in oratory and rhetoric for which Rhodes was to become famous. The great Roman orator, Cicero, was said to have spent time in Rhodes in the first century B.C. and had come here where he'd been taught the discipline of curbing his impetuous and exuberant nature. Julius Caesar had also come when, as a young man, he'd felt the need to perfect his oratory, realizing it was his most powerful weapon for swaying public opinion.

I left the stadium and asked a couple of Greek men lounging under a tree – were they guardians of the site, or labourers taking a break? – if there was more information to be had about the acropolis. They pointed to a small building some fifty yards further down where they told me I'd be able to get any information I needed – the second piece of Greek misinformation that morning.

It turned out to be a small well-lit room whose walls were lined with photographs of the acropolis. I learned that the whole vast area had been set apart for the people of the city for religious, educational, and recreational purposes.

So where was the sanctuary of Zeus Polieus and Athena Polias (the two epithets meaning protector and protectress of the city)? I enquired of the same lounging men, and one of them promptly waved a hand at a random pile of ruins nearby. "There," he announced, and went on chatting to his companion.

Was it just! There was no notice to verify his words, and I asked a woman who had an identification tag pinned to her shirt and looked like a tour-guide. She spoke good English and promptly told me that the sanctuary was to be found along the road to the east. I must go up to the road again and turn right. It was a bit of a walk, and there was little to be seen when and if I did find it, she warned.

Did I want to walk in the midday heat for a pile of stones? No, I didn't. I sat under a juniper again and read up about it, and learned that on a higher terrace had been a large temple of Zeus Polieus and Athena Polias which could be seen from every part of the city, and from far out to sea. It had been there that inscriptions had been found regarding the city's treaties. I also read that it was there, according to literary sources, that a Colossus had been erected – though whether that had been *the* Colossus it didn't say. But it had been an important sacred site.

From where I sat close to the temple of Apollo I looked out over the terraces, to the town and sea beyond, then up to the great vault of blue sky where the sun glittered. Apparently, it had been up here that a second century B.C. astronomer had set up his observatory. He'd been a great mathematician and had calculated such things as longitudes and latitudes, and when and how and what were equinoxes, and catalogued eight hundred fixed stars.

I thought how I would like to come up here again at night. Surely, away from the town, the stars in the night sky would be like a burst of fireworks. It would be romantic with the columns of the temple as dark silhouettes against the myriad stars in the heavens.

But it was early afternoon and Helios was riding his chariot overhead. I was ready to take a taxi back to the cool of our hotel. I went and stood by the roadside waiting for a taxi – one of the numerous ones which could be had, or so I'd been told. After ten minutes one did arrive and I waved it down only to be informed it had come to pick up a family and there was no room for me. No problem, the taxi-driver told me, I had only to walk down into the town, and there I'd find a taxi rank, a mere ten minute walk.

And so I walked – and walked. After twenty minutes I was in a built-up congested street but could see no taxi anywhere, let alone a taxi rank. I asked a woman with a push-chair. A taxi? She advised me to ask at a nearby *kafeneio* to phone for one.

Greek misinformation that day had excelled itself. As usual things eventually worked out, and I was finally deposited near the Archaeological Museum. There, rather by luck than ability, I came across the wrought-iron gates to our hotel. Harry and the Stoic were seated under a lemon tree, shaded from the afternoon sun.

"She's come!" said the Stoic. "I told you she'd find her way back, she always does." She looked at her watch meaningfully. "So late! Poor Harry has been fretting, imagining the worst!"

"Where the hell have you been?" Harry didn't mince his words.

"To the temple of Apollo, of course. I said that's where I was going."

"Two minutes there and you would have seen it," he said.

"Well, maybe you would have, but I need time at such places." I changed the subject. "So how were the Knights of the whatever and the Grand Palace?" I asked.

They forgot my lateness, and I was immediately bombarded about the wonders of the Inns, the 'tongues', the Palace of the Grand Masters and its small museum, and the numerous floor mosaics brought from nearby Kos. They'd walked the palace walls and from there had seen the minarets and mosques left over from the years of Turkish occupation.

"Oh, your lunch!" the Stoic announced, and she rummaged in her bag and produced a cheese and spam roll for me.

"We've already eaten," she said. "And now I must retire to my room to regather my strength." And she gave a great stretch and yawned. After several attempts, she struggled up from her deep and comfortable basket chair, and was soon mounting the exterior stairway step by step with frequent pauses to her bedroom. On the top step she called down to us: "And I really advise you to do the same after the rigours of this morning and the heat."

We followed her advice.

It is our last evening here in Rhodes city, and the Stoic has today produced her latest acquisition, an ipad. "So necessary in this day and age! Ask me any question and this will provide the answer!"

We have just visited the Archaeological Museum and we all feel bog-eyed as a consequence. I say wearily: "Ask it where the best taverna is for supper tonight."

The Stoic taps in some suitable question, and sits poised over the small screen waiting for answers to come up.

"The best value-for-money place," Harry prompts.

"Oh, we must get value for money," the Stoic agrees. "It's surprising how much money you can save by investing in a little gem like this," she says, and pats her ipad as if it is her favourite dog. "It takes no room at all – like the brain – but holds so much more information."

"And then ask your i-thing how to get to our new apartments tomorrow," Harry says.

"I will willingly, but later," the Stoic says. "As yet this little brain-child can only do one thing at a time."

Before homing in on the recommendations of the Stoic's ipad, we decide to visit the old Jewish quarter of the city. There were Jews here as early as the second century B.C., possibly escaping from the Seleucids who ruled Palestine at that time.

On our way we pass through the arcaded Ippokratos Square with views to medieval buildings. In its centre is an ancient looking stone fountain with carved panels around its stone base and an owl perched on a stone dove-cote-type structure supported by a sturdy stone column. We come to the Square of the Jewish Martyrs where there is another fountain with large bronze seahorses on top, and coloured square inserts to its base depicting sea creatures. Here there is a memorial honouring the one thousand and sixty-four Jews from Rhodes and Kos who were massacred by the Nazis in World War II. It is a sombre reminder of the brutality of man. But our mood is soon lightened by colourful parrots who are being handed to tourists by young men (are they Jews?) They attract many onlookers with their bright plumage and comical antics. It is a cheerful scene.

"Herod the Great was made King of the Jews here in Rhodes," I announce.

"What, the bad boy who massacred all the male infants in Bethlehem?" the Stoic asks.

"Yes. He was a pal of Antony and Cleopatra. But when Antony was killed, Herod feared sinking without trace into oblivion and came here to Rhodes to meet Caesar Augustus to swear eternal loyalty to him. Augustus was so impressed that he declared him King of the Jews there and then – or something of the sort."

"My dear wife is a little shaky on her Roman history," Harry warns.

The Stoic is kindly: "Maybe, but I'm sure there's a pearl of knowledge somewhere there."

We leave the Jewish quarter, and go up to the old Turkish area where we rub shoulders with the many tourists ambling along the pebble-cobbled streets and alleyways; we pass ancient doorways, and shuttered or iron-barred windows, and stroll under numerous stone arches which appear to stretch across to keep the old buildings from falling forward on each other. The bustle and brightness of the little shops and stalls draw the eye away from the throng of bare-legged, bare-armed tourists; it is the medieval architecture not the people that attract.

"Here it is!" The Stoic stops in her tracks by a notice which gives the name of her ipad's recommended taverna offering good value for money.

We pass under an arched entranceway and find ourselves in an attractive landscaped garden with small trees and streams, discreet lighting and the sounds of trickling water, and background Greek music. This must surely cost a bomb?

But no, not at all. It is surprisingly cheap considering how exclusive it is. Our spirits rise with the ambience of this taverna. While we eat delicious value-for-money food, I tell Harry and the Stoic about some of the Hellenistic marvels I came across in the Archaeological Museum while they were visiting the medieval galleries. They didn't see the beautiful marble figure of the crouching Aphrodite holding out her locks of hair, I say. They also missed the ancient, sea-washed Marine Venus written about by Lawrence Durrell in his book *Reflections on a Marine Venus*.

No, but they'd enjoyed the walk around the building itself, they tell me. They saw the great cloistered courtyard with its monumental statue of a lion holding the head of a bull between its front paws, and looking up as though startled by the intrusion of the visitor. They saw grave-stones and coats of arms of the Hospitallers which were of great historic interest. I tell them about the head of Helios with holes around the crown where spikes for sun rays would have been; it had been found in the neighbourhood of the Palace of the Grand Masters. But they're not interested, and rave on about the mosaic floors brought from early Christian churches, and the Museum garden.

And so our last evening in Rhodes city passes pleasantly, and we round it off by brewing our own coffee and sitting out under the stars at our hotel. The evening is balmy and warm while Helios makes his night journey. What we look forward to is Helios rising up at dawn and giving us another day of his light. Tomorrow we collect our hired car from the airport and drive to Lindos.

No four-wheeled vehicles were allowed into Lindos, now classified as a village, so we had to park our car down near St. Paul's bay. It was mid-afternoon when we arrived and the Stoic (thanks to her ipad) discovered that our pre-booked apartment was about three hundred yards up the hill from the car park. We strung our belongings about ourselves and began the long haul up the cobbled road, trundling our luggage behind us.

By the time we arrived we were hot and tired, and I was in a foul mood, ready to find fault with everything. There was, in fact, quite a lot to find fault with. Our room was spartan with a black and white pebbled floor patterned in the customary Rhodian design, with accumulated dust and dead insects between the stones. There were no cupboards or chest of drawers so we could only hang our clothes on the bedposts. The one mirror was placed so high on the wall I could only see the top of my head. Harry could find no fault with the place, but only because he didn't want me to cause a furore. A spartan room was better that no room at all, he said.

I flopped onto my bed with a cup of tea, found my notebook where I made a list of my grievances, then as quickly forgot them as I wrote about our morning's activities.

We had visited Ialyssos, one of the three cities of antiquity named after a grandson of Helios. Ialyssos had been about half an hour's drive from the airport, and was situated on a pine-clad hill known as the hill of Filerimos. It had a certain charm of its own, though in their recent occupation of Rhodes the Italians had left their Roman Catholic stamp on the place by creating a long avenue of juniper trees marked out with the Stations of the Cross. For me that had spoilt the ancient site. I found the crucifixion, the sorrow, the Christian emphasis on sin and repentance gloomy. How much more entertaining were the escapades of the pagan divinities, and the 'laughter of the gods' as the ancients had put it.

Yes, Ialyssos had once been a thriving pagan site; and yes, it was a fine location overlooking the extreme north-west tip of the island; and yes, we'd found two pagan sanctuaries, one of Zeus Polieus, and another of Athena Polias – dedications similar to the ones on the upper acropolis which I hadn't found at Rhodes city; and yes, there were some fine peacocks strutting around to be admired, as well as the remains of an early tenth century Byzantine church and the later Monastery of Filerimos; but no, the pagan site did't compare with Rhodes city, and the natural setting for the temple of Apollo Pythias on its acropolis –

I must have dozed off because I was awoken by Harry with another mug of tea. He had more things to collect from the car, and did I want to come, he asked? Yes, I wanted to go down to the bay of St. Paul to see the little white-washed chapel there. The Stoic said she didn't want to go down a hill since it meant coming up again, so would stay where she was and amuse herself with her ipad.

Despite the foundation of Rhodes city, ancient Lindos had remained the religious centre of the island with its spectacular temple of Athena on its high rocky acropolis visible to all passing ships. Regarding St. Paul's bay: the story is that in 58 A.D. on one of his voyages, St. Paul's ship was blown off course in a wild storm and he was miraculously saved from shipwreck by a flash of lightning which had split asunder the rocks at the mouth of this bay thus providing a safe passage into its haven.

St. Paul's bay was extraordinarily picturesque with a curve of white sand, and its small chapel on the right with its view to the temple of Athena, and to the left a taverna looking across to the chapel. We could see a bridal couple and their guests in its courtyard. We were to learn that weddings there were a thriving business, and over seven hundred couples pledge eternal love there every year. St. Paul would approve.

We paddled in the warm lucid water, then sat at the taverna with cool drinks while we watched the evening light change the sky from dark blue to duck egg blue to amber.

We saw the bridal pair descend to the water's edge and together with their few guests board a small passenger-boat which chugged away into the sunset through the narrow gap, the miraculous opening which had appeared for St. Paul.

Seeing how demanding the climb up to the acropolis would be, the Stoic decided to explore the alleyways and wander down to the Great Harbour where we could meet later at a taverna. She would take her ipad, she said, and catch up with the world news, see a film, perhaps, and in general while away the time.

Harry and I began the slow, demanding climb up the shallow steps. Pairs of donkeys bearing tourists were led up a parallel donkey trail nearby. There had been defence walls up there in antiquity, but the medieval Knights had built higher and thicker ones so that the temple columns and other sacred buildings were barely visible from below, only the massive crenellated walls. Harry was a lover of the crusading Knights who could do no wrong, but I thought them intrusive here on this sacred site.

Close by the steps going up to the ticket-office there was a carving in relief on the high rockface. It was of a new type of *trireme* which had both sails and oars and was capable of great speed – a second century B.C. new design of war ship. The carving, in fact, had been the base for a statue (now lost) of a victorious admiral, and on the ship's prow those in the know (and able to get close enough) would have been able to detect the faintest image of the goddess Athena. The carved ship and statue had been both a memorial to the admiral, and a thanksgiving to the goddess for her assistance in victory.

We mounted the modern flight of steps to the ticket-office, and could see on our left cut out of the rockface the few remaining well-worn ones up which the ancients would have passed.

Ignoring the Knight's castle (bother the Knights) I went straight to the corner of the acropolis and stood before the temple of Lindian Athena. The sky was blue, the sea was blue, and the acropolis rock was a mixture of beige and greys. Was I a little disappointed with the Italian restoration and what appeared to me to be pseudo-sandstone columns?

To fit into its landscape its overall size had been twenty-two metres by eight metres wide. Its original columns would have been stunning as a landmark visible from all directions both out at sea and inland. Unusually it had a north-south alignment instead of the west-east commonly found in temples and churches.

But what a grandiose history! The island had sent nine ships to the Trojan War, believed to have sailed from Lindos. Athena had favoured the Greeks throughout the Trojan War. She'd been worshipped in Troy too, but she had chosen to give victory to the Greeks.

It was Athena who'd inspired the Greeks with the Trojan horse idea. A priest of Poseidon at Troy had warned the Trojans not to trust the Greeks with their gift of a wooden horse intended for Athena, Troy's patron goddess, and he'd thrust a spear into its side with devastating consequences as two sea serpents had risen up from the deep and strangled both him and his two sons. Believing this to be a divine punishment for violating this gift intended for their city's goddess, the Trojans dragged this so-called 'gift' into their city, and the Greek heroes who'd been hiding inside it, leapt out and so brought about the downfall of Troy.

"Do you know who I mean by Cassandra?"

"Cassandra? I've heard of him – her – "

"Her. She was the daughter of King Priam of Troy and went around full of woe, warning the Trojans to keep away from the wooden horse. But they all thought she was mad, thanks to Apollo."

"Apollo, why?"

"Well, he fancied Cassandra and tried to win her affections by giving her the gift of prophecy. But because she rejected him he became angry and laid a curse on her so that, although she could see the future and all impending dangers, no one would believe her warnings."

"So what became of Cassandra?" said Harry in a vague only-half-attending tone.

"A typical Greek tragedy. When Troy fell, Cassandra was raped and dragged off to be Agamemnon's concubine. Agamemnon was, of course, killed by his wife on his return, as was Cassandra."

"The Crusaders were far more single minded – Christianity – a clear objective. They never went to war because somebody's love-sick wife ran off with some wretched prince. Absolute nonsense. Ten years of war and they all died anyway."

I was getting nowhere with Harry who, in fact, quite enjoyed the old Greek stories but was a Crusader fan, an admirer of Christian values, of peace and love – which, in fact, hardly existed where the Crusaders were concerned.

"And wasn't the old girl born from the head of Zoos, or something ridiculous like that?" Harry asked, more as a statement than a question.

It rankled. Goddess, an 'old girl'? I found myself defending Athena. "Goddess of wisdom? Goddess of weaving and arts and crafts? To be born from the head from where wisdom and creativity are born I think extraordinarily appropriate. Much better than the normal way."

I turned my attention back to the temple buildings. In the third century B.C. a *propylaea* had been built before Athena's temple. A pilgrim would have ascended a wide stairway to this *propylaea* (a massive entranceway) flanked by columns, and then would have passed through a hall from which he would have had his first close up glimpse of the temple with its magnificent backdrop of sea and coastline. The cult statue would have been in the inner *cella* (the holy of holies) facing him as he'd approached. A sacrificial altar would have stood in the centre of the *temenos* with another for bloodless offerings before the cult statue of Athena.

There had been epiphanies of the goddess here on her acropolis. For instance, in 490 B.C. when the Persians had been besieging the island, the islanders had gathered within its fortified area, but soon had suffered from a severe water shortage. One night Athena had appeared in a dream to a magistrate telling him that she would intercede with Zeus and water would come. Sure enough a few days later there'd been a cloud-burst (above the acropolis only) which had provided them with all the water they'd needed. When the Persian admiral learned about it, he'd been so impressed by the goddess Athena's intervention, that he'd presented all his personal possessions to her.

Two marble plaques have been found on one of which was a list of the priests who had served the goddess, and on the other her miracles and a list of the names of people who had come here.

Heracles (Hercules) had come, as had Alexander the Great to offer gifts to the goddess. Helen of Troy and King Menelaus (her husband) were also mentioned. Had they come together before she'd run off with Paris? Or had they come separately to seek wisdom from the goddess regarding their marital problems?

"Poirot!" Harry said. "You expect to see Poirot appearing from behind a pillar." Harry had recently seen an Agatha Christie on T.V. whose location had been on Rhodes at Lindos. I dismissed Poirot and remembered instead reading how Athena Lindian had been assimilated with the even older goddesses worshipped in a cave beneath this temple. Similarly today Christianity had absorbed Athena into the cult of the Virgin Mary. In Athens, the Parthenon under the Byzantines had been turned into a cathedral and dedicated to Agia Sophia (Holy Wisdom); later it had become known as Panagia Atheniotissa (the All Holy Lady of Athens). The word 'parthenos' means virgin, so the great virgin goddess Athena slipped naturally into her new Christian role.

It was Harry's turn now to pursue his interest in the Knights and the medieval ruins left on this holy site. While he went down to the castle, I did a quick sprint to the ruined Byzantine Church of St. John which was on the usual west-east alignment. I overheard a tour-guide call out to her troupe that in the Middle East the custom had been to address their gods (and certainly God) as 'Lord' thus implying their human servility, whereas the Greeks had addressed their deities by name and had been on a more familiar footing with them. The ancient Greeks, she went on, had been united by both their language and their gods.

I found Harry admiring the coat of arms of the Grand Master d'Aubusson above the castle gate. I myself was more interested in the highly polished surface of the few remaining ancient steps, caused by the numerous pilgrims in antiquity who'd passed that way to honour the great goddess.

It was time to leave the acropolis and join the Stoic in the Great Harbour. We went down the less demanding donkey trail, a gentler slope with no steps. I thought the donkeys looked forlorn, their eyes lack lustre. Back in the busy Lindos street, the oder of donkey was overpowering, their droppings shovelled away swiftly before tourists trod in the mess. We saw the numerous listless animals penned up awaiting their next turn to climb to the acropolis again.

We left the depressed looking creatures, and were soon cheerful as we joined the Stoic at a taverna beside the Great Harbour with its small bright boats on a sparkling sea.

We're on a one-hour coastal cruise, seated in a glass-bottomed boat. The Stoic has enjoyed her morning browsing the many tourist shops, and idling with her ipad beside the Great Harbour – it was she who spotted this hour-long boat trip – "Not long enough to start feeling sea-sick," she'd said. The sea beyond the harbour looks choppy and I hope she's right.

We have two other families on board, one with a lively seven year old son who is glued to the glass bottom watching shoals of small fish above the silver-gold sand of the seabed. I hope to see larger ones, something spectacular. We are told by the girl in charge that the turquoise blue appears where there is silver-gold sand and where the depth of the sea is only six metres; the true blue of the sea is where it is deeper.

We are told to look at the rocky cliff-face where a black goat can be seen poised perilously on a ledge, reaching out to nibble some plant. It has no sense of danger balanced as it is on its two hind legs, its front two stretched out, its neck extended. There is a sheer drop of about a hundred feet beneath it.

And there now, we are informed, is the wild rocky coastline with precipitous cliffs which was used for the location of the film *The Guns of Navarone*.

A white egret is pointed out as we chug along, and a grey heron, then a pied kingfisher on a wild stretch of volcanic barren rock. The sea is choppy and occasionally spray flies up from the bows. We come to Athena's temple on its massive rocky acropolis; the eroded cavities beneath it are clearly seen where prehistoric religious rites once took place.

Next we pass outside St. Paul's bay where we see the split in the low rocks (not so easily seen from the shore) through which St. Paul had sailed to safety.

Too soon we have completed this outward journey and turn about for the return, though not before we are told to look at small, treacherous rocks protruding as islets, one of which looks like a lion's head, another a lion cub, and another a crocodile.

The skipper picks up speed, amused by his passengers clinging to the railings as his flat bottomed boat smacks the waves. It is quite exciting but, as he goes faster and faster and spray flies through the air, the smacking of the waves becomes uncomfortable. The boat rises and crashes with a wallop against the next wave. I hope Harry is alright, and I glance and see he is smiling but oh, God! as we crash-wallop and hit the next trough it feels as if my spine has impacted into my skull. I cling with both hands and brace myself for the next one, eyes shut. The big smack, thankfully, is not repeated and now I worry that when it comes to getting off the boat I may not be able to stand.

The skipper has another amusement for us (or himself); we are coming to the Great Harbour and here the water is calm, so once more he opens up the throttle and in a James Bond style keels the boat right over as he takes a sweeping curve at high speed into the harbour.

I am amazed after the battering I have had that I can get to my feet, that I can stand upright, that I don't feel any pain in my spine or have a splitting headache. We say our 'thank yous' and are soon helped from the boat and walk away.

"Well, that was memorable," said the Stoic. "I think a little rest at that taverna again might steady my nerves and settle my stomach."

Harry, who before the trip had quibbled at what he regarded as an exorbitant expense for just one hour, says rather surprisingly: "It was worth every penny! If it wasn't so expensive I'd do it again. Are you alright?" He turns to me. I hang on his arm and say: "Surprisingly, yes, I think I am."

It is evening and we stroll down to St. Paul's bay again. The Stoic wants to read her book, and we arrange to be back by seven-thirty so we can all return to a taverna we like, where guests dine on the roof-top with a view to the acropolis and the temple of Athena.

As we leave the road and descend the long concrete path to the chapel, we can see it is preparing for yet another wedding. There are rows of chairs in the courtyard, and we can see the door to the chapel is open.

Harry thinks we shouldn't intrude and continues down to the sandy beach for a swim, but as it looks open I hope to see inside the chapel and, if I'm lucky, watch the wedding. I can see two black robed, bushy bearded priests amongst the several people busy preparing the chapel and courtyard for the occasion, as well as a couple of photographers who are setting up their cameras. The time is about six forty-five. When is the wedding due, I ask one of the organisers? He says about seven o'clock and makes a rocking movement with his hand indicating it to be an approximate guess only.

The white linen covered chairs in the courtyard are so arranged that there is an aisle between them for the bride and groom to walk to the chapel entrance. The aisle is bordered with brown hessian laid along the ground overlaid with whorls of cream coloured gauze. There are pots of green plants and tall white lobster-pots with candles inside them. Along the low whitewashed wall on the left are sea shells, candles in glasses and cream-coloured starfish. From a conifer close to the chapel entrance hang streamers of white satin ribbons and starfish. On either side of the chapel door are massive candles entwined in the same hessian and cream gauze. Beneath the conifer is a table with numerous little packages tied neatly with fine gold thread which I assume are small gifts for the guests.

One of the priests, portly in his long black garment with a large gold cross on a chain resting on his stomach, stands grinning broadly with his arm around a friend's shoulders as he poses for a photograph. The second priest is sitting on a ledge talking on his mobile. I ask someone if I can look inside the chapel and I am given the go-ahead.

The little chapel is barrel-roofed and very beautiful with frescoes and icons. It is mystical with its lighted candles, but I only stay briefly before I am back in the courtyard. A table is carried from the chapel and placed before the entrance; it is covered with a red satin cloth, and on it is placed a decanter of red wine and a Bible encased in an ornate gold cover. One of the priests enters the chapel and comes out again holding a censer with bells attached which he swings forwards and sideways over the table sending up clouds of incense.

The evening light is magical. There are a few small boats in harbour and a larger one flying the Turkish flag. I can see Harry with his head sticking out of the water as he basks in the shallows. I look at my watch, and notice it's already nearly seven. We don't want to be too late for the Stoic. But I must see the bride! The guests are beginning to arrive; it is a long walk from the top road for those in high-heels. I can see the cars as they approach Lindos down the rocky hillside. I can also see shacks where the donkeys are penned for the night; one of them is braying which has drawn my attention to them.

And now I hear horns being sounded repeatedly, and I watch as several cars zigzag down. Things are happening at last. The chapel bell clangs briefly. Soon I see a tall, cheerful young man in a light coloured suit, and gold silk tie and shoes to match. He is the groom arriving with his close friends, and he waves a bouquet of cream coloured roses he is carrying as he greets the guests already here. He poses with a tall young woman wearing a gold brocade jacket and skirt, and I ask a woman beside me if she's the bride. No, I'm told, she is his sister. Is he a fisherman, I ask next, and I indicate the decoration of shells and starfish and lobster-pots. No, I am told, it is just the decorations chosen by the bride. It's lovely, I tell the woman.

I can see Harry now dressed and pointing at his watch as he catches me looking at him. But nothing can move me from this wedding. I must stay to see the bride. So I make gestures to him to wait longer. Soon car horns blare again. The bridegroom raises an arm and waves vigorously at the hillside. I glimpse a large black limousine, white ribbons flying from it. The evening light, the shadows of the black silhouetted rocks, Athena's temple on its acropolis, the sea still as a membrane – the setting is perfect. At the taverna at the other end of the bay there is now a hurricane lamp set on each table, and there are many more laid along the sandy shore.

At last! I see the bride emerging from her car which has been allowed to descend the long narrow approach road and is now only about twenty yards away. The bridegroom is all smiles, and waves happily at his wife-to-be while the train to her wedding gown is prepared suitably so it spreads out behind her. She slowly approaches on the arm of her stout father.

Oh, how beautiful she is! She is a little nervous but quite composed. Her white gown is exquisite with vine-leaf patterns in rhinestones worked into the material; it has a tight-fitting bodice and a simple V-shaped neckline. Her thick, wavy dark hair is held tidily in place by a white fillet encircling her brow, the two ends of which hang loosely from her left temple. As she passes me on the arm of her father I am her greatest admirer; she has such poise, such shy serenity. I watch as the bridegroom seizes her father's hand and kisses it ardently, his lips pressed to his hand for half a minute. Then he does the same to the hand of the bride's mother and another half minute passes. His beautiful bride waits, her long, wavy, dark hair cascading over her shoulders with the simple white fillet. There is such love and respect in the air this evening. And I see Harry is now watching from beside the bridal car; he too is joining with the well-wishers for this age-old ceremony.

Reluctantly, we know that we must leave these celebrations; we must return to the Stoic who is waiting for us. The reality of everyday matters takes over as we make our way up the long steep hillside to the road. We turn and take a last look at St. Paul's bay. The scene is like a backdrop to a dramatic opera – the dark outline of rocks, the silky sea with its boats and hurricane lamps, but above all the vignette of wedding guests, bride and groom and priests outside in the candlelit courtyard of St Paul's chapel.

It is now late evening – ten thirty-five to be precise because I check the time. We are unexpectedly seated on tiered stone seats facing an open space where local people are dancing. The musicians are young and play an assortment of instruments such as a fiddle, bazooki, accordion, and there is an older man conducting them. He has just made the announcement in English (for the benefit of the many tourists seated watching) that we should be aware that they are performing a dance which over two thousand years ago would have taken place in the ancient theatre of Dionysos behind him. We look beyond the musicians to the remains of the small semi-circle of tiered seats cut out of the acropolis rockface. I am glad to have had my attention drawn to it.

There is an eccentric looking man leading them. He is wearing brown tweed trousers and a matching waistcoat with a gold watch chain (like a Victorian gentleman) and a small felt hat (which no English gentleman would have been seen dead in). He prances and is very nimble with his legs as he draws his line of followers across the open space. I love the Greek music and want to dance too but stay seated. There are many toddlers straying from their watchful parents and twisting and turning to the rhythm. The line of dancers comprises all ages from great-grandmothers to children as young as six.

The evening is balmy, the sky is velvety, the ancient theatre dimly perceived in the shadows, the acropolis a dark outline with a haloed pinnacle where the floodlit temple is hidden from view.

I have a great urge to take part. I cannot bear this inertia. I prod Harry who refuses to budge. I poke the Stoic, but she is even less inclined to move. In the end I just get up and join the line. You don't have to be expert as you would in ballroom dancing, here you jerk along as best you can with the others; so long as you keep roughly to the beat when the line moves on it doesn't matter if you have your foot forward, across or behind at the wrong moment. I have an ample woman on my right, and soon a sticky handed teenager on my left. The eccentric man in his waistcoat and hat is performing trick movements as he sometimes pirouettes, sometimes leads the line drawing his neighbour by the hand, sometimes kicks up his heels and does his own thing.

Oh, it is fun! but I feel I may drop dead in my tracks if I have to hop sideways much longer. Mercifully, the music soon stops and I return to Harry and the Stoic.

"My dear, what stamina! What endurance! Not just you, but that old man in his hat!" She stretches her legs out before her, declares they are not made for dancing, and thinks they might just get her back to our apartment.

She holds both arms up, and we help her to her feet. The music starts again but we know we must leave; we have to pack and prepare ourselves for the following day when we move on to the west of the island.

We arrived at Embonas mid-afternoon, and booked in at a small hotel. Embonas is a village set in the wine producing area of the island. The rooms of our hotel had balconies with views to the hills, and there was a swimming-pool. Soon the Stoic suitably garmented flopped into the pool, did a few aquatic somersaults before emerging like a seal to bask by the water's edge.

We were there at Embonas in order to visit Kameiros, the last of the three earliest cities named after the grandsons of Helios.

I wrote up my notes while Harry had a siesta. We had driven across Rhodes, through forested hills which had suddenly turned to miles of blackened tree stumps the result of some earlier forest fire.

We'd stopped off at a landmark called Monolithos, a hill on top of which was a medieval castle. Harry immediately set off to walk up to it. The Stoic and I found ourselves chatting to an enthusiastic woman at a stall selling trinkets and tawdry touristy things. She had three donkeys tethered in the shade of a nearby tree, and a young man in attendance. She looked slightly Indian with raven hair and a dark skin, but told us she was an Australian Greek.

She was very vivacious and bubbly. We mentioned the miles of burned trees we'd driven past. When had that happened, we asked? Five weeks ago, she said, and she'd nearly been a victim of it. She showed us the video evidence of the raging forest fire on her mobile, and told us how they'd escaped in their car (I wondered who 'they' had been – a husband, a child, the young man hovering around, was he her lover?). The car had become dangerously hot and she'd been terrified it might explode, she went on. The flames had taken giant leaps carried by a scorching wind. Certainly the video of it looked like hell on earth.

"And, you know, the flames reached the roof of the monastery (I didn't catch the name of it) and it was a miracle the building didn't burn. I do believe that miracles happen. I know there is something out there which stopped that fire from destroying the building. I saw the flames on the roof."

The Stoic said: "I expect the tiles were asbestos." But the woman wanted miracles. "There is something mystical about Greece," she said. "I feel it here in my heart. The myths, the gods! I have only to go to places like Olympia or Delphi and I get goose-bumps. I feel the energy rising from the rocks. I get very emotional in such places. You know the ancients were closer to nature than we are today. They didn't choose temple sites at random but because they could sense the sacredness of places. I can sense it too. It is why I come back every summer. Don't get me wrong, I love Australia, but Greece is where my heart is, where my roots are."

I told her about my books, and she'd immediately taken both my hands and searched my face. She could see I had soul, she said. That was very gratifying. I thought everyone had soul.

The Stoic felt she'd been left out, and said later: "She never looked at me at all! I feel I have no soul, or one so negligible it didn't catch her attention. Miracles! I expect the monks were hosing down their rooftop as any sane person fearing an approaching fire would do."

I didn't argue the matter because I, like the woman, liked to think that miracles could occur.

I closed my notebook and went and sat on the balcony. Embonas was dominated by a great mountain, Mt. Atavyros, which I could see to my left. Its barren summit had what looked like a giant golf ball on it (to do with radar, I'd read). On its peak there had once been a temple of Zeus. The story was that the nearby village of Kritinia had been founded by King Minos of Crete's grandson (hence the name Kritinia). The young man had felt so homesick that he'd climbed this barren mountain, and there on its summit had built a temple in honour of Zeus. From this vantage point he'd been able to glimpse Crete, his birthplace, as well as the birthplace of the god.

I was to find that this barren mountain could be glimpsed from many points far and wide as we explored the western side of Rhodes.

So barren were its upper reaches, so high was it, that I knew I would never get up, I could only stare and admire it from below.

No, we had more important things to do with the little time left to us on the island. The following day we planned to visit Kameiros.

When we arrived at Kameiros about twenty tour coaches were already lined up. Yet the many visitors were barely noticeable walking among the ruins of this vast and ancient city.

With the help of a site-plan we found ourselves in the city's *agora*, or market place, which had also been used for religious occasions and had in it sacrificial altars. A straight road led from it through the residential area with its numerous small ruined houses. From here looking up towards the acropolis, a temple of Athena would have been seen magnificently in profile. To the east of this market place were the ruins of a temple dedicated to an unidentified god, and to the west a temple of Apollo Pythia.

The central straight street led to what was termed the Fountain Square – no city can survive without a reliable water supply. The Fountain Square was an area with many inscribed votive bases in it, its facade marked out by six short columns.

Walking on up, the slope became steeper till we came to a *stoa*, once a six hundred and sixty feet long colonnaded building. From there steps would have led up to the all important temple of Athena on its acropolis. A massive earthquake in the third century B.C. had destroyed much of the earlier buildings, including Athena's temple, which had then to be rebuilt.

We picked our way up the steep slope. By now it was midday and very hot. There was to our right a large old juniper where we paused to cool down and drink bottled water. We were all drawing breath when a German couple huffed and puffed their way up and joined us under the tree. The man had on a T-shirt with the words 'Great Wall' on it. As we were sharing the same shade I asked him if he'd been to the great wall of China. "Ya, ya, great vall!" I smiled at his wife who at once said they'd been in China for five years. Five years? Were they working out there – the diplomatic service, perhaps? "Nein, nein," said the husband. "My vife, she means that ve vere in China five years ago. Ve vere there only tventy days." It is interesting how the misuse of words in language can make such a difference to the meaning of a sentence.

We left them resting on a couple of boulders, and made our way on up to what remained of the great temple on the summit. If this approach were a musical score, what a crescendo and climax this was! The extensive views beyond to the south were of mountainous hills and agricultural land – olive groves and vineyards. To the north we could see the sapphire blue of the sea and the distant landmass of Anatolia. Apparently, in its heyday, Kameiros had been a peaceful city in a rural setting, inhabited by farmers and craftsmen. Ceramics had become its speciality, together with the export of such things as olive oil, figs and wine.

What better location than here for the goddess Athena. From here she could look down over her citizens in their small houses, to the temple of Apollo Pythia, and the one to the unknown god.

I was interested in the latter because when St. Paul had been in Athens he'd noticed an altar to an 'unknown god'. This anonymous dedication was in order that citizens could give thanks to a deity for some benefit received but whose identity was uncertain. When St. Paul addressed the Athenians in the first century A.D. he'd said: "'Men of Athens, I perceive that in every way you are very religious. For as I passed along, and observed the objects of your worship, I found also an altar with this inscription, 'to an unknown god.' What therefore you worship as unknown, this I proclaim to you. The God who made the world and everything in it, being Lord of heaven and earth, does not live in shrines made by man...'" (Acts 17:22-24).

I wondered how long St. Paul had stayed on Rhodes. Today there is a great summer festival in honour of a somewhat mysterious saint named Agios Soulas. Lawrence Durrell in his book *The Marine Venus* put forward the theory that Soulas was a variant of Saul and, therefore, the festival was in honour of St. Paul who had been born Saul. I have only recently discovered the reason for this change of name. His father, a Jew and pharisee, had also been a Roman citizen, so Paul (as his son) would automatically have had Roman citizenship too. In this capacity he had been given a second Roman name, Paul. After his blinding vision conversion on the road to Damascus, the then Saul (persecutor of Christians) wanted a name acceptable to the Gentiles to whom he was to preach this new religion, so he discarded the Jewish Saul for his Roman name Paul.

"Finished here?" Harry asked.

I supposed I had. To remain in a state of crescendo and climax was not something that could be continued for ever. From crescendo inevitably comes dimuendo.

"For myself," said the Stoic, "I feel the need for food and a dip in the sea."

We drove to the small fishing village of Skala Kameiros. There we sat at a beachside taverna with a cooling breeze and our favourite *tsaziki* (yoghurt, cucumber and garlic). Afterwards, while the Stoic paddled, Harry and I wandered along the harbour and watched four fishermen seated patiently on their stools, casting and recasting their lines. There was a bite, and a grizzled fellow reeled in his line – from the look of the end of his rod which was bending to the weight of the catch it would be a big fish. But out came a sprat. The fisherman, who knew we were watching, gave us a shrug and an apologetic smile. Nevertheless, he unhooked the floundering creature, wrapped it in a yellow cloth and placed it in the saddlebag of his old motorbike. It was, after all, a mouthful of food for someone in his family.

It is early morning and Harry and I are in our dressing-gowns sitting out on our hotel balcony with mugs of tea. I am looking out across to the wooded slopes of hills; in the foreground are the silver-grey-green of olive trees, a little further are the darker emerald green of oak, and the bottle green of juniper trees. The sea is just visible through a veil of early morning haze. The barren summit of Mt. Atavyros to our far left is receiving the first rays of the sun. I think of Helios in his chariot being drawn up into the heavens by his four fiery steeds heralded by Eos the dawn.

"You remember the story of Phaethon?" I ask Harry.

"Never heard of Phaethon." Harry says the name as though he is spitting.

"He was a son of Helios, and made a wish that he'd be allowed to drive his father's chariot. Despite his doubts as to his son's ability to control the horses, Helios had made a promise to grant him any wish, and this is what Phaethon most wanted."

"And what happened? I suppose another tragedy?"

I put my feet up on the balcony railings. The early morning warmth in Rhodes was pleasant. "Yes, of course!" I said. "Poor little chap wasn't strong enough and the horses bolted. They first galloped up to the heavens, leaving a path which some say became the Milky Way. They then charged earthwards, scorching the world and turning all people near the equator black. Then Zeus, seeing catastrophe looming, threw a thunderbolt and poor Phaethon fell in flames into a river where he perished. His sisters, who'd been watching the whole sorry story, stood and wept till they were turned into poplars, and their tears became amber."

"The moral to which, I suppose, is never to have an unreasonable wish."

"Or never promise to grant one without laying down sensible conditions," I say.

We watch sparrows flitting around the swimming-pool below. Some of them stand poised on the edge and dip their beaks into the water to drink. A cock begins to crow somewhere to our left. To the right are houses, and nearby a woman is already picking figs from a tree beside her house, and placing them on a cloth spread out on the ground in preparation for the sun.

Harry points to the chimney on the woman's house. "An owl!" he says.

I look and see a small owl, a symbol of the goddess Athena, perched on the chimney top. A moment later it flies with extended wings and glides down to land on a telegraph wire nearby.

Today we leave and somehow the owl (Athena), Helios rising up into the heavens drawn by his four fiery steeds, and the barren Atavyros mountain with its temple of Zeus on its summit, are all reminders why I came to Rhodes and why I'd like to stay. But there are other islands of interest that I must visit, and so I must be patient. I hope once they've been done perhaps we will return.

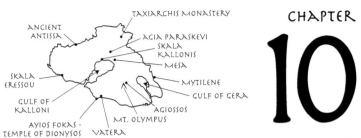

LESBOS (MYTILENE)

We are seated at a taverna at the water's edge in Mytilene, the main city and harbour of the island of Lesbos, also known as Mytilene. The light tonight is magical as the sun sinks low in the evening sky. It is so bright that the sea is like a sheet of quicksilver. It is no wonder that the island has inspired musicians and poets. I am on this island for two famous names that have come down from antiquity – for Orpheus whose singing was divine, and for Sappho and her lyric poems about love.

The harbour is horse-shoe shaped, and we are on one side of it looking across the bay at a long low hill (the ancient acropolis) where today the defence walls of a Genoese fourteenth century *kastro* can be seen. In antiquity that hill was a small islet with a narrow channel separating it from the main island, and it was there that the city was first built. In time the channel silted up and the expanding population spilled over to the main island.

Had we been here several millennia ago we would, from where we sit now, be looking across the harbour to the islet and seeing the soaring columns of a temple of Demeter and Persephone – Demeter, goddess of corn and vegetation, and her daughter who'd been abducted by Hades and, at Lord Zeus' command, had been destined to return to the upper world for eight months of the year and back to the kingdom of Hades for the other four of winter.

In the sixth century A.D. a Christian basilica dedicated to John the Baptist had been built over the ancient temple of Demeter, and death and resurrection were given a new significance in their new Christian role.

Later still under Ottoman rule a mosque and minaret were built there, as well as a *madrassa* (school), and a *tekke* for mystics where whirling dervishes performed their rites. And so the acropolis has seen many changing faces of religion.

Wandering around the old town of Mytilene is to see a mixture of new and old, prosperity and poverty. The architecture in general is of red tiled roofs, solid small houses with wrought-iron balconies, and steep cobbled side streets. Then, as you think you've got the measure of the town you come suddenly on mansions on a grand scale, some with a flavour of the Renaissance, or houses of Turkish influence with overhanging upper storeys. Or, amongst the crowded houses and churches, you as suddenly see a bare concrete wall scrawled with graffiti in garish colours.

When two days ago we'd flown over the island, we'd had a bird's eye view of Lesbos and its pine-covered hills and mountains, extensive olive groves and its two enormous almost landlocked inland gulfs with narrow openings to the Aegean sea.

Tomorrow we move on to self-catering rooms in rural Skala Kalloni which overlooks the Gulf of Kalloni, it will be a convenient central place for us from which to set off on our daily trips. When I say we, I mean me, Harry and the Stoic. We've asked the unflappable Stoic to join us again because we know we need a car as Lesbos is a large island, and the places I want to see are far-flung. I've mentioned the fact that we will be close to salt marshes where migratory birds are to be seen, and the Stoic tells me she's brought her bird book with her. "And! My new mobile has a Satnav which I've tried and tested," she says. "This little thing will tell us how to get everywhere." She retrieves her marvel of technology from her large, colourful shoulder-bag and looks at it lovingly.

I duly admire it before turning my gaze back to the harbour and the darkening evening light. The great Florentine looking greeny-grey dome of a church, set back centrally amongst the buildings crowding the harbour, is now floodlit, as are the great *kastro* walls.

Greeks of all ages stroll along the harbour front in the cool of the evening. I am surprised how many families are seated at the many tavernas, and how few tourists there seem to be. The sea is now dark, and reflects the street lights of yellow balls one above the other in evenly spaced stretches of orange streaks around the bay.

I soak up the atmosphere and the tranquillity. A man seated at a table behind us is throwing pieces of bread into the sea which bring fish up from the depths. To our left is a line of squid hanging along a stretched wire between two uprights. The peaceful scene belies the violence that has overtaken the island in the past. Tonight, though, is poetic, and I think of Sappho, whose renown is still with us from so many centuries ago, from the seventh century B.C. to be exact. It was here in Mytilene that she used to play the lyre and sing to spellbound listeners. I hope to visit Eressos her birthplace in the far west of the island. I have planned many things and as yet Harry has only seen the island as a map, not as a large island with geological upheavals of mountains to be got up or around. Most other Aegean islands are quite small in comparison.

'After thirty metres turn right,' said the irritating voice.

We were driving along a rough track surrounded by agricultural fields, some with baled straw, others with vegetables and fruit trees. We had left the main road half an hour earlier, and were being directed by this disembodied, demented female voice along one dirt road and then another.

"If only one was able to judge the length of thirty metres – or ten – or a hundred – " murmured the Stoic as the car pitched and rolled as it went around and over large stones and hit potholes.

"Why don't we ask someone?" I suggested.

"Satnav will get us there," said Harry, knowing how much this new toy meant to the Stoic.

"Yes, but asking a local will get us there quicker," I said. I didn't want to be difficult but if we didn't know the length of a hundred metres but turned left or right at the first track that came -

'Turn left after twenty metres," instructed the voice.

We passed a truckful of women and children with cheerful faces, who looked like gypsies. They waved at us – to see a new clean car on their dusty dirt road must have been an unexpected novelty for them.

"This can't be right," said the Stoic eventually.

"Why don't we ask that woman there," I said more forcibly. The woman was standing outside the gate to her house. "I'll ask. They love to tell you the way, and she'll know!" I said.

The Stoic obligingly drew alongside, and I got out and tried in my best stumbling Greek to ask the way to the address I showed her. The woman threw up her head in acknowledgment, and said something incomprehensible. But she then beckoned to me to follow her. In the mid-afternoon heat I hurried after her for about a hundred yards followed by the car, and the woman then pointed down a turning to the left, and indicated a tall house on the right at the far end.

"Well, it got us nearly there," the Stoic said, whose Satnav could do no wrong. "And we would never have seen those farms and fields if we hadn't gone off piste, as you might put it," she added.

After unpacking I sat out on our balcony, and wrote up my notes. It was important to jot down the main events of the day, before other things crowded in and obliterated them.

As we'd driven up the hill out of Mytilene, we'd stopped briefly by the ancient amphitheatre whose concave shape was landscaped naturally into the hillside. It was believed to have been third century B.C. and had, apparently, seated fifteen thousand. It was fenced off behind a wire-mesh fence but its solitude amongst pine trees whose branches sheltered us from the hot sun made it a pleasant place to linger.

Driving on we'd soon come to the first of the two great inland gulfs, the Gulf of Gera with its distant hills and mountains. We drove on through pine forests, then olive groves extending to the far distance either side of the road. Then, suddenly, we'd emerged to see a flat plateau and the Gulf of Kalloni, its inland sea a sort of grey turquoise, its surrounding mountains veiled in a light haze.

I'd spotted a signpost pointing to Mesa where I'd read there was an ancient temple of Aphrodite, goddess of love. Sappho with her turbulent love affairs would surely have come to the temple to beseech the goddess? The Stoic had responded to my shout and, fortunately, Harry's grumble that all sites were closed on Mondays (and it was Monday), had his attention distracted by a large turkey strutting along the road followed by two fluffy chicks.

It had only been a mile out of our way and the site had been open. The ruins were in a quiet location in beautifully kept grounds with flowering oleanders and well laid flagged pathways. I had questions to ask, and a cheerful girl was called from some distant gardening task because she spoke English. My belief that Sappho had come here to beseech Aphrodite was immediately quashed because excavations had shown that it had almost certainly been a centre for the worship of Zeus, Hera and Dionysos.

Why a sanctuary so out of the way, I'd asked? Because it was the centre of the island, and all pilgrims would have had the same distance to cover to come to it, came the answer.

She'd then pointed out the roofless ruins of an early basilica church which had been built over the pagan temple or temples. In the ruins of the apse there was a simple altar on which were several small icons, an incense cup and a candle. Apparently, a priest came annually to hold a service in what remained of the church.

We'd left that isolated sacred site and had soon come to the stretch of salt marshes before the town of Kalloni. There we'd seen what we thought were cranes, and a small dark bird standing on one long, thin leg.

It was after that that the Stoic's Satnav had gone berserk and had led us off the main road into the fields. I put away my notebook. It was time to go out to find somewhere to eat.

Another tranquil evening at the water's edge with the gentle repetitive swish of small waves breaking on the beach. The Gulf of Kalloni stretches out before us to distant pine-covered mountains and soaring above them is a barren, ashen coloured oval peak which is Mt. Olympus, called after the great Mt. Olympus in northern Greece, the mountain of the gods. A small boat chugs in from the far side of the gulf, and another goes out from the harbour and a fisherman is casting out his nets. As it darkens, the Stoic points to a strand of purple cloud. I've never seen a purple cloud before. But now the evening light turns the sea indigo blue, and the azure sky darkens making the mountains into black silhouettes. The waiter lights torches along the sea front set in tall bamboo sticks split at the top to hold the lights.

"So where to tomorrow?" the Stoic asks.

"Ah," I say. "Well, as this is Sappho's island, I think we should start with her and go to Eressos – Skala Eressou," I correct myself. "It's Sappho's birthplace where she spent her childhood."

I do not add a few other places I hope to visit afterwards while we are in that area. Harry has already laid out the road map on the table and announces it's a long drive.

The woman in the small museum at Skala Eressou was like a cork popping out of a champagne bottle whenever I approached her desk to ask something. She flew to the display cabinet to point out perfume bottles, and then to a file to show me early coins with the head of Sappho on them, then to a sarcophagus –

I asked about any early temples where Sappho might have played her lyre and sung, and this helpful, eager woman popped out to the pavement to point out the ancient acropolis behind the museum which, she said, had a path up it. But the heat, she warned – it was by now midday – and there were many snakes, she added, regarding our open sandals.

"You don't need to see it," Harry said. "You've already seen that ancient thingummy." He waved an arm vaguely.

The woman looked non-plussed, and I said: "The church ruins and its mosaics there."

"Ah, the early Christian basilica Church of Agios Andreas," she said."

"The apostle Andrew?" I asked.

"No, this Andreas came from Crete," she said. "The church, we think, was built on a sanctuary of Apollo and Dionysos. I cannot leave my desk, but you can see a little of the temple remains in the south-west corner."

Another couple entered the museum, and she returned to her desk to issue them with tickets. She was soon flying this way and that, explaining the exhibits to her new arrivals. I took another look at the various small perfume bottles and thought how Sappho might have used one of them. She loved all things of beauty, and one of these was small and exquisitely shaped, decorated with small flower heads.

We left the museum and I led Harry to the path at the base of the tree-covered conical hill, the ancient acropolis. I felt I had to give it a go. The Stoic was relaxing at a taverna, and wouldn't worry that we were taking our time exploring Sappho's home territory.

It was a goat-track more than a path, partially concealed by wild flowers and dried grasses, which wound up gently around the pine-clad acropolis. We'd go just a little way only, I told Harry – to the corner where it made its way around the hill, I suggested. I used my trekking stick to beat back the tangled plants, and hook away odd fir branches. Yes, I was wary of snakes.

"It's too hot," Harry said. And I had to agree with him.

"No further than that corner," I promised.

We beat our way to the corner where there was a convenient log to sit on in the shadow of a pine tree. We drank from our water bottles.

"Shall I read you one of Sappho's poems?" I said. I didn't wait for an answer, and Harry didn't say no, so I opened a slim book of her work and began to read:

'In all honesty, I want to die.'

(I acted the part with an exaggerated gesture of an arm).

Leaving for good after a good long cry,
She said: 'We both have suffered terribly,
But, Sappho, it is hard to say goodbye.'

(Harry began idly tapping his stick against a rock. Using what acting skills I had to keep his attention, I went on):

I said: 'Go with my blessing if you go
Always remembering what we did. To me
You have meant everything, as you well know.'

Harry interrupted. "What did they do?" he asked.

I hesitated, then said: "It doesn't matter what they did. Just listen!" I read on:

'Yet, lest it slip your mind, I shall review
Everything we have shared – the good times, too:

'You culled violets and roses, bloom and stem,
Often in spring and I looked on as you
Wove a bouquet into a diadem.

'Time and again we plucked lush flowers, wed
Spray after spray in strands and fastened them
Around your soft neck; you perfumed your head

'Of glossy curls with myrrh – lavish infusions
In queenly quantities – then on a bed
Prepared with fleecy sheets and yielding cushions,

'Sated your craving...'

"Um," I said, and closed the book. "It ends there."

"Queer sounding fellow," Harry said. "Soft neck – perfumed black curls – picking flowers and all that. Bit of a pansy, I'd say." He got up stiffly. "Have I sated your craving for this place? I could do with a yielding cushion right now!"

Obviously Harry knew nothing about Sappho's penchant for young girls. For some reason I didn't like to mention it as I wanted to keep him on side with her as a poetess. Since we were there on Sappho's acropolis, however, and there was something about her which

I thought hypnotic, I didn't want to be rushed. I remained seated, and opened the book again. I selected another poem, one I thought suitable for the occasion in which Sappho was beseeching Aphrodite. She was a deity who encouraged love in all its shapes and forms. It was only under Christianity that love between a man and woman consummated in marriage became the rule, and those who deviated were in danger of hell fire. St. Paul had come briefly to Lesbos and must have held his hands up in horror at the mortal sins going on if he ever learned about them.

I read to myself this time.

> *Subtly bedizened Aphrodite,*
> *Deathless daughter of Zeus, Wile-weaver,*
> *I beg you, Empress, do not smite me*
> *With anguish and fever.*

I remained absorbed as I read the verses, oblivious of the heat and Harry nearby.

> *Come to me now. Drive off this brutal*
> *Distress. Accomplish what my pride*
> *Demands. Come, please, and in this battle*
> *Stand at my side.*

In a trance-like state I closed the book and looked up to see Harry standing impatiently, swinging his stick from side to side like a pendulum. Apart from the sound of that as it beat against a rock on one side, and swished against tinder-dry grasses on the other, I became concious of the gentle soughing of the breeze in the branches of the pines behind me, the chirrup of birds, and the barking of a dog in the far distance. From where we were there was a view over the terra-cotta tiled roof-tops of the square houses of Skala Eressou to the sparkling sea.

"Ready?" It was Harry speaking.

It was too hot to stay there. Reluctantly I turned my back on the enticing path which would have taken us up the acropolis and, instead, with a cautious eye out for snakes, we beat our way back along the way we'd come.

Back on the road, we walked down a narrow cobbled alleyway to the ancient port, then strolled along the old jetty which jutted out into the blue sea glittering in the sunlight. We sat on a convenient wooden seat which overlooked the harbour and its colourful fishing boats.

"Look," said Harry, waving his stick up at the acropolis, the back of which we could now see. On its top was the remains of a small tower, a Genoese structure masking what had once been the ancient landmark as Sappho would have known it.

One of the stories about Sappho was that Aphrodite had caused her to fall hopelessly in love with a good-looking young ferryman who'd brought the goddess from mainland Greece to Lesbos. The result of this story (or so I'd read) was unrequited love on Sappho's part and, in her state of frustrated despair, she'd thrown herself from a cliff to her death. That, however, hadn't been here, but on an island in the Ionian sea.

Leaving this ancient harbour, we rejoined the Stoic at the taverna where we'd left her. She was in animated conversation with a dynamic young waitress who was fluent in English. The Stoic said: "At last! If you want to know anything about your Sappho you've only to ask Maria who's lived here all her life."

Maria had an attractive personality, a down to earth, no nonsense, what you see you get sort of air about her. She had a dark complexion and shortish dark hair giving her a slightly impish look. She was efficient, and went at speed about her work.

She fetched menus and, as she handed them to us, she said: "Sappho was born and lived here till she was fifteen." She then hurried away and returned with a paper cloth for our table, and carried on where she'd left off: "She would go up the acropolis over there and play her lyre and sing while watching for her father's return because he was in the navy." (Later I read it was her brother who, as a merchant trading with Egypt, was often at sea.)

Maria shook out the paper cloth, and fixed it with clips on the sides of the square table. As she did so, she said: "Then her father died and her mother took Sappho to Mytilene where she founded a school for girls. And she fell in love with one of her students but had to restrain herself." She shrugged her shoulders with a defiant expression challenging us to disapprove, then quickly left to attend to new visitors who'd just sat down.

"Sappho was a lesbian," the Stoic explained. Harry wasn't used to such frank discussions about sex and became engrossed in his menu. The Stoic glanced at me and realized that the subject was off limits. But Maria was back almost at once with salt and pepper, saying: "It is why here on Lesbos we get many lesbian visitors. It is from Lesbos that your word lesbian comes – from Sappho." And she was gone again.

Harry had never taken such an interest in a menu before. I noticed a couple of women hand in hand walking along the beach. There were two other females seated at a nearby table. But there were several heterosexual couples also.

The waitress returned with a pad of paper to take our orders, and said: "Sappho was an aristocrat, and so mixed with aristocrats in Mytilene. She taught her girls poetry, singing, and the lyre. They say she performed with her girls at symposiums, weddings or at special functions and religious festivals. Do you know yet what you want to eat?"

We dithered about which dishes to order, and finally decided on a couple of communal salads, and Maria said as she swept up our menus leaving Harry with nowhere to hide: "*Up, my lute divine, and make thyself a thing of speech...* That is all that I remember learning when I was at school," she explained.

"How poetic!" I remarked. Maria gave a fleeting smile, and was gone to hand our menus to the guests at the next table.

As swiftly, she returned with oil and vinegar, saying: "Sappho married and had a daughter called Cleis. But her husband was unfaithful and the marriage ended. She took part in politics but was an anarchist so was sent into exile."

"Quite a colourful life," the Stoic remarked when Maria was gone again. "So what plans do you have for this afternoon?" she enquired.

"Fossilized trees," said Harry. I had pointed out this tourist attraction to him on the map; it wasn't too far from where we were on the west of the island and they were my sweetner for his morning of Sappho.

"Not too many miles, I do hope?" said the Stoic. "We've been on the road two hours already to get here." The remark came out in such an accepting-the-inevitable way that we didn't give it any thought. Harry unfolded the map and pointed to the road we would be taking. The petrified forest looked reasonably close.

Maria returned with our salads, and continued speaking as though the subject had never ceased: "Sappho lived at Paphos in Cyprus for many years where she worshipped Aphrodite," she said, placing the dishes, and plates on the table. (I'd read it was Sicily). "And because Sappho didn't want to grow old," Maria went on, "she sacrificed herself to Aphrodite and jumped off a rock." (Another wrong piece of information. She'd leapt off the cliff at wherever it was because of her rejection by the ferryman she'd fallen for).

But I preferred Maria's Aphrodite version of the Sappho story.

She disappeared briefly, then returned with our cutlery wrapped in paper table napkins, and said: "*Lo! Love the looser of limbs stirs me, that creature irresistible, bitter-sweet...* That too I learned in school. Enjoy your meal!" she said, and was gone.

While we helped ourselves from the salad dishes, the Stoic said: "My dears, what other poems are there, I wonder?" I caught Harry's eye which I could see was forbidding me to get out my book.

Maria with a full tray for the next table, bent down to us in passing, and recited –

> *You were at hand,*
> *And I broke down raving –*
> *My craving a fire*
> *That singed my mind,*
> *A brand you quenched.*

And she swept past with an impish smile.

"I suppose she learned that at school also," the Stoic remarked. "Do you think she's a lesbian?"

Harry shot a glance at me, the Stoic, and the others in the taverna. I changed the subject to St. Paul which somehow led back to love and whether it was better to marry than to burn, or to just get on with it, which somehow also led to the possibility that Helen of Troy had visited the island because after the war she'd been reunited with her unfortunate (or was he lucky?) husband King Menelaus of Sparta, who'd come to Lesbos with Odysseus to discuss how best to get home.

Within an hour all was forgotten as once again we were driving off heading north-west. "Petrified forest," Harry read from a booklet. "It's twenty million years old and preserved after a volcanic eruption. That'll be really interesting!" he said.

We're back at our apartments again having an hour or two's respite before going out to a taverna for supper. The Stoic has hinted that, perhaps, a little less driving in one day might be better; if it hadn't been that she'd wanted to look out for a stork standing on its nest on top of a telegraph pole which we'd seen on setting out, she would most decidedly have fallen asleep.

I realized I must select the essentials with more care, and not embellish them with other attractions. The drive, though, had been worthwhile; the scenery had varied from conifer forests, to extensive olive groves, the trees pruned so each was identically oval shaped, to low mountains scattered with unusual, large tan coloured muffin shaped rocks like elephant dung, to a tree-filled gorge pierced with huge assortments of russet-coloured volcanic pinnacles, to a barren lunarscape.

Harry had been happy with his petrified forest, though we'd arrived with only half an hour before the site closed for the day, having visited a monastery on a pinnacle first, the Ipsilos Monastery. The petrified forest covered a large area which needed a great deal of time for the various trunks of ancient trees which remained rooted where they'd petrified in the volcanic upheaval those twenty million years ago. Many tree stumps were fifty metres or so from one another, reached only by a number of well kept pathways. It really required a whole day to do the site justice.

My thoughts are now interrupted as Harry asks me what my plan is for the following day.

"Orpheus," I say, and I point out where Ancient Antissa is on the road map. "I'll cut out heading east afterwards, and driving up and over a mountain, much as I would like to do it," I add, in order to appear considerate. "But Ancient Antissa is a positive," I say with emphasis.

"It's important not to tire the Stoic."

"No, we mustn't tire the Stoic," I agree.

"So what should we know about this Orpheus fellow?" the Stoic enquired as we turned down a dirt track as directed by a signpost – after the Satnav debacle it was never used again.

"I don't know where to start," I said.

"Start at the beginning," said the Stoic manoeuvring around a large stone. "Was he a god? A mere mortal? Or what?"

"He was a sort of god – a sort of man – a hero/god, perhaps. He played the lyre – "

"Like your Sappho woman?"

"And sang so beautifully that animals would draw near, even fish would leap from the sea to listen, and mountains bow down."

"My dear wife is bringing us here to the back of beyond because legend has it he was torn to pieces on mainland Greece, and his head – still singing – what gibberish! – came floating here to Lesbos."

"His head still singing and attached to his lyre which was still playing," I corrected.

"And why not? This is the island of poetry, music and imagination," said the Stoic kindly.

"And the cave we were looking for just now, where they were blasting the mountainside, was apparently the fellow's oracle," Harry scoffed.

The mountainside we'd passed was certainly being quarried, and the rockface had been a rather beautiful deepish pink. I knew there should be a cave somewhere on that mountainside, but could see nothing. The cave was where the head of Orpheus had ended up, and it had been regarded as the oracle of Orpheus until Apollo had expressed his anger that Orpheus (his son) was usurping his oracular powers and so silenced him.

"Turn down here," instructed Harry where a sign indicated a taverna. "I could do with a drink, and we can ask about this cave. My wife won't be satisfied until somebody has told her something."

We soon arrived at a taverna where several people were seated at peace with the world. We ordered freshly squeezed orange juice and sat at a table aware of the curiosity of the others that anyone should come at all to this isolated spot. I asked the waiter if he spoke English, and he at once turned to a couple seated nearby.

"Hello, I am English," said the man. "What can I do for you?"

English? Here? How wonderful not to have to struggle with the language!

I told him we were looking for Orpheus' cave, and he immediately called over a relaxed and smiling forty year old and spoke to him in fluent Greek. After a while he turned to me, and said: "He knows the cave. It's not far, but it's difficult to get to." He turned to the man and made more enquiries. "He says he goes hunting up there and he has been into the cave but there's nothing to see."

"Not worth visiting, thank God for that!" said Harry.

The man spoke again to this personable young man, then turned to me, and said: "It has been thoroughly explored. Archaeologists have been up there but have found nothing. It's very inadvisable to try to walk up there in this heat, he tells me."

"And not worth it when you get there, so that decides it," Harry added with finality.

It was then that I noticed that the young man being questioned had said nothing at all. How extraordinary. With a cheerful smile he returned to his friends, and the Englishman told us that he was a deaf/mute. What is more he had a deaf/mute brother and through internet dating, they had both married deaf/mute Russian girls. They'd had children who, fortunately, hadn't inherited the condition, and everyone was happy.

With detailed instructions how to get to the spot where Orpheus' head had floated to the island, we set off again. In no time we were driving alongside a river whose river banks were lush with tall reeds and, amazingly, had water flowing in it. We had seen many dry river-beds on the island, but only one other that had had any water. That had been near to Skala Eressou and, from the bridge, we had seen many small turtles. Some had been sunning themselves on rocks, but most had been idly swimming with their four legs extended from their shells, their heads with inquisitive eyes looking out for crusts of bread which people threw to them (this bit of information the Stoic had gleaned from Maria the waitress). Harry had counted three hundred of them.

In this river there were no turtles, only extreme tranquillity with a gentle breeze rustling the rushes and tall grasses. I walked over rocks and pebbles to the water's edge and tried to imagine Orpheus singing. The thought of a floating head attached to a lyre was quite horrible to contemplate – a voice singing, and a lyre playing, yes, but not a decapitated head.

We drove over a ford as instructed, and were soon driving parallel to the sea. We arrived at Ancient Antissa, an isolated small promontory with the ruins of a *kastro,* and a tiny chapel, outside which were a few ancient column drums, and one with a marble capital.

Harry tried to climb up to the *kastro,* but found the path blocked by fallen walls. We spent a while at the small chapel with its courtyard of ancient columns, and also a massive old oak tree.

"I like it," said the Stoic, sitting on a low stone wall. "There's a certain mystique to the place, a certain *je ne sais quoi,* if you know what I mean. So this Orpheus character of yours – " She indicated that since we had driven so many miles to get here, I'd better tell her more about my reasons for it. "What did he do? Why do we all know his name but know nothing except that his beloved wife, Euridice, died from a snake bite and went down to the underworld? Couldn't he as a god or hero have prevented it?" she asked.

"All the singing in the world didn't bring the woman back," said Harry, joining forces with the Stoic in ridiculing my hero of the moment.

I rose to the occasion in defence of Orpheus, and said: "His singing and playing got him down to the underworld. It charmed Cerberus the monster dog who guarded the entrance to Hades so he was able to pass; and Charon the ferryman was so enchanted he left his boat and followed him to Hades where the judges of the underworld – one of them King Minos of Crete – wept at the beauty of his singing. And Persephone – you remember Demeter's daughter who became the great god Hades' queen? She was so overcome by the purity of Orpheus' playing and singing that she allowed Euridice to follow him back to the upper world on the understanding that he didn't look back at his beloved. But poor Orpheus, as they were nearing the upper world, forgot and glanced back at his dear bride so the spell was broken and he lost her for ever."

"As I've always said, those old Greeks had vivid imaginations," Harry said.

"Vivid? I'll say. But so clever," went on the Stoic. "So clever at making real the unreal. So what else should we know about your hero/god?" she invited.

"Well, he was the son of Apollo, and his mother was the muse Calliope," I said. "I suppose he got his musical and poetic talents from them." And I went on to tell her how legend had it he'd been one of the Argonauts and had sailed with Jason to retrieve the Golden Fleece; how he'd been indispensable to them because Jason and the crew depended on his fine singing to outshine the Siren voices who otherwise would have lured everyone to their deaths; that even the other hazards, such as the Clashing Rocks had been held back by the power of his voice, instead of crushing them as they'd sailed between them; and how his voice had finally lulled to sleep the dragon guarding the Golden Fleece so that Jason had been able to get it back and thus regain his kingdom.

"After the loss of his beloved Euridice," I went on, "he ignored women altogether and only wanted to be in the company of men."

"Which is why that English chap at the taverna just now said he was a homo."

"Which I think is quite untrue and unfair. He was just inconsolable after Euridice died. Anyway, what actually happened was that the Maenads, the women worshippers of Dionysos, resented the fact that he paid no attention to them and tore him to pieces and his head, still singing, floated over the sea from northern Greece, to here." I stared out to sea, trying to imagine a singing head floating across to this island of poetry and music. But the vision somehow didn't fit the charm and beauty of the place.

"He left sacred writings, and had quite a following," I continued, "but only scraps of his doctrine remain. It's thought he believed in good and evil and the immortality of the soul. He taught that each life was an opportunity through righteousness to bring the soul closer to the divine. Really rather Christian," I said.

"Nothing Christian about it," said Harry firmly. "Just fanciful nonsense!"

"As is so much in all religions," said the Stoic. "We have to give Orpheus the benefit of the doubt, and give credit to the wonderful imagination of those minds that lie behind the stories. I wonder if he was tenor, baritone or bass?" she mused.

I entered the little chapel, put a few coins in the donation box and lit a candle, the holy in me saying a silent 'thank you' for having got to this off-the-beaten-track corner of the island. There was a certain magical quality, a serenity about this spot that no amount of scoffing or sarcasm could eradicate.

As we drove back the Stoic said: "May I make a suggestion?" She regarded me in the rear-mirror.

"Of course," I said, hoping what she was going to say wasn't going to scupper the plans I'd come up with for the following day.

"We'll be passing the salt marshes, so it would be nice to spend a little time there. I have my bird book."

"No question about it," Harry said. "We'll do it now."

We were fast approaching the salt marshes which we could see stretching out serenely into the far distance as we came down from the hills.

Soon we had turned down a track which ran alongside a canal, beyond which were the shallow man-made rectangular stretches of water. And so the day ended with a fascinating assortment of migratory birds: flamingos, thin-legged wading birds, some white with black wings and long fine black beaks; some white with a black head with black wing tips; one with a black stripe on its body; a duck with a yellow chest and ten ducklings; a lapwing – The Stoic spent as much time consulting her book as she did looking at the birds. A great white mound which I took to be a marquee turned out, in fact, to be heaped up salt. There were watch-towers for bird fanciers – it was decidedly a place for enthusiasts to spend the day, if not the entire season.

Today we are driving south to a place called Vatera, to see a temple of Dionysos. We are at the moment taking a short break, and sitting under tamarisk trees on a gravelled terrace looking out over a sand and shingle beach to the sea. There is quite a wind and there are small glittering wavelets. To our left can be seen the foothills of Mt. Olympus rising beyond the town of Plomari.

This is a family-run hotel, and the young man who has brought us our drinks speaks good English. He should by now, he tells us, because he spent four years studying International Relations at Nottingham University.

The temple of Dionysos, I ask? Yes, we have only to keep driving; we will then come to a bridge and, after crossing that, we just follow the signs.

We are soon on our way again and, yes, there's a bridge across the river with a surprising depth of green water. We stop, and for a while listen to the rustling of the tall rushes and reeds in the light breeze, and watch the slow swimming of more small turtles enjoying the warm sun shining down on their submarine world.

We drive on and see the sign pointing to the temple of Dionysos, also to an early Christian church and, unexpectedly, another with the words Well of Achilles on it. In no time we see this ancient round stone well on our left, ringed with notches around the inside of the rim. We stop to take photos. We are surprised there is no lid to this well, no safety precautions to prevent small children or animals falling in.

The Stoic says: "Why is it Achilles' Well? Are we talking Achilles of Achilles' heel fame?"

"I'm sure we are," I say.

"Remind me why he was famous for his heel?" she asks.

I tell her how as an infant his mother, Thetis, a minor goddess, had tried to immortalize him by dipping him in the river Styx. But, because she'd held him by his heel, it hadn't been submerged and, therefore, remained for ever mortal and vulnerable. "And this," I say, "eventually caused his death because he was wounded in his one vulnerable spot."

I am curious about this well and wonder what the locals have to say about it. Harry drops a stone into it. There is no water and, from the sound of the stone hitting the bottom, we judge it to be about fifty feet deep.

We drive on, heading for a promontory. Here we find another taverna overlooking a small fishing cove. The beach to the left of this little cove with its few fishing boats is sand and shingle, and two people are swimming. When we walk up to the headland to the temple of Dionysos, we see on our right that there are black rocks with white crested waves crashing over them, not dissimilar to the north Cornish coast.

So here we are at the temple of Dionysos Bresagenes, and I try to draw inspiration from the various columns and paving stones amongst the dried flowers and grasses. Apart from his strange birth, I am only aware of the fact that Dionysos, the son of Zeus, was said to have been torn to pieces, as had Orpheus, the son of Apollo – both of them sons of gods. There seemed to be a certain link between those two ancients and Jesus who was a son of God who had also been mutilated and put to death by men.

"Do you know," I say to Harry, "that there's a seal or an amulet portraying what you would think was Jesus on the cross, but which at the base is inscribed with the name Orpheus and Bacchus?"

"Is there?" Harry doesn't sound surprised or very interested.

"It was third century A.D.," I say. "A.D.!" I emphasize. "Christ was never depicted crucified until the fifth century. Don't you find a depiction of a crucified Orpheus and Bacchus – Bacchus being another name for Dionysos – odd?"

Harry is unexpectedly inspired with brilliance. "It was obviously made by a Christian wanting to portray the old pagan gods as crucified," he says. I regard him with surprise. He warms to his idea and goes on: "And what was resurrected was the new Christ."

Encouraged by Harry, the-newly-inspired, I say: "And it's interesting that Jesus in St. John's Gospel said: 'I am the true vine'?" (John 15:1)

"You mean wanting his followers to regard him as the new Dionysos?" Harry suggests.

"Well, yes, I suppose so. As for Orpheus," I go on, "he was often portrayed with a lamb slung around his neck, and Jesus, as the Good Shepherd was shown in exactly the same way as Orpheus."

"Stands to reason," says Harry, the new thinker. "Jesus the Good Shepherd. It all adds up – the grand finale taking up all the old pagan strands, and turning them into the one God, the one Son and the one Holy Spirit. So there!"

So there! No more discussions!

We go down to the small modern whitewashed chapel of Agios Phocas standing just outside the wire mesh perimeter fence to the temple. There are a few column drums outside the chapel. The Agios Phocas dedication is suitable to Lesbos because the saint was believed to have been a market gardener, and of all islands we've seen so far Lesbos is the most fertile and cultivated. During the persecution of the early Christians, Phocas had invited those who had come to kill him into his house, and had persuaded them to stay the night. While they'd slept, Phocas had dug his own grave. In the morning he'd offered himself up as a willing martyr, and told his persecutors to go ahead and kill him then to bury him in the grave he'd dug ready for them. This they had done but with sorrow and regret.

The Stoic, who has been meandering quietly and bending to study the odd small flower, approaches, and declares that she will die if she doesn't have some sort of sustenance to keep her upright, and she is going down to the nearby taverna now. Harry says he will come too. I am ready also, but just want to walk to the other side of the headland, a matter of forty yards.

I give a last long look around the church and temple ruins. Why a temple in honour of Dionysos built here? And why Dionysos Bresagenes? The 'genes' part I can understand, but Bresa? What does that mean? I have no answer to the question.

I wander down to the perimeter fence, and squeeze through between two wire mesh sections which have been pushed apart. I begin walking but realize quite soon that it is private property and there is a farmstead on my right. I note goat-droppings. I then spot a large, lone white billy goat with long curved horns who has his big green goat eyes on me watching my approach. Much as I would like to get down to the Cornish-type rocks and crested crashing waves, I don't want to be torn apart as Orpheus and Dionysos were. I turn tail and make a quick getaway.

After a salad lunch at the nearby taverna, and the Stoic is fortified for the drive back, we once again pass the Well of Achilles. I ask the Stoic to stop at the family-run hotel/taverna where I can pick the brains of the ex-Nottingham university student.

I find the young man seated at the reception desk and greet him again. Fortunately, he is free to give me his whole attention when I ask him about the Achilles Well.

Tradition has it, he tells me, that the beautiful slave girl, Briseis, who'd been won in battle by Achilles at the start of the Trojan War, had come from the nearby village of Brissa. Because King Agamemnon had had to forfeit his own slave girl won in battle and return her to her father (who happened to be a Trojan priest of Apollo), he'd seized Achilles' girl. The result was that Achilles had gone into a sulk, and had immediately withdrawn his fleet from the war, and had come here to the port at Vatera.

I can only see the young man's head and shoulders above the reception desk; his eyes blink at me behind horn-rimmed spectacles. He looks learned and knowledgeable, and he tells me there is evidence to support this story. The local farmers, when ploughing their fields, have turned up ancient arrow heads, even helmets. And also, when deepening the harbour at Agios Phocas, artefacts have been found from that same period. His eyes continue to blink solemnly at me as he tells me there are many local girls called Briseis after the slave girl of Achilles.

I suddenly remember the dedication of the temple, Dionysos Bresagenes. I realize that the 'Bresa' part might well be because of the village Brissa, or the girl Briseis.

I am very excited by what I've been told, and thank the young man for his information. We say goodbye, and he turns back to his computer screen.

"This is so stressful," the Stoic said. We were somehow lost in a maze of streets in the heart of the small town of Agia Paraskevi.

Harry said calmly as though he were air traffic control giving instructions to a pilot about to crash-land: "You're on course, keep her steady, then ease in to your right."

"Ease to my right? My dear Harry, I can't ease anywhere, I'm quite hemmed in. Don't let another car come up this road, dear God!"

"It's one-way. That's good, you're doing just fine. Just keep her steady."

"I wonder where the church is." I said.

"We're not doing any church, we're getting the hell out of here," the Stoic said.

"Good. Now turn right here – "

We somehow got out on to a main road which Harry said was the right one. After a while the Stoic asked: "So what was so special that you wanted to see that town?"

"Agia Paraskevi? Because they have a spectacular festival when they sacrifice a bull."

"Oh, I wouldn't want to see that."

"And have horse races down the streets. At least, I think they are in the streets."

"And the streets so narrow!"

"I'd like to see the bull sacrifice. Very pagan."

"The last bull you saw sacrificed," said Harry, "you couldn't stop crying."

"Life – then sudden death. Horrible."

"So when do they hold this great festival?" the Stoic enquired.

"February 10th," I said. "In honour of St. Charalambos. I think he was martyred at the end of the second century. He is usually portrayed with his foot on a female demon who has fire blowing out of her mouth."

"So where are we going now?" the Stoic enquired.

"The Taxiarchis Monastery at Mandamados," I said. "Everyone says we should see it."

"What happens there? Another god? Another hero?"

"An archangel," I said.

"An archangel?"

"The Archangel Michael, to be exact," I said.

"My dear, tell me about him. I know so little about archangels."

"He took over from the Roman god Mercury in conducting the souls of the dead to the next world. Mercury took over from the Greek god Hermes. And so on, and so forth," I said vaguely. "But, of course, unlike archangels who have large wings, Mercury and Hermes only had tiny ones, and not on their shoulders but on their feet and their hats."

"My dear, I can't wait to see your Archangel Michael."

And the Stoic put her foot on the accelerator till we sped along the main road as if we too had wings.

The Taxiarchis Monastery was the proud possessor of a miracle-working icon made from human blood. It dated from the tenth century as the result of a Saracen pirate raid. The chief pirate, according to an account I was to read later, was a huge fellow: 'Gold rings were hanging from his nose and ears... and, while talking, a row of big, bright white teeth would show which quite often would also serve as weapons in terrible battles. His hawkish one eye, since his other eye was always covered by a black cloth tied behind his left ear, would spew fire when staring at you.' Harry particularly liked this passage, and has since quoted it back at me when I am being particularly difficult about something – 'my hawkish eye spewing fire!' he'll say.

Early one morning when the monks were at their dawn prayers, the Saracens attacked and slaughtered all the monks except one young novice who attempted to climb through a window to the roof. But he was spotted, and they were about to kill him too when a 'wind and a roar was to be heard from the church roof. The roof was instantly transmuted into heavy sea and on the whitened waves there was a huge soldier... The pirates' hair raised like pins with terror...'

The Saracens consequently fled, and the novice monk passed out. When he finally came round and saw the slaughtered bodies of his fellow monks, he could only beseech what was then the icon of the Archangel Michael for help and guidance, with the result he was moved to create the icon we were looking at, using the blood of his slaughtered fellow monks. A very strange story. But his thinking was that he didn't want their blood to have been shed in vain. He collected two bowls of it, mixed it with clay till it was like plaster and a dark rose colour, and 'His initially shaky hands gradually became stable, working with certainty, speed and grace as if some invisible power were helping them.'

When there was no one queuing up to kiss the icon, I went up to it. The icon stood on an ornately carved and inlaid stand with an arched canopy, and the dark face of the archangel (painted in human blood) was in bas-relief, and was surrounded by embossed silver with a crown of the sort the Magi are sometimes depicted wearing.

I had no desire to kiss it, though I felt I should make the sign of the cross – which I didn't do either – but studied the face staring from its silver mount, with its strange crown, not forgetting his archangel wings, and his sword.

Sometimes, it was said, the eyes were seen to shed tears, or the lips to smile; or, if someone unworthy approached, he would be held back by his divine power. I was happy that I was allowed to come near and wasn't given any sign of disapproval as an unrepentant, curious spectator. There was no particular gruesome evidence that the face was created with human blood. It just looked like a moulded dark brown face.

I became aware of someone waiting behind me, so stepped aside for a soldier in combat dress to make his devotions. He was the third one I'd seen there. We'd passed an army camp on the way here, and I wondered whether the archangel, a warrior saint, was appealed to for courage and protection by these young men. It wasn't till later that I learned he was protector of soldiers.

I noticed another young man seated to one side taking a video of the shrine and the people coming to it. Close to the shrine was a large bronze bowl filled with olive oil, with lighted night-lights floating on it. I sat nearby and watched as people came with small wads of cotton wool which they dipped into the oil then put into slim plastic envelopes to take away with them. I'd seen this done elsewhere in Greece on a feast-day at a church dedicated to the Virgin Mary. On that occasion those who had fertility problems converged on the church to take away this holy oil in the hope of conceiving. I supposed this was the reason people were doing it here.

There were a number of rather strange pairs of metal shoes arrayed at the base of the brass bowl of oil. I have since learned these are presented to the Archangel Michael, and some time later the soles are examined to see if they are worn down which is sometimes the case. If so, then the archangel has been actively engaged in looking for a solution to the particular problem which has been put to him by the devotee.

Before leaving the church the young man who had been sitting to one side videoing the comings and goings, approached the icon as a penitent – or was he a devoted pilgrim? He was tall and lean, and wore old faded jeans. He fell to his knees and bowed his head before the shrine. He shuffled sideways on his knees and, after making the sign of the cross, bowed his head for a while over the silver shield at its base. He shuffled sideways to the opposite side absorbed in his own devotions. What had he done to be so intense? Was he in the army? Had he deserted, or had he defied his company commander?

He was totally unselfconscious and in no hurry, being oblivious of everything else. He then stood and laid his head against the glass which covered the face of the archangel. He seemed to be at one with the icon, glued to it in despair or in devotion – pleading silently, or giving thanks. There was more of an air of despair about him, and I felt sorry for his plight whatever it was. He was too young to be suffering whatever torment it was. I felt sure it must be some military offence.

While we sat outside on the monastery terrace with drinks, we saw the young man walking past deep in thought. I wanted some excuse to talk to him, and thought he might know the whereabouts of a marble fountain I'd been reading about which had miraculous holy water. I seized my opportunity when I saw the young man returning.

"Do you speak English?" I asked.

He stopped in his tracks, and looked surprised at this interruption to his solitary stroll. No, no English. So I tried Greek, knowing that 'holy spring' in Greek was something like *'Agios Pygi'*. The young man looked perplexed, then suddenly his face cleared and he beckoned to me to follow him. He led me back into the courtyard, to the far wall where an arched marble frame had within it a couple of brass taps. He turned on one of them and showed me the running water. I caught some of it in my cupped hands and drank it – a symbolic gesture only. He then indicated to me to wait there and went to speak to a woman before returning with two small stoppered bottles so I could take some of the holy water away. He levered off the tight fitting stopper and I filled my bottle. He then filled his. Not knowing at the time that the archangel was protector of soldiers, I asked him whether the archangel's icon was of particular significance for the army. Unfortunately, I'd forgotten the correct word for army and the word *'stavros'* came to mind which made my poor young man look thoroughly confused. In the end I just thanked him very much for showing me the marble fountain, and said goodbye, feeling mildly frustrated that I hadn't been able to think of an opening gambit regarding why he'd spent so much time on his knees before the icon.

"Now where has she been?" the Stoic questioned, directing her remark to Harry. "Your dear wife has an air of triumph about her. What were you doing with that poor young man?" she asked.

I produced my small bottle of holy water. "Holy," I said. "I am now well armed against all the evils of the world."

"I wish I had your faith," said the Stoic.

"My wife in truth is a great believer," Harry said. "She says she's agnostic, even an atheist, but in reality – " He took the small bottle of water and studied it, but I took it back quickly before he did an unholy act by pouring it away.

I then took out my pocket dictionary and looked up the word 'soldier'. Ah, the word I wanted was not *'stavros'* which I now remembered meant 'cross', but *'stratos'* or *'stratiotys'* (army). I saw my young man on another pensive stroll and, as he passed, called out to him that I'd wanted the word *'stratos'* not *'stavros'*. He smiled and came to join us. I stumbled on as best I could with his language and asked him whether there was a special reason for soldiers coming to the icon of the archangel (most of the words I got right). He sat down and attempted to explain. With a certain amount of miming, he told us that they came to gain confidence. The Stoic was more on the ball and understood him at once. "To be successful – get promotion," she declared, as the young man placed a finger on his shoulder, then two, then three and gestured the act of climbing a ladder. He smiled suddenly and his eyes lit up; they were the colour of honey bees on a sunny day. He didn't appear depressed, or to be suffering in any way.

"Such a nice fellow," I said ruminating about him, as we finally drove away. "I wonder why the poor man was sidling about on his knees all around the archangel's shrine. He looked as though he was in agony about something. I wish I'd managed to ask him what his problem was." I was later to read that the monastery took in troubled visitors who could stay on site to find peace and recover from mental stress, bereavement, or any such emotional trauma. I came to the conclusion he was staying there for one of these reasons.

I felt ridiculously triumphant at having got my small bottle of holy water. I removed the stopper and passed it to Harry to sample. "Holy water," I said. "Blessed by the Archangel Michael. Go on, drink it."

And the great believer rejected it at once. "Holy water? Ooooof! I wouldn't touch it with a barge pole. You don't know what germs are in the water."

"Well, I've drunk it," I said, relaxing back on the seat in a state of purity."

"Don't blame me if you get an upset stomach, then."

I felt momentarily anxious. But decided firmly that holy water, even if full of impurities, was still holy and, therefore, would dispel any toxics. Only good could come from it.

Tonight we are eating in. It is our last night on Lesbos and we have yet to pack, pay our bill and prepare for an early morning departure. Breaking in on our late siesta is the sound of a wind picking up; in no time it is howling round the building. Harry slides open the shutters of one of our windows to look out, and the sound increases fourfold. Voluminous sulphur-coloured clouds are overhead, and turbulent grey-black clouds can be seen over Mt. Olympus in the far distance. Fortunately we do not have to go out in what we feel sure will be a deluge as we have already bought wine, cheese pies and peaches.

We pass the evening at the doors to our balcony with glasses of wine, watching sheet lightning over Mt. Olympus, and listening to the distant roll of thunder. The whole area is obliterated by grey cloud. We are glad the storm didn't strike when we were in the area after our visit to Vatera and the temple of Dionysos. From Vatera we had returned via the small town of Agiassos at the foot of the mountain. We had explored its steep cobbled streets flanked by stone houses with terra-cotta roofs, wrought-iron balconies and Turkish-style architecture. I'd hoped to climb a little way up the mountain, but none of us really had the energy to look for the track. Instead, we'd visited its beautiful church dedicated to the Panagia Vrefokratoussa (the all holy protectress of infants). The church is the proud possessor of an important icon of the Virgin Mary which is believed to have been painted by St. Luke no less, and was brought from Jerusalem to Ephesus, and thence to Lesbos in the early ninth century. On the 15th August, the feast-day commemorating the Virgin Mary's Assumption, there is a great gathering of pilgrims in the town and, according to a Glaswegian couple we met who live on Lesbos, the icon is taken on horseback to the top of Mt. Olympus. If that is the case it is very demanding for those following behind, as the last part is a steep and difficult ascent to its barren summit. On leaving Agiassos we'd spotted the blue dome of a church rising above the conifers on a lower level, and thought that the icon was more likely to be carried there.

Despite the storm raging over Agiassos and the mountain, here we have no rain, only the gale-force wind. I am happy that, despite the distances we've had to cover, I've seen all that I've come out for. I raise my glass and say: "Here's a toast to Lesbos!" And Harry and the Stoic raise their glasses also. There is something unique about the island, not just Lesbos itself but the islanders. We've been impressed by how industrious they are; every part of the island is put to good use. They do not depend on tourists but work the land and, despite the centuries since Sappho, there is still something lyrical hanging over the landscape.

I raise my glass again and, as this is Sappho's island, I say spontaneously: *"Up, my lute divine, and make thyself a thing of speech..."* And even Harry raises his glass with a slightly shame-faced smile, and repeats: *"Up my lute divine!"*

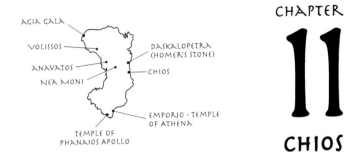

AGIA GALA

VOLISSOS

DASKALOPETRA
(HOMER'S STONE)

ANAVATOS

CHIOS

NEA MONI

EMPORIO - TEMPLE
OF ATHENA

TEMPLE OF
PHANAIOS APOLLO

CHAPTER

11

CHIOS

The uniqueness of Chios made the time and trouble of getting there well worth the effort. The cheapest way (or so we'd been advised) was to fly to Izmir in Turkey, get a taxi transfer to Cesme, spend the night there, then travel on by ferry-boat to Chios early the next morning (less than an hour's journey away).

At last! To sit on deck and see the island's outline increase in visibility as the boat sailed nearer over a glittering gentian sea, caused all the inconvenience of the journey to fade into oblivion.

Most people who visit the island for its ancient past know that Chios claims Homer for its citizen – Homer, the blind bard of the ancient world, from whom *The Iliad* and *The Odyssey* have come down to us.

Chios is an island just forty-eight kilometres long, and at its widest twenty-four. We hired a car and thought driving would be easy. It never occurred to us that down the centre of the island were wave after wave of mountains around which the road went in loops and coils. What might have been twenty-four kilometres as the crow flies in reality became three or four times further.

We arrived on the west coast mid-afternoon. Our apartment was part of a long, low house with its own small terrace where jasmine bloomed together with a morning glory, a vivid blue flower which came out only when the sun had risen and appeared to die in the afternoon, hence its name.

From our terrace we looked out to a low hill whose slopes descended to stretches of sea. On either side a road led down to a cove. On this trip Harry wanted to be near the sea, somewhere not crowded by tourist hotels but with a sandy beach. What, he demanded, was the point of visiting Greek islands if he didn't take advantage of the sun, the sea and never swam?

Later that afternoon we walked down the left-hand road to a small fishing village in its cove, and soon Harry was in the water doing the crawl, one white arm swinging over his head, followed by the other; he then lay on his back and floated, enjoying the warmth of the late afternoon sun.

When travelling around the islands I do things in order of importance for fear of any of the myriad hazards in life which might prevent us from seeing what I've come for.

So today we're back in the outskirts of the town of Chios, the port where we arrived, to see what is known as Homer's Stone. It is a difficult-to-find site and we are in a network of possible streets of which only one can be the correct one. Divine intervention suddenly steps in – a goddess in the guise of a stout housewife in a green dress. She crosses the road to her car with her shopping bags and I intercept her to ask the way to the *Daskalopetra* (the Teacher's Stone). She tells me to follow her and she will lead us to it.

After driving for about a kilometre with frequent left and right turns, she eventually stops and waves her hand in the direction where we can park our car beside the site. So here we are! I am fulfilling what has so far only been in my imagination, except there is suddenly a problem: a metal chain is looped across the footpath leading through fir trees to the Stone with a notice telling us to keep out.

But we haven't come all this way to be defeated by that. Divine intervention gets me hopping over it, and Harry follows. If some angry Greek appears I can pretend I do not know the language so do not understand what the notice says.

There are three small terraces each reached by a dozen or so steps only, and on the first I am so eager to identify Homer's Stone that I immediately rave about a boulder that I see, and then another. My mind is cast back in time – my imagination is so fluid that it is able to conjure up whatever I want it to, although I'm being impetuous and very foolish. Harry, who is far more practical, calls down from the second terrace: "Here it is! I recognize it from the photograph you showed me!"

How is it that I can make the wrong boulders play the part? I swallow my pride and join Harry. This terrace is a pine-needled area about fourteen metres square, and within this there is a low round rocky platform about five metres in diameter. To one side but rising from it is a waist-high rough stone, the *Daskalopetra*. Tradition has it that it was here that Homer taught his pupils, here that he played his lyre and sang *The Iliad* to an audience seated spellbound on the ground nearby.

Some scholars believe this Stone is, in fact, a throne of the near-eastern goddess Cybele, an ancient fertility goddess, because there are traces of lion's paws at its base which were a customary feature of her thrones. I run my hand over it. It is a creamy pinky-grey and rugged, but I can detect in it slither-like patches of cream which have a high patina and could be marble.

The sun shines, illuminating and accentuating the grandeur of the grey-pink crags to one side, great arching rockfaces, with high mountains looming behind them which have surely been there since the beginning of time? And, turning the other way, between emerald green, loose-branched fir trees, I see the broad sweep of glittering sea with the landmass of Turkey rising on the horizon. North along the Turkish coast is where the Trojan War took place, the subject of *The Iliad*.

Today the blind bard Homer doesn't sing, instead cicadas do. I think their sound is telling me something: they are an echo from Homer in antiquity, a divine hum from the ancient past. It is an unexpected bonus.

I've brought a copy of *The Iliad* with me. To me *The Iliad* is inspiring, a sort of bible in which human emotions run high, and warriors are tested to their limit. In it gods and men intermingle, and divine wills aid their favourite heroes.

We sit and I read a little of my *Iliad* to Harry which I've marked for the occasion, a piece I think he'll like about Achilles' two horses. Achilles, I explain, is refusing to fight because King Agamemnon stole his beautiful slave girl Briseis. But now the Greek army is in dire trouble, and Achilles relents a little by sending his best friend Patroclus to fight on his behalf, giving him his armour, chariot and his charioteer.

"To cut a long story short," I say to Harry as I sit down on the flat, round rocky platform, "Patroclus is killed. With Patroclus dead the charioteer, Automedon, needs to get the horses away from the battle, but the pair refuse to budge. Now listen!" I begin to read:

...they stood motionless in front of their beautiful chariot, their heads bowed to the earth. Hot tears ran down their eyes to the ground as they mourned for their lost charioteer (Patroclus), *and their luxuriant manes,*

falling to the ground from the collar on both sides of the yoke, were soiled in the dust... (Iliad 17: 437-441) "Don't you think that's incredibly sad?" I ask.

"Horses don't cry," is Harry's response.

"But the idea that they can," I say. "Two horses hanging their heads and weeping 'hot tears' for their master's dead companion is tragic. Even Lord Zeus seeing their distress was unhappy for them." And I tell Harry how Zeus is determined that Hector, the Trojan prince who killed Patroclus, will not have the added glory of driving Achilles' chariot. Instead, he 'breathed energy into the horses' and they rejoined the battle with Automedon.

"When was the Trojan War?" Harry asks.

"They think about 1200 B.C."

"And Homer?"

"Some time between the ninth and seventh century B.C."

I can see Harry is thinking of the time lapse between the war and Homer's epic poem, and I say: "There was no such thing as writing at the time, but the Trojan War was such a momentous event that the story was spun verbally down the generations, and the main events of it were depicted on pottery or other artefacts which kept the memory of it alive."

Another couple appear through the trees and wander around Homer's Stone and rocky platform. Without the trees obstructing the view to the sea in the east, and the pinky-grey craggy rocks rearing up to the west, not to mention the port along the coast which, in Homer's day, would not have had a sprawling suburb, this quiet spot where now the cicadas sing, would have been spectacular for its tranquillity and its grandeur – a reflection of the love-affair of Helen and Paris, and the tumultuous struggles of the war.

It is said that Homer was the first to give the gods human form and emotions. He is the first ever author known to the western world. *The Iliad* was passed down by word of mouth and wasn't a written text before the fourth century B.C.

"Why did old Zoos back the Trojans?" Harry asks.

I also wonder why, but say: "Just to be contrary – probably because his wife Hera supported the Greeks. And that, may I say, was because Paris, the Trojan prince in The Judgement of Paris, chose Aphrodite as the fairest and rejected Hera and Athena."

"So Athena backed the Greeks too?"

"And Aphrodite helped the Trojans. But you really ought to

read *The Iliad*," I say. "It's so inspired! It's so like Life when you find yourself moved to act, as though something unseen is forcing you to do whatever it is. The gods and goddesses were always, according to Homer, intervening: wrapping someone in a thick mist, or turning aside the point of a spear – "

"Putting energy back into the horses," said Harry.

"Exactly."

"How did they know which god was supporting whom?" Harry asks.

"Ah." I ponder the question and can find no answer. "It just says so," I say.

I have always liked the ancient Greek idea of a god or goddess each taking care of one area of human life and making no demands on being worshipped. Yes, Zeus was all powerful and the supreme god of the heavens, and he might throw thunderbolts if displeased, but Zeus had a family who put the brakes on him whenever he became too dictatorial. His authority was kept in check. In contrast God in the Old Testament had no other God but himself, and what he willed was what he expected to get.

And so I sit and dream of the far ancient past, of the mighty warriors battling it out on the plains of Troy; of the watching deities and their swift interventions when their favourites faced dire peril.

And all the while, as I sit in this quiet idyllic spot, the cicadas sing their song.

Evening. We were seated at a taverna, and I was busy scribbling in my notebook because I didn't want to forget anything I'd seen or heard so far. Harry had an early morning swim today, and saw a full moon setting in the west behind a promontory while the sun was rising in the east. This island is so full of grandeur and beauty with its dramatic mountains, and tranquil coves, I am bewitched. After Homer's Stone we'd taken another road back across the mountains via a tiny village called Pityos which had once claimed the honour of having Homer's house, but the claim was dropped, presumably because it wasn't true. Certainly for a blind bard a house in the mountains some twenty kilometres or so from his *Daskalopetra* was unlikely.

We'd also stopped off at Volissos, a small town with a ruined Genoese castle on its hilltop. Its inhabitants claim to be the descendants of Homer, and call themselves Homeridai. It was a pleasant town where we'd had lunch at a taverna filled with Greeks. If they were descendants of Homer there was nothing about them to make it evident. We'd later bought groceries in the small supermarket, and were then directed to the town's bakery; we could smell the bread as we approached down little side streets of huddled houses, and down steps behind a small sleepy looking police station. But it was closed. It was siesta time for those descendants of Homer. Many houses had strings of tomatoes hanging out to dry.

Now, within easy walking distance of our apartments, we were seated under one of many big white umbrellas set up beside the sea. The evening light was magical as the sun set behind a promontory to the west, and the full moon rose above a mountain to the east sending a shimmering path along the darkening sea. A young waiter with an attractive personality stood hovering by our table speaking remarkably good English. We later learned he was only fifteen, but he was already coming up with remarks such as 'I think you'll find it very tasty'.

By the end of the meal night had fallen and the harbour lights were winking red and green. To my left it was as if fireworks were going off; it was the light from the full moon, by now half way up into the heavens, glittering on the numerous small wavelets.

Dramatic power and energy revealed by the mountains by day, and quiet romantic beauty by night. No wonder Homer was inspired by his island.

We didn't pause in our climb up the acropolis. It wasn't the ruins of the small houses of the ancient settlement on the right side of the flagged track which drew us up, or the remains of the defence walls to be seen on our left, but the all important temple of Athena on a higher level. The temple, it is thought, was built several centuries after the altar found up there dating from the eighth century B.C. Homer might have walked this way to pay his respects to the goddess who played such a prominent role in his epics.

"Don't forget Athena was on the side of the Greeks in *The Iliad*," I told Harry as we climbed the track – there was no pausing for fear of not continuing in this midday heat. "You have to remember she was anti-Troy because she and Hera had been spurned by Paris in the all important Judgement."

"Remind me whose side old Zoos was on?" Harry asked.

"He was a bit of a turncoat was Zeus. He kept weighing the

outcome of things in his gold scales, and whoever or whatever weighed the heaviest and tipped the balance downwards was doomed."

"Didn't he have control over who lived or died?"

"Not really. It was the Fates who spun the threads of human life in ancient Greece. One held the distaff, the other drew off the thread, and the third cut the thread of life at death. Zeus might have been all powerful, but he didn't interfere with the Fates because he didn't want to overturn the natural order of things."

Harry stopped, turned towards the view and waved his stick. "Look at that!" Rugged slopes descended to the vivid blue sea with its shoreline of coves and inlets. Above was the vivid blue of the sky with a few small listless white clouds. The aroma of rosemary, thyme and lavender heated by the sun wafted up to us in waves. A few small emerald green conifers dotted the hillside either side of the track.

We were at a place called Emporio in the far south of the island. My map-reading had been impeccable once we'd got on to the correct route south. As ever, the road went in loops up and around mountains, giving us occasional glimpses of the sea, before eventually straightening out as we'd approached the gentler hills in the south of the island; there the road ran parallel with the coast for a while before finally going inland to the mastic-growing area. This part of the island was unique because it was the only place in the world where a certain species of the mastic tree could grow. Mastic gum is a clear resin-like substance that seeps from the trunk and branches of the tree where incisions are deliberately made to release it. It is used in cosmetics, or drunk as an aperitif, and it also has medicinal qualities. We'd driven through groves of them and had seen this dew- or bubble-like substance welling from the bark. The trees take five years before they begin to 'shed tears' as it is described.

We continued with our upward climb and finally reached what remained of the temple of Athena. It was, of course, like all excavated ancient sites. But it wasn't the ruins but the location that was worth all the effort of getting there. No temple was ever built for the convenience of its devotees as churches later were for citizens in populated areas; they were built on sites known to have sacred qualities. They were built where the gods were thought to be. Even Harry sat on a boulder and said he could feel there was something about the place, a certain energy perhaps.

I did my duty, examining what was left of what was once the *naos* (the holy of holies) but now only cream-coloured blocks of stone; and the stand where the cult statue of Athena would have stood, and the rectangular altar. But soon I turned my attention to the much higher loose-bouldered conical hill which looked as though it was held together by rooted scrub. It was known as the Profitis Ilias, as were most high mountain peaks in Greece. At its summit I could detect a ruined shack and beside that a tall metal cross claiming the triumph of Christianity.

A chugging sound brought my attention around to the sea where one motor-boat with an awning was towing another back to harbour. Further out were two container ships; they were so close they were clearly not *triremes* with sails as I'd mistakenly thought on Kos when my imagination had taken over.

"So what did your goddess do in the Trojan War?" Harry asked, as I sat beside him on the boulder.

"Athena was very good at divine intervention," I said. "When the Greeks were being driven back by the Trojans to their ships King Agamemnon, realizing the perilous situation for the Greeks, tried to win back Achilles by promising him great wealth as well as the return of his beloved Briseis if he would only fight again. But Achilles became even more enraged that Agamemnon could think he could be bought with money, and in his fury was about to kill him, when Athena quickly intervened by grabbing his arm which held the spear, and speaking 'winged words'. Don't you think that's poetic? 'winged words'?"

"Was Agamemnon's thread of life not ready to be cut then?" Harry queried.

"No. The thread was cut when he returned home after the war, and was murdered by his wife," I said.

I still had my *Iliad* with me and pulled it out of my shoulder-bag. I'd marked some passages concerning Athena and told Harry about another of her interventions regarding Achilles. How she'd thrown her tasselled *aegis* (her impregnable defence) around his 'mighty' shoulders, and crowned him with a 'golden cloud' so that he shone with a 'blaze of light' and, when he gave a shout, Athena also 'raised a war-cry' so that the Trojans were panic-stricken.

"So when did Achilles die?" Harry asked.

"Not till later. Xanthos, Achilles' horse, is given the power of speech by Hera and, hanging his head so his mane falls forward over his head again like when he was mourning for Achilles' companion, warns Achilles that he too is soon to die. He then anxiously tells him that it won't be due to any slackness on his part as his horse, any more than it was when Patroclus was killed. Patroclus' death was due to Apollo, he says.

"Or due to one of the Fates?" Harry put in, and he too hung his head as Xanthus the horse had, and peered down at the ground. He had no mane, what hair he had was under his sun-hat.

"Time to leave," I said. "We've a temple of Apollo to see next." And, as though on cue for our departure, suddenly the cicadas sang as they had at the *Daskalopetra,* Homer's Stone.

Harry was in a state of nervous shock. He hadn't been in danger from a charioteer with a sword or dagger, or from a Trojan brandishing a rock, but from a humble two-inch long centipede-like creature with multiple legs as thick as the scribble of a crayon which had run up from under a loo seat when I'd pulled the chain. I'd quickly flicked it into the pan where I'd left it swimming frantically. When I'd told Harry he'd taken pity on it and had gone to fish it out, whereupon it had run up his arm and into his shirt.

"It's only frightened," I'd said as Harry had yelped, expecting me to ferret around looking for it. But by now it had raced up the nape of his neck and hidden under his hat.

"Ouch! Yah! It's up here!" And Harry had thrown his hat away and rummaged through his hair; the terrified creature was last seen scurrying away as fast as its many legs could take it into undergrowth.

We were now driving along a dirt-track, and we'd been going for over four kilometres with Harry quivering and occasionally still ruffling his hair. "I can still feel it. Ugh, ugh, ugh!" The rough track was taking us into a wilder and increasingly more isolated area with no reassuring car or sign of habitation. The road was on the flank of a scrubby hillside which eventually joined what looked like a widening gorge. If the car broke down, or if Harry suddenly swelled up because he'd been bitten by the 'creature', how would I cope? What could I do?

We crossed a dry river bed, and continued through olive groves.

"Why, in God's name, are you bringing us here?" Harry demanded, giving another ruffle to his hair as the ghost of the 'centipede' ran over him.

"Apollo," I said. "Phanaios Apollo, meaning some sort of divine epiphany. The worship of Apollo here goes back to the ninth century B.C. It's very important."

Before I allowed the scenario of a flat tyre or some other mishap to take a hold, to my great joy we suddenly arrived. My 'great joy' being partly because about two hundred metres further along this dry river-bed estuary, I'd spotted a number of cars glinting in the sunlight, and the gentian blue sea glittering between two mountain slopes.

So here we were, still isolated but within hailing distance of humanity. To be totally out of range of help and human life was somehow alarming – enough to send the blood pressure soaring.

We got out of the car and explored this holy site of ancient Phanai. I'd read that a temple here had been dedicated to Apollo Phanaios, not because Apollo had appeared here ('phainomai' is Greek for 'to appear'), but because it was here that it had been revealed to Apollo's mother Leto that the tiny island of Delos was to be raised from the sea-bed for her confinement – Hera, in her jealous rage against Zeus for having had a fling with Leto, a mortal woman, had forbidden anywhere on earth to allow the birth to take place. Because of this epiphany, this area was known as the Delos of Chios. Certainly, the temple of Phanaios Apollo was believed to have been of the greatest importance here in this gloriously isolated spot at the mouth of a gorge where it opened out to the sea.

"So what was Apollo's role in the Trojan War?" Harry asked, leaning on his stick, then suddenly shuddering as the ghost of his 'centipede' ran up him again.

"It was Apollo who helped Hector kill Patroclus. Why he supported the Trojans I don't know. Maybe it was because he had a temple on King Priam's citadel. But also he and Poseidon had helped build the walls of Troy, so obviously he wouldn't want them destroyed."

I sat on a column drum, thumbed through my *Iliad* and read the passage aloud to Harry:

...He (Apollo) stood behind Patroclus now and, striking his back and broad shoulders with the flat of his hand, he made Patroclus' eyes spin and knocked the helmet off his head... (Iliad 16: 791-793)

"So there!" I closed the book.

"But the Trojans didn't win the war?"

"No, because Achilles was so grief-stricken and enraged by the death of his friend, he finally decided to fight. And then Lord Zeus weighed the future in his golden weighing scales, balancing the death of Achilles against the death of Hector, and Hector's pan went down indicating he was doomed. Apollo deserted him, leaving Achilles able to strike the fatal blow. *TheIliad*," I said, "is brilliant at describing the way humans and deities interact with one another."

"Thank God now for Christianity!" Harry said.

"Probably the same unseen energies, but going by a different name?" I suggested.

Here on this ancient temple of Apollo, an early Byzantine church had been constructed using many of the old temple blocks.

Pagan temple or Christian church – as we began to take our leave, as if on cue for our departure, once more the cicadas in high chorus sang.

Early morning, and we are breakfasting out on our terrace where the morning glory greets us, a vivid blue in sharp contrast with the white sweet smelling jasmine through which it climbs. Harry is making coffee, and I'm staring at the sea. It is the palest of blues like a young bridesmaid's frock with a dark blue band along its horizon like a velvet ribbon. Above that the faintest outline of the island of Psara is visible; it is almost transparent as if outlined on tracing paper. The sky too is colourless. I can see a small slither below the blue band which I take to be a fishing boat. All is tranquil, and the island is at peace, belying the horrific events of its comparatively recent historical past.

Yesterday, while Harry was having his late afternoon swim, and I'd been scribbling my notes, a woman had approached over the soft sand and greeted me. She'd heard us speaking English, she said, and she hoped I didn't mind being disturbed. Not at all, I'd replied. She invited me to join her and her husband.

They had, they'd told me, bought a property nearby, and her husband had then gone on to say how he'd been researching his Greek forebears and had discovered that in 1822 his great great great grandfather (or however many generations went back to that date) had been caught up in the Greek War of Independence on Chios. Before it the islanders had accepted Turkish rule, and his forebear and other merchants had had good business relations with them. But when the Greek mainland and other islands rose up in rebellion, the Greeks of Chios had become caught up in the troubles. His forebear had been one among fifty volunteers from the wealthiest families on the island to offer himself as hostage in order to reassure the Turks that the Chiots were not planning an insurrection. But then Samos had joined the war and had stirred up trouble on Chios, and the Turks had reacted with violence; they'd massacred the hostages, and whole villages had been decimated.

I'd been so caught up in the lyrical, poetic side of the island that these atrocities struck an unexpected strident chord. From now on we became aware of the darker side of this idyllic island.

Harry was now interested in wars and uprisings and read up about the Greek War of Independence and the atrocities carried out by the Turks on Chios. There was an entire village whose inhabitants had been killed, and whose empty shells of houses still stood on a high pinnacle overlooking a ravine which he now wanted to visit. The day was set aside for it together with Nea Moni which I'd been told should be seen.

Another swings and roundabouts drive to get to the monastery which was in the middle of the island. Here were forested mountains and, yes, the monastery was superbly situated overlooking the lower mountain slopes to the east. But, as soon as we set foot inside it, I felt a sense of dejection. It had suffered from the Turks in 1822 who'd sacked and looted it, and then in 1881 from an earthquake which had caused the church's dome to collapse. It was still proclaimed a landmark to be visited for its ancient Byzantine mosaics. But, despite restoration work, so little of its ancient splendour was to be seen. I'd been spoiled for Byzantine mosaics when visiting the Monastery of Dafni outside Athens. But here only scraps were left on arches in the *katholikon*.

There seemed to be no one with a welcoming smile; people looked listless as they wandered around. I wanted the monastery shop where I hoped to buy a book about its history but it was locked. When I enquired of a woman through an open doorway, she was annoyed and said impatiently that her room was private and to please go. And so I left feeling unholy and cross that this once famous monastery had long lost its beauty yet was still attempting, against all the odds, to keep up appearances.

"Ready?" Harry asked. He was already back at the car waiting for me.

"Now to your Anavatos?" I asked.

"I've found it on the map. It won't be difficult," came the answer.

Apparently, tradition has it that Anavatos had been founded by Byzantine lumberjacks who'd come to make scaffolding for the construction of Nea Moni – a rather odd belief since it was so inconveniently placed on a high pinnacle of rock some ten or so kilometres from the monastery. Its location was certainly ideal for looking out for any threat along the west coast, together with the Genoese watch-towers built at intervals along that coast.

We saw the rocky pinnacle at the end of a ravine, with the shells of stone houses climbing to its summit. It was dramatic. We were able to drive up to the foot of this abandoned ghost village where a taverna was open for visitors.

We walked up between the tightly-packed cubic, flat-roofed stone buildings with their empty holes for windows, and doorless entrances. There was a warning that these buildings were dangerous and it was advised not to explore inside them. Their doorways were low, and the whole impression was eerie. Many of the villagers had thrown themselves over the walls into the ravine below rather than await death at the hands of the Turks.

We left this ghost town and had a picnic by the side of the ravine where we sat on rocks and gazed back at those sightless eyes of windows and ruined buildings climbing their craggy peak. It was a sad reminder of what men could do when provoked and mutual tolerance ceased to exist.

This, our last day, and we were in the north of the island. As we climbed the steep stone-flagged steps which led up to the tiny ancient Church of Agio Gala, I didn't know I was in for a big surprise. The small church had been visible from the ravine below, nestling against the high rockface, its whitewashed round drum pierced with small arched windows under a terrocotta-tiled roof.

The flagged steps became steeper and so narrow it was difficult to get a firm footing so, as we climbed higher, I grabbed the arm of the strong young man who had presented himself as a guide on our arrival and was leading the way. We reached the small church's terrace and our guide unlocked an outer door. As he did so he told us that before the nearby village was called Agio Gala it had been known as Agios Thelenis or Agia Eleni. This wasn't the big surprise, not yet, since St. Helena, the pious mother of Constantine who, in the fourth century A.D., first recognized Christianity as a true religion, had had many churches dedicated to her. The big surprise came when the guide went on to say that long before Christianity, tradition had it that Helen of Troy had visited the island and had been worshipped as a goddess in the locality.

Helen of Troy? Really?

I was astonished, even though I'd recently learned that she'd been looked upon as a goddess at Sparta where she'd grown up and had married King Menelaus. Being the daughter of Zeus, supreme Olympian god, it shouldn't have been a surprise that she'd been regarded as divine. That she'd become the victim of Aphrodite's wiles and had run off with Prince Paris of Troy had merely shown she was also human. With a father like Zeus what else could you expect? In a way I rather admired her daring.

We were led into the church. Its sanctuary facing east was built on the projecting rocks, while its western end was in a cave. Its most striking feature was its heavy, intricately carved wooden *iconostasis* depicting flowers and foliage, angels, strange Dionysiac figures, mask-like faces, animals and birds and bare-breasted females. Above the central Royal Doors which had a two-flap opening to the sanctuary, was an icon of Christ, and to its left another of the Virgin and Child, below which were strung votive offerings from grateful devotees whose prayers had been answered.

Light entered this small church from two small windows in the main body of the church and from four arched windows around the dome. The scant remains of a depiction of Pantocrator could be seen in the dome, and below it were plaster cherubs.

We were taken to an inner cave which was dedicated to Agia Anna which, in comparison to the first church, had a very plain modern looking sanctuary screen and unexciting icons. We were then led on to the innermost cave. This was a sort of womb-like area with udder-shaped stalactites (called 'mastoid stalactites') from which dripped calciferous water resembling breast-milk. This was believed to have miraculous healing qualities and was collected in wide bowls placed beneath these 'udders'. This was where the earliest worship had taken place.

The three successive caves starting from this innermost womb-like one with its mastoid stalactites, then the Chapel of Agia Anna (St. Anne who'd given birth to the Virgin Mary), and finally the amazing small church on its rocky ledge with its icon of the Virgin Mary holding the Christ Child seemed to me a symbolic graduation from pagan to Christianity.

"So that was interesting," Harry said when we were down below again and seated under the plane trees in the tree-filled ravine. A young man who was selling refreshments brought us Cokes, and also filled a jug with water from an overflowing pipe beside the stream – pure spring water, he told us. We'd had to cross the stream to get here from the car-park.

There was no one else sitting at the tables set beneath the plane trees whose shade sheltered us from the mid-morning sun. Harry said: "What was all that about the early name of the village being Aggi Heleni or something, and about Helen of Troy?"

I eyed him for a moment before replying. I didn't want my goddess scorned. "He said Helen of Troy had been worshipped here on Chios," I ventured. "But under the Byzantines the village became Agia Eleni after Constantine's saintly mother."

"Well, that makes sense, I suppose," Harry remarked. "You wouldn't want your goddess Helen hanging around when there was a Christian saint with the same name. She was the one who found the True Cross, wasn't she?" Harry asked. "Well done her! A Christian!"

"Well, she was certainly no Helen of Troy," I agreed, slightly irritated by Helena's saintly life. Then I remembered that, in fact, she hadn't always been a woman of virtue, and I threw a small pebble into the pious waters. "Your saintly Helena," I said, "before she married Constantine's father, worked in an inn and was believed to have been a prostitute, so there! That's how they met, your pious Helen!"

"Oh, I don't believe that!" Harry said. "And even if she was, she more than made up for it when she trod the straight and narrow," he added easily.

I kept quiet about my secret admiration for my Helen the goddess – Helen, the woman who'd dared, but said: "How dull the world would be if everybody was pious like your precious Helena. There'd be no stories, no epic poems – no *Iliad!* What would Homer have sung about?"

"He'd have found something," Harry said. "Poets always do. The mountains – the heavens – something or another."

"Well, he had his *Hymns,* I suppose," I agreed.

"Did Homer write hymns?"

"Yes, the *Homeric Hymns.* In pagan times people prayed and sang hymns at their temples much as they do today in churches. The difference being the priests were usually drawn from the laity and served for a year, and they had no dogma, no 'thou shalt nots' or 'thou shalts', and certainly no emphasis on sin and repentance.

"Hm. That was their trouble. They never repented. Just got deeper and deeper into some quagmire of their own making having given in to some temptation."

"And what wonderful dramas as a result! There'd have been nothing worth writing about without mad or wicked females! Helen of Troy was the very first to hit the literary scene! Your St. Helena pales into insignificance in comparison."

"My St. Helena, as you call her, will have reaped her reward in heaven. God knows where your faithless goddess has gone!"

We left the shady plane trees, crossed the wooden bridge and braced ourselves for a fifty metres very steep (almost vertical) ascent in the car to the road above. I volunteered to stand up at the top to flag down any approaching cars while Harry came up. I expected the usual punishment from on high for my defence of the wayward Helen of Troy and for blabbing about the sins of the saint. But there were no cars and Harry with the maximum revs shot up and out like a bullet and missed me. As a result I was able to sit back and enjoy the scenery as we returned by an inland route.

When driving northwards that morning, we'd taken the road on the coastal side of the mountain range, and had been surprised by the olive groves which filled the valleys and extended up the mountain sides. We'd then spiralled up a mountain road where there'd been a ruined windmill, and then passed the ruins of a Genoese castle on a hilltop silhouetted against the sunlight. For a while there'd been a strange range of chocolate coloured mountains with dark shadows on them like the interior of chocolate fondants, and behind them the hazy outline of a higher range of mountains. Now, on our return journey via the interior road, we passed closer to the range of chocolate fondant mountains. They were at that moment shadowed in the afternoon light and looked mysteriously velvety like moleskins. We could see tracks curving up along their sides, and a solitary, centrally placed whitewashed chapel in the foothills.

I thought sadly how this time tomorrow we would be preparing to catch the ferry-boat back to Turkey. Harry and I both agreed that, of all the islands, this was the one we would most like to return to.

We are now at our usual taverna seated under one of the large white umbrellas beside the sea, listening to the rhythmic swish of the wavelets on the shore a few feet from our table. Over the past days we have become the best of friends with the family who run it. The young waiter's mother is the cook and we are told what she is preparing for that evening. Her English too is good, if more hesitant than her son's who has picked up linguistic phrases like 'I think you'll find it to your liking', and 'I will be waiting for you,' when I'd said that I hoped one year to return. I suspect he watches American films and has picked up the phrase from the hero waving goodbye to his heroine. His mother tells us he is the youngest of her four children. Her husband has the open, cheerful countenance of one well contented with his lot.

Even Harry is happy to eat what the mother recommends. For some unaccountable reason he trusts her cooking, maybe because she says she grows her own vegetables; or maybe because there is something comfortably reassuring about her. This evening I question her about the atrocities the Chiots experienced in the 1822 War of Independence. Had her family been involved, I ask? She tells me that she herself comes from Athens, but that her husband's grandfather was involved in the Great Catastrophe of 1922 (the exchange of the Christian and Moslem populations). And a shadow clouds her face as she tells me how then the inhabitants of Chios had gathered on the beach right here because a boat was coming to take them off the island to safety. But the boat hadn't come and all those waiting had been slaughtered. The sea, she says, had turned red from the blood of those who'd been killed.

This evening the sea is a deep sparkling cobalt blue and dead calm except for the regular swish as it breaks on the sand. The sky is a pale colourwash of greens and apricot. As the sun sets behind the headland, the promontory darkens till it becomes a black silhouette. The outline reminds me of our dog with her head down on her front paws, her nose sniffing a small rock rising just out of reach; and there are black trees which are her eyebrows; I can imagine her eye looking at me from under them.

Gradually the sea turns black as night comes on and the promontory merges with the night; we glimpse a small white light of a boat gliding across the blackness, while the full moon rises above the promontory to the east.

War? What war? Catastrophe? What catastrophe? Tonight all is as tranquil and sublime as it is possible to be.

Chios town, and we have time on our hands before our ferry-boat this evening. We are seated at another taverna, this time overlooking the port. We've just visited the Archaeological Museum where we were shown finds from Emporio and ancient Phanai, small figurines, as well as columns and entablatures from the temples. We were also shown exhibits of the great fertility goddess Cybele, with her lion's paws at the base of her throne. My favourite exhibit was a small head wearing a finely decorated warrior's helmet which I liked to think was from the time of the Trojan War – a bottle-stopper, we were told.

A cruise-liner has just docked and we watch idly as the passengers disembark. Middle-aged and silver-haired couples wander past in expensive casual clothes. A few sit at our taverna bringing with them an air of opulence. I am captivated by a woman whose short dark hair has been swept back and upwards in controlled spikes. I can only see her in profile, her eyes concealed behind dark glasses; she wears a very simple yet elegant top, her make-up is subtle, and she has an air of mystery and quiet about her. Her companion looks as though he enjoys a wealthy lifestyle; He is a dark-haired young man wearing a black and white striped, long-sleeved top; he is never off his mobile which he holds permanently clamped to his ear.

An hour later and we watch the cruise-liner passengers return from their perambulations, and re-embark up the gangway to appear like ants as they walk the upper deck. I can imagine their conversation with friends when they return home: 'And we visited Chios, at least I think we did – we saw so many places it's difficult to remember exactly. Of course, we had interesting lectures but don't ask me anything about them now. So many wonderful places, but it's all become a bit of a blur, you know what it is!'

And now the hour comes for our departure too. We go through security checks because we are leaving Greek territory and crossing into Turkish. Soon we are on the ferry-boat drawing away from the island we love. I study the faces of the Turkish men, looking for ruthless streaks behind their pleasant expressions. Do I detect an underlying malevolence behind those smiling eyes? *Anger – sing, goddess, the anger of Achilles son of Peleus, that accursed anger, which brought the Greeks endless sufferings and sent the mighty souls of many warriors to Hades, leaving their bodies as carrion for the dogs and a feast for the birds...*

Those are the first lines of *The Iliad*. They were sung by Homer calling on his Muse to fill his soul with inspiration, with words and song to keep alive the memories of the violence that erupts from the abuse of hospitality or the abuse of power; about the heroes who did battle in the Trojan War, and the woman over whom the war was fought – Helen. Some say her name derives from 'helios' (meaning 'sun', 'a beam of light'), while others that it comes from the word 'Hellene' ('of the ancient Greek race').

I look back to the island we have left, and search along the suburbs of the port to see if I can detect the *Daskalopetra,* that landmark where the blind bard sang his epic poem to the world. But I can see no Homer's Stone. And soon Chios becomes just the outline of an island, a memory only. We turn back to the Turkish landmass, and the more pressing matter of arrival as the past recedes.

THE END

GLOSSARY OF GODS & HEROES

ACHILLES

Son of Peleus and Thetis, and Greek hero of the Trojan War.
He was furious when King Agamemnon stole his slave girl and,
as a consequence, refused to fight. Only when the Greeks were on the
point of defeat and his best friend Patroclus was killed, did he consent
to rejoin the battle and, by his strength and valour, brought victory to
the Greeks.

AEGEUS

Legendary king of Athens, and father of Theseus.

AGAMEMNON

King of Mycenae and leader of the Achaeans (Greeks) in the Trojan
War. He was murdered by his wife, Clytemnestra, on his return.

ALEXANDER THE GREAT

(356-323 B.C.) King of Macedonia, son of Philip II and Olympias.
He was a keen admirer of Homer's *Iliad* and carried a copy of it with
him throughout his campaigns.

AMPHITRITE

Wife of Poseidon.

APHRODITE

Goddess of love.

APOLLO

Son of Zeus and Leto, and twin brother of Artemis. He was god
of music, archery and prophecy.

ARES

God of war.

ARTEMIS

Daughter of Zeus and Leto, and twin sister of Apollo. She was goddess of wild life and hunting.

ASCLEPIUS

God of medicine, son of Apollo and Coronis, a mortal woman.

ATHENA

Daughter of Zeus. She was virgin goddess of wisdom, arts and crafts.

CALLIOPE

One of the nine Muses, identified with epic poetry.

CENTAURS

Strange beings who were half horse, half man.

CHIRON

A Centaur who was both wise and kind and knowledgeable in music and medicine.

CLYTEMNESTRA

Wife of Agamemnon, king of Mycenae. Clytemnestra murdered her husband on his return from the Trojan War.

DEMETER

Goddess of corn and agriculture.

DIONYSOS

Son of Zeus and Semele, a mortal woman. He was god of wine and drama.

EURYDICE

A beautiful nymph who married Orpheus and died tragically soon afterwards from a snake bite.

FATES

See Moirai.

FURIES

Greek spirits of vengeance who harassed those who committed murder, especially family members. They were often portrayed as winged women, and could be regarded as symbolizing pangs of conscience.

GAEA

Personification of the earth.

HADES

Brother of Zeus and god of the underworld.

HELEN

The beautiful wife of Menelaus, king of Sparta. She was seduced by Paris and ran away with him to Troy which triggered the Trojan War.

HEPHAESTUS

Lame son of Zeus and Hera. He was god of fire and a master craftsman in all metal work.

HERA

Wife of Zeus, goddess of women and marriage.

HERACLES

Best known of the Greek heroes for his twelve labours. He was renowned for his courage, strength, endurance and compassion. Under the Romans he became Hercules.

HERMES

A messenger of the gods. He conducted the souls of the dead to Hades.

HESTIA

Goddess of the hearth, symbol of the home and family.

HIPPOLYTUS

Son of Theseus and the Amazon queen, Hippolyta. Theseus' second wife, Phaedra, fell hopelessly in love with him with disastrous consequences.

HYGIEA

Daughter of Asclepius, god of medicine.

JUDGEMENT OF PARIS

A legend in which Strife, during the course of a marriage-feast, threw down a golden apple inscribed with the words 'for the fairest'. The three goddesses, Aphrodite, Athena and Hera, each thought the apple was intended for her and it was left to Paris, son of the King of Troy, to decide who was to receive it. Each of the goddesses offered him a bribe to persuade him to choose her, and he settled for Aphrodite as she promised him Helen, the most beautiful woman in the world.

KORE

See Persephone.

KRONOS

Married to Rhea. He was father of Zeus and many other Olympian deities.

LETO

Mother of Apollo and Artemis by Zeus.

MEDUSA

One of the Gorgons. They were all hideous with glaring eyes and snakes around their heads for hair.

MENELAUS

King of Sparta, married to Helen who ran off with Paris to Troy.

MINOS

King of ancient Crete, who became one of the judges of the dead.

MINOTAUR

Offspring of Pasiphae. He was half man, half bull and was kept in a labyrinth. See Pasiphae.

MOIRAI

The Fates. Three in number: the first assigned man's lot at birth, the second spun the thread of life and the third cut it at the end of the allotted life-span.

MUSES

Nine daughters of Zeus and Mnemosyne (personification of Memory). Each presided over one of the arts or sciences.

NEREIDS

Sea maidens.

NIKE

The Greek personification of victory.

ODYSSEUS

A hero of the Trojan War in Homer's *Iliad,* and his subsequent adventures in *The Odyssey.* He is courageous, resourceful and able to overcome crises.

OLYMPIAS

Mother of Alexander the Great.

ORESTES

Son of King Agamemnon and Clytemnestra. He was hounded by the Furies after he killed his mother in order to avenge his father's murder by her.

ORPHEUS

Founder of the mystic cult of Orphism. He was the son of Calliope one of the Muses and possibly Apollo, and became renowned for charming wild beasts with his singing. He married Eurydice and was distraught when she died soon afterwards from a snake bite.

PANACEA

Daughter of Asclepius, god of medicine.

PARIS

Son of the King of Troy. Aphrodite helped him to seduce the beautiful Helen which triggered the Trojan War.

PASIPHAE

Wife of King Minos of Crete. To punish King Minos, Poseidon caused Pasiphae to fall in love with a bull and she gave birth to the Minotaur.

PELEUS

King of Thessaly, married to Thetis, a Nereid. Achilles was their son.

PERSEPHONE

Daughter of Demeter. She was a beautiful young goddess who was abducted and carried off to the underworld by Hades and became his queen.

PHAEDRA

Wife of Theseus who fell in love with Hippolytus, her step-son, with tragic consequences.

POSEIDON

Brother of Zeus. He was god of the sea as well as of earthquakes and horses.

PYTHIA

The priestess of Apollo at Delphi through whom the god gave his oracles.

PYTHON

A monstrous serpent (or dragoness, according to Homer) who inhabited Delphi before Apollo came and killed it.

RHEA

Wife of Kronos and mother of Zeus and many other Olympians.

SIRENS

Weird women who lured sailors to their doom by their singing.

THEMIS

Mother of the Fates.

THESEUS

Son of King Aegeus of of Athens.

THETIS

A sea-nymph, married to Peleus. Their son was Achilles. To make him immortal Thetis held him by the heel in the river Styx. Where she gripped him, however, remained for ever mortal – hence the saying someone has an 'Achilles' heel', a vulnerable spot.

TROJAN WAR

A war waged by the Achaeans (Greeks) against the Trojans in order to recover Helen who had run off with Paris, son of the King of Troy.

ZEUS

Supreme god of the ancient world. God of the heavens and controller of the weather. In classical times he was regarded as protector of civic law and justice.

BIBLIOGRAPHY

Attwater, Donald: *Dictionary of Saints.* Penguin Books, 1983.

Baumann, Hellmut: *Greek Wild Flowers and plant lore in ancient Greece.* The Herbert Press, 1993.

Constantinidou-Partheniadou: *A Travelogue in Greece and a Folklore Calendar.* Athens, 1992.

Dodds, E.R: *The Ancient Concept of Progress.*

Durrell, Lawrence: *Reflections on a Marène Venus.* Faber and Faber Ltd., 1960.

Eusebius: *The History of the Church.* Penguin Books, 1965.

Ferguson, Everett: *Backgrounds of Early Christianity.* William B. Eerdmans Publishing Co., Michigan, 1987.

Frazer, J.G: *The Golden Bough.* Macmillan Press Ltd., 1983.

Grant, Michael & John Hazel: *Who's Who in Classical Mythology.* Weidenfeld & Nicolson, 1993.

Graves, Robert: *The Greek Myths:* I & II. Penguin Books Ltd., 1986.

Greece, *The Blue Guide.* A & C Black Publishers Ltd, 1990.

Greece, *The Rough Guide.* Penguin Books, 1995.

Grigson, Geoffrey: *The Goddess of Love.* Constable & Co. Ltd, 1976.

Hanson, Richard: *Studies in Christian Antiquity.* T. & T. Clark Ltd, 1985.

Herodotus: *The Histories of Herodotus*, translated by Harry Carter. Oxford University Press, 1962.

Harvey, Sir Paul: *The Oxford Companion to Classical Literature.* Oxford University Press, 1974.

Hesiod: *Theogony,* translated by Richard Clay. Penguin Books Ltd, 1985.

Homer: *The Iliad,* E.V. Rieu translation published 1950, revised and updated by Peter Jones and D.C.H. Rieu, 2003.

Homer: *The Odyssey,* translated by Walter Shewring. Oxford University Press, 1980.

Homer: *The Homeric Hymns,* a new prose translation by Andrew Lang, 1899.

Kerényi, Carl: *Dionysos.* Princeton University Press, 1996.

Kerényi, Carl: *The Gods of the Greeks.* Penguin Books Ltd, 1958.

Lane Fox, Robin: *Pagans and Christians.* Penguin Group, 1988.

Lyra Graeca, Volume I, translated by J.M Edmonds, William Heinemann, 1922

Norris, R.A: *God and World in Early Christian Theology.*

Norwich, John Julius: *Byzantium, the early centuries.* Penguin Books, 1990.

Pausanias: *Guide to Greece,* volumes 1 & 2. Penguin Books Ltd, 1971.

Plato: *The Collected Dialogues of Plato,* edited by Edith Hamilton and Huntington Cairns. Princeton University Press, 1961.

Radice, Betty: *Who's Who in the Ancient World.* Penguin Books, 1973.

Rahner, Hugo: *Greek Myths and Christian Mystery.*

Rodd, Rennell: *The Customs and Lore of Modern Greece.*

Sappho: *Stung with Love: Poems and Fragments,* translated by Aaron Poochigian, Penguin Classics, 2009.

Scully, Vincent: *The Earth, the Temple, and the Gods.* Yale University Press, 1962.

Ware, Timothy: *The Orthodox Church.* Penguin Books, 1964.

Warner, Marina: *Alone of all Her Sex.* Picador, 1985.

INDEX

Achilles 197, 199, 209, 210, 214, 216
Achilles, well of, Lesbos 197, 199
Adonis 12
Aegean, sea 36, 62, 66, 67, 79, 100, 182
Aegeus, King 4, 36
Agamemnon, King 168, 200, 209, 214
Agia Anna, chapel, Chios 220
Agia Eleni, Chios 219
Agia Irini, church, Santorini 68
Agia Paraskevi, Lesbos 201
Agia Paraskevi, church, Lesbos 200
Agia Sophia, cathedral, Athens 169
Agia Triada, Crete 23
Agiassos, Lesbos 206
Agio Gala, Chios 219-222
Agios Andreas, church, Lesbos 186
Agios Dionysios, saint 47
Agios Georgios, church, Naxos 44
Agios Ioannis, monastery, Kos 150
Agios Minas, church, Iraklion 2
Agios Nikolaos, church, Naxos 49
Agios Nikolaos, monastery, Zaros 20
Agios Nikolaos, Crete 12, 15, 16
Agios Phocas, chapel, Lesbos 199, 200
Agios Soulas, festival, Rhodes 178
Agios Stephanos, archaeological site, Kos 149
Agios Stephanos, ancient church, Santorini 67
Agios Titos, church, Iraklion, Crete 2, 25
Airs, Waters, Places, The 136
Akrotiri, Santorini 62, 68-70
Alcestis 114
Alexander the Great 66, 169
Aliko, Naxos 42, 46
Alioi Games 160

Allah 134
Amazon 53
Ampelos, mountains, Samos 96, 97
Amphitrite 123
Anatolia 151, 178
Anavatos, Chios 218-219
Annunciation 117
Annunciation, Church of the, Santorini 67
Anoyeia, Crete 34
Anthony, St. 12
Antimachea, Kos 150
Antissa, ancient, Lesbos 192, 194-196
Antony, Mark 163
Aphrodite, goddess 12, 53, 85, 88, 145, 156, 164, 184, 188, 189, 190, 191, 210, 220
Apo Sangri, Naxos 41
Apocryphal, Gospel of Bartholomew 14
Apollo, god 23, 25, 36, 46, 50, 54, 56, 57, 67, 90, 92, 93, 101, 104, 134, 135, 137, 151, 156, 158-161, 165, 167, 177, 178, 186, 193, 195, 198, 200, 215-217
Apollo, St. 48
Apostles' Creed 14
Ares, god 84
Argonauts 195
Argos, Peloponnese 93
Ariadne 4, 35, 36, 38, 47-49, 53
Ariadne, St. 47
Artaxerxes, King 139
Artemis, goddess 56, 101, 104, 109, 135, 151
Asclepiads 136, 140
Asclepius, god 114, 134, 136, 137, 138, 141, 153
Asclepeion 56, 113, 135-139, 141, 145, 151-152

Aspronisi, island, Santorini 65

Assumption 127, 206

Atavyros, Mt., Rhodes 176, 179

Athena, goddess 23, 43, 54, 104, 122, 156, 160, 165, 166, 169, 170, 171, 177, 178, 180, 210, 212-215

Athens 1, 4, 53, 54, 57, 72, 97, 103, 109, 122, 126, 131, 139, 178, 218

Athos, Mount 73, 80

Atlantis 60, 61, 63

Automedon 209, 210

Axos, Crete 27

Bacchus 198

Baptism 125

Barbarossa 128

Basil, St. 72

Battle of the Gods 8

Bay of Fourni 56

Bodrum 150, 151

Briseis 199, 200

Brissa, village, Lesbos 200

British 6, 11

Britomartis 15, 17

Bulls 1, 4, 38

Byzantine 2, 16, 21, 22, 49, 67, 68, 85, 87, 122, 146, 155, 165, 169

Cadmus, King 40, 67

Caesar Augustus 163

Caldera 59, 64-66, 78

Calliope 195

Cassandra 167, 168

Centaur 135

Cesme 207

Chaos 63

Charalambos, St. 201

Chares 157

Charon 195

CHIOS, island, Eastern Aegean 207-225

Chiron 135

Chora, Naxos 35-39, 46-50

Chora, Patmos 101, 103, 109

Christmas 15

Chrismation 125

Christ 13, 14, 15, 21, 22, 24, 45, 54, 71, 99, 102, 103, 105, 106, 122, 134, 151, 198, 220

Christian 3, 13, 15, 16, 20, 21, 22, 24, 20, 21, 22, 30, 37, 40, 42, 47, 55, 57, 71, 95, 97, 101, 112, 113, 114, 119, 122, 123, 134, 137, 141, 146, 151, 153, 156, 164, 168, 169, 181, 186, 188, 196, 197, 198, 214, 217, 219, 220, 221, 223

Christian Fathers 55

Christmas 15

Christodoulos, Osios 103, 104, 146

Cicero 160

Clashing Rocks 195

Cleis 190

Cleopatra 163

Collyridians 112

Colossus, Rhodes 156-157, 159, 161

Constantine the Great 15, 111, 112, 129

Constantinople 112

Coptic 14

Coronis 135

CRETE 1-34, 35, 54, 61, 68, 86, 176, 186, 195

Croton 92

Crusaders 134, 146, 150, 151, 156, 158, 168

Curetes 8, 29

Cybele, goddess 209, 223

Cyclopes 8, 63

Cynthos, Mt. 52, 54, 55

Cyprus 6, 122, 190

Dactyloi 29

Daniel, prophet 93

Daskalopetra, Chios 208-211, 225

Day of Atonement 15

Day of Judgement 99, 100

Delia, festival 56

Delian Games 53, 56

Delian League 57

DELOS, island, Cyclades 36, 50, 51-58

Delphi 9, 24, 68, 90, 92, 159, 178

Demeter, goddess 8, 41, 42, 43, 46, 146, 181, 195

Demetrios, St. 47

Diktaon, cave 7-10, 22, 29

Dionysios, St. 37, 47

Dionysos, god 36-41, 46, 57, 117, 126, 174, 184, 186, 195, 197-200, 206

Dorians 136

Doric 18, 111, 141, 159

Dreros, Crete 18

Easter 10, 79, 82, 86
Egypt 53, 68, 86, 93, 157, 189
Eileithyia, goddess 53
Ekatondapiliani, church, Paros 111-115
Eleusian Mysteries 42
Elevation (see Exaltation of the Cross)
Elijah, prophet 71
Elounda 15-18
Elysium Fields 26
Embonas, Rhodes 175,176
Embros Thermi, Kos 142-144
Emporio, Chios 213-215, 223
Eos 155
Ephesus 96, 101, 151
Epidaurus 135, 136
Epimenides 10
Eressos, Lesbos 183, 185
Eupalynus, tunnel, Samos 84
Euphorbus 93
Euridice 114, 194, 195
Europa 1, 20
Exaltation of the Cross 15, 19, 20, 30, 31
Ezekiel, prophet 93

Fates 70
Feast of Weeks 15
Filerimos, Monastery of, Rhodes 165
Filoti, Naxos 42
Fira 59, 70, 75
Flerio, Naxos 45-46

Gaea 63, 159
Gabriel, angel 14, 117
Galilee 21, 22
Genoese 181, 189
Gentiles 21, 178
Germans 11, 34
Gnostics 14
God 25, 33, 40, 54, 71, 97, 101, 107, 109, 120, 122, 123, 137, 146, 178, 198
Golden Fleece 195
Gortyn, Crete 20-27
Gospels 13, 83, 120
Graces, minor goddesses 88
Great Catastrophe 223
Greek War of Independence 117, 122
Grotto of St. John, Patmos 101-103

Gulf of Gera, Lesbos 184
Gulf of Kalloni, Lesbos 182, 184, 185
Gyroulas, Naxos 41

Hades 8, 41, 114, 181, 195
Hector, Prince 210, 216
Helen of Troy 169, 191, 219, 221-222; 224
Helena, St. 15, 111, 129, 219, 221-222
Helios 155, 156, 157, 158, 159, 161, 164, 165, 175, 179, 180
Hellenic 22, 52
Hephaestus, god 84
Hera, goddess 8, 40, 41, 51, 52, 53, 79, 82, 85, 90, 92, 93, 184, 210, 212, 216
Heracles 67, 114, 145, 169
Heraion, Samos 82-85
Hercules (see Heracles)
Hermes, god 85
Herod, King 14
Hestia, goddess 8,12
Hippocrates 135-139, 142, 151, 152
Hippocratic Oath 133-134, 139, 153
Hippolytus 114
Holy Land 15, 111
Holy Sepulchre, Church of the, Jerusalem 15
Holy Spirit 117
Holy Week 79
Homer 37, 53, 93, 104, 207-212, 221, 224, 225
Homeridai 211
Horae (see Graces)
Hospitallers 156, 164
Hundred-handed giants 8
Hygiea 134, 137

Ialyssos, Rhodes 155,165
Ida, Mount, Crete 29-33
Idaion, cave, Crete 29-33, 42, 86
Iliad, The 207, 209-211, 212, 214, 216, 221, 224
Ipsilos, monastery, Lesbos 192
Iraklion,Crete 1, 2, 3, 6, 25, 33, 34
Irene, St. 68
Iria, Naxos 39
Iris 53
Isis, temple of 54
Isles of the Blest 6, 109
Israelis 29
Ixion, King 84

Jason 195

Jerusalem 21, 111

Jesus 14, 15, 53, 85, 137, 198

Jews 40, 106, 153, 156, 162-163, 178

John the Theologian, Monastery of, Patmos 99, 101, 103, 104, 106-109

John the Evangelist 57, 96, 99, 101, 146

Judgement of Paris 210

Jouktas, Mt., Crete 3, 10

Judaea 21

Judas, Gospel of 14, 15

Julius Caesar 160

Kali Limeni, Crete 22

Kalloni 185

Kameiros, Rhodes 155, 175, 177-178

Kameiros Skala, Rhodes 179

Kaniaris, Captain 122

Kardameina, Kos 143

Kechrovouni, convent, Tinos 119-123

Kefalos, Kos 149

Kerkis, Mt., Samos 90-96

Knights of St. John 134, 141, 152, 156

Knossos, Crete 2, 3-6

Kore (see Persephone)

KOS, island, Dodecanese 133-153, 162, 163

Kouros of Flerio, Naxos 45-46

Kreipe, General 6, 11, 34

Kritinia, Rhodes 176

Kritsa,Crete 7, 10, 12, 15

Kronos, god 7, 8, 63

Kynops, magician 101

Lasithi, plain, Crete 10

Lato, Crete 11, 12

LESBOS, island, Eastern Aegean 181-206

Leto 51, 52, 53, 54, 56, 104, 216

Lindos, Rhodes 155, 157, 164-175

Luke, St. 14, 118

Lygdamis 37

Macedonian 54

Maenads 195

Mandamados, Lesbos 201

Mandraki, harbour, Rhodes 156-157, 159

Marathokampos, Samos 96

Mary, mother of Jesus (see Virgin Mary)

Menelaus, king of Sparta 169, 191

Mercury 201

Mesa, Lesbos 184-185

Michael, archangel 14, 106, 201-205

Minas, St. 2

Minoan 5, 9, 29, 31, 61, 68

Minos, King 2-6, 9, 10, 17, 22, 25, 176, 195

Minotaur 1, 4, 35, 36, 48, 54

Mnemosyne 41

Moirai (See Fates)

Moni, Naxos 44, 45

Monolithos, Rhodes 175

Monophysite 14

Monte Smith, Rhodes 158

Moslem 40, 134, 151, 153

Moss, W. Stanley 11

Mother Goddess 5, 7, 9, 79

Muhammad 40

Muses 41, 224

Mytilene, city 181-183, 184, 189, 190

Naiads 126

Naoussa, Paros 128-131

NAXOS, island, Cyclades 4, 35-50, 53, 86

Nea Kameni, Santorini 59, 63, 64-66, 71

Nea Moni, Chios 218

Neochori, Samos 96

Nereid 123

New Testament 22, 57, 99, 121

Nida, plateau, Crete 29, 31

Nike 69

Nisyros 143

Nymphaia 159

Ocean 155

Odysseus 191

Odyssey, The 6, 207

Oia, Santorini 63

Old Testament 93, 107, 121, 211

Olous 17

Olympia 12, 178

Olympian gods 5, 9, 57, 60, 63, 112, 220

Olympus, Mt.,Thessaly 8, 37, 38, 53

Olympus, Mt., Lesbos 185, 197, 205, 206

Omphalos 9

Oracles 90, 151

Orestes 104

Orpheus 114, 181, 192-196, 198, 199

Orthodox 14, 27, 49, 72, 79, 113, 120, 121, 141, 153

Orthodox Church 15, 19, 28, 45, 105, 107, 108, 113, 120, 121, 141

Osios Christodoulos, monk 104, 146

Ouranos 28, 63, 159

Palatia, Naxos 35

Palestine 162

Palia Kameni, Santorini 65

Palio Pyli, Kos 144-147

Pan 88

Panacea 134

Panagia Atheniotissa, cathedral, Athens 169

Panagia Drosiani, church, Moni, Naxos 44

Panagia Episcopi, church, Santorini 68

Panagia Evangelistria, church, Tinos, 116

Panagia Kera, church, Kritsa, Crete 12-16

Panagia Vrefokratoussa, Lesbos 206

Pandroso 96

Panathenaea 139

Paphos, Cyprus 190

Parikia, Paros 111-115, 116, 128-131

Paris, Prince 169

PAROS, island, Cyclades 42, 111-115, 116, 128-131

Parthenon 169

Pasiphae 25, 48

Passover 15

PATMOS, island, Dodecanese 57, 96, 99-110, 146

Patroclus 93, 209, 210, 215, 216

Paul, St. 2, 10, 21, 22, 94, 151, 156, 165, 166, 170, 178, 188, 191

Paul, St., of Latrino 95

Pausanius 53

Pelagia, Agia 117, 119, 121

Pentecost 15

Pericles 139

Perissa, Santorini 68

Persephone 41, 181, 195

Persians 57, 139, 168

Petrified forest, Lesbos 191, 192

Phaedra 53

Phaethon 179, 180

Phanai, ancient, Chios 215-217, 223

Phoebe 159

Pirates 57, 117, 128, 131

Pirgos, Samos 96

Pityos, Chios 211

Plato 6, 60, 61, 63, 124

Plomari, Lesbos 197

Polycrates 84, 85, 86, 92

Portara, Naxos 35, 39, 49

Poseidon, god 4, 8, 25, 48, 52, 60, 61, 63, 123, 143, 167

Potami, Samos 87

Priam, King 167, 216

Prochoros 102

Profitis Ilias 30, 214

Profitis Ilias, Monastery of, Santorini 60, 63, 64, 66, 68, 70-74

Ptolemies 66, 67

Pyli, Kos 144, 146, 147

Pythagoras 89, 90, 91-93

Pythagoras, cave of 89, 90-96

Pythagorio, Samos 82, 84, 85, 86

Pythaïs 90

Pythia 90

Python 24, 68, 159

Raphael, archangel 80, 81

Resurrection 86, 87

Revelation 99, 102, 103, 109

Rhadamanthys 6

Rhea, goddess 5, 7, 9, 112

Rhodes, city 155-164, 165

RHODES, island, Dodecanese 155-180

Rhodos 155

Roman 85, 102, 134, 160, 163, 178

Roman Catholics 45, 49, 165

Salt marshes, Lesbos 185, 196

SAMOS, island, Dodecanese 79-98

SANTORINI, island, Cyclades 3, 59-78

Sappho 181, 183, 184, 185-191, 192, 206

Saracens 117, 146, 201

Saul 178

Semele 40, 41

Serapis, temple of 54

Sinai 29

Siren, voices 195

Skala Eressou, Lesbos 185-191, 194
Skala, Patmos 99, 101, 104, 105, 108, 109
Smith, Sir Sidney 158
Smyrna 152
Snakes, sacred 138
Socrates 54, 55
Sparta 67, 191
Spinalonga, island 16
Spinalonga, peninsula 17
St. Paul's bay, Rhodes 164, 165-166, 170, 171-174
St. Paul, chapel, Rhodes 164, 171-174
Stephen, St 67, 149
Styx, river 52, 197
Sun 48
Synoptic Gospels 15

Tartarus 6, 8, 109
Taxiarchis, monastery, Lesbos 201-205
Thelenis, Chios 219
Therassia, Santorini 59, 61
Theodosius II, emperor 141
Theotokos 111
Theras 67
Therassia, Santorini 59, 61
Theseus 4, 35, 36, 46, 47-49, 53, 54
Thira (See Santorini)
Thira, ancient 66-68, 74
Timios Stavros, church, Mt. Ida, Crete 30
TINOS, island, Cyclades 115-128
Titans 41, 63
Titaness 159
Titus, bishop of Crete 21, 22, 26
Tria Dontia, basilica, Heraion, Samos 85
Trojan War 93, 104, 167, 199, 209, 212, 214, 216, 224
Troy 93, 167, 211
True Cross 111
Turks 2, 134, 182, 217, 218, 219
Turkey/Turkish 80, 86, 95, 133, 139, 147, 150, 151, 163, 207, 209, 222
Tyche 112

Vatera, Lesbos 197, 205
Vathy, Samos 79, 80, 81, 86, 96
Venetian 2, 3, 16, 35
Virgin Mary 14, 44, 45, 49, 85, 94, 96, 111, 112, 113, 114, 117, 118, 121, 122, 123, 127, 128, 169, 203, 206, 220
Volissos, Chios 211
Votsalakia, Samos 87, 89-96

World War II 6, 33, 163

Xanthus 214, 215

Yom Kippur 15

Zaros, Crete 19, 20
Zas, Mt., Naxos 42, 43, 45
Zenia, Crete 11
Zeus, god 1, 3, 7, 8, 9, 10, 16, 17, 20, 22, 29, 30, 31, 33, 40, 41, 42, 43, 45, 51-54, 63, 67, 71, 79, 83, 84, 85, 86, 109, 112, 137, 146, 155, 156, 160, 165, 168, 176, 179, 180, 181, 184, 198, 210, 211, 212, 213, 216, 220
Zoodochos Pigis, church, Chora, Naxos 49
Zoodochou Pigis, monastery, Samos 79

ALSO BY JILL DUDLEY:

Ye Gods!
(Travels in Greece)

Ye Gods! II
(More travels in Greece)

Holy Smoke!
(Travels in Turkey and Egypt)

Gods in Britain
(An island odyssey from pagan to Christian)

Mortals and Immortals
(A satirical fantasy & true-in-parts memoir)

Holy Fire!
(Travels in the Holy Land)

JILL DUDLEY'S

NEXT BOOK

DIVINE WILLS
& TROJAN HEROES
(IN THE FOOTSTEPS OF THE ILIAD)

BIOGRAPHY

Jill Dudley was born in Baghdad and educated in England. Her first play was performed by the Leatherhead Repertory Company, since when she has written plays and short stories for radio. She returned to Iraq in 1956 when her husband was working out there and after the Iraqi revolution they came back to England where they bought a dairy farm. When they retired from farming in 1990 they travelled extensively around  Greece, Turkey and Egypt and a number of her travel articles have appeared in the national newspapers followed in quick succession by her popular travel-writing books.